# THE WOMEN'S LIBERATION MOVEMENT IN AMERICA

# The Women's Liberation Movement in America

Kathleen C. Berkeley

Greenwood Press Guides to
Historic Events of the Twentieth Century
*Randall M. Miller, Series Editor*

Greenwood Press
Westport, Connecticut • London

**Library of Congress Cataloging-in-Publication Data**

Berkeley, Kathleen C.
    The women's liberation movement in America / Kathleen C. Berkeley.
        p.   cm.—(Greenwood Press guides to historic events of the
    twentieth century, ISSN 1092–177X)
    Includes bibliographical references.
    ISBN 0–313–29875–0 (alk. paper)
    1. Feminism—United States—History—20th century.   2. Women's
rights—United States—History—20th century.   I. Title.
    II.  Series:  Greenwood Press guides to historic events of the
    twentieth century.
    HQ1421.B47   1999
    305.42′0973—dc21            99–25007

British Library Cataloguing in Publication Data is available.

Library of Congress Catalog Card Number: 99–25007
ISBN: 0–313–29875–0
ISSN: 1092–177X

First published in 1999

Greenwood Press, 88 Post Road West, Westport, CT 06881
An imprint of Greenwood Publishing Group, Inc.
www.greenwood.com

Printed in the United States of America

The paper used in this book complies with the
Permanent Paper Standard issued by the National
Information Standards Organization (Z39.48–1984).

10 9 8 7 6 5 4 3 2

*Front cover photo:* A women's liberation march, Washington, D.C., 1970. Library of Congress.

*Back cover photo:* A pro-ERA rally in Raleigh, North Carolina, 1982. Used by permission of Raleigh, North Carolina, *News and Observer.*

## Copyright Acknowledgments

# Contents

CONTENTS

*A photo essay follows page 80*

# Series Foreword

As the twenty-first century approaches, it is time to take stock of the political, social, economic, intellectual, and cultural forces and factors that have made the twentieth century the most dramatic period of change in history. To that end, the Greenwood Press Guides to Historic Events of the Twentieth Century presents interpretive histories of the most significant events of the century. Each book in the series combines narrative history and analysis with primary documents and biographical sketches, with an eye to providing both a reference guide to the principal persons, ideas, and experiences defining each historic event, and a reliable, readable overview of that event. Each book further provides analyses and discussions, grounded in both primary and secondary sources, of the causes and consequences, in thought and action, that give meaning to the historic event under review. By assuming a historical perspective, drawing on the latest and best writing on each subject, and offering fresh insights, each book promises to explain how and why a particular event defined the twentieth century. No consensus about the meaning of the twentieth century emerges from the series, but, collectively, the books identify the most salient concerns of the century. In so doing, the series reminds us of the many ways those historic events continue to affect our lives.

Each book follows a similar format designed to encourage readers to consult it both as a reference and a history in its own right. Each volume opens with a chronology of the historic event, followed by a narrative overview, which also serves to introduce and examine briefly the main themes and issues related to that event. The next set of chapters is composed of topi-

cal essays, each analyzing closely an issue or problem of interpretation introduced in the opening chapter. A concluding chapter suggesting the
long-term implications and meanings of the historic event brings the
strands of the preceding chapters together while placing the event in the
larger historical context. Each book also includes a section of short biogra-
phies of the principal persons related to the event, followed by a section introducing and reprinting key historical documents illustrative of and
pertinent to the event. A glossary of selected terms adds to the utility of each
book. An annotated bibliography—of significant books, films, and CD-
ROMs—and an index conclude each volume.

The editors made no attempt to impose any theoretical model or historical perspective on the individual authors. Rather, in developing the series,
an advisory board of noted historians and informed high school history
teachers and public and school librarians identified the topics needful of exploration and the scholars eminently qualified to examine those events with
intelligence and sensitivity. The common commitment throughout the series is to provide accurate, informative, and readable books, free of jargon
and up to date in evidence and analysis.

Each book stands as a complete historical analysis and reference guide to
a particular historic event. Each book also has many uses, from understanding contemporary perspectives on critical historical issues, to providing
biographical treatments of key figures related to each event, to offering excerpts and complete texts of essential documents about the event, to suggesting and describing books and media materials for further study and
presentation of the event, and more. The combination of historical narrative
and individual topical chapters addressing significant issues and problems
encourages students and teachers to approach each historic event from multiple perspectives and with a critical eye. The arrangement and content of
each book thus invite students and teachers, through classroom discussions
and position papers, to debate the character and significance of great historic events and to discover for themselves how and why history matters.

The series emphasizes the main currents that have shaped the modern
world. Much of that focus necessarily looks at the West, especially Europe
and the United States. The political, commercial, and cultural expansion of
the West wrought largely, though not wholly, the most fundamental changes
of the century. Taken together, however, books in the series reveal the inter-
actions between Western and non-Western peoples and society, and also the
tensions between modern and traditional cultures. They also point to the
ways in which non-Western peoples have adapted Western ideas and technology and, in turn, influenced Western life and thought. Several books examine such increasingly powerful global forces as the rise of Islamic

fundamentalism, the emergence of modern Japan, the Communist revolution in China, and the collapse of communism in eastern Europe and the former Soviet Union. American interests and experiences receive special attention in the series, not only in deference to the primary readership of the books but also in recognition that the United States emerged as the dominant political, economic, social, and cultural force during the twentieth century. By looking at the century through the lens of American events and experiences, it is possible to see why the age has come to be known as "The American Century."

Assessing the history of the twentieth century is a formidable prospect. It has been a period of remarkable transformation. The world broadened and narrowed at the same time. Frontiers shifted from the interiors of Africa and Latin America to the moon and beyond; communication spread from mass circulation newspapers and magazines to radio, television, and now the Internet; skyscrapers reached upward and suburbs stretched outward; energy switched from steam, to electric, to atomic power. Many changes did not lead to a complete abandonment of established patterns and practices so much as a synthesis of old and new, as, for example, the increased use of (even reliance on) the telephone in the age of the computer. The automobile and the truck, the airplane, and telecommunications closed distances, and people in unprecedented numbers migrated from rural to urban, industrial, and ever more ethnically diverse areas. Tractors and chemical fertilizers made it possible for fewer people to grow more, but the environmental and demographic costs of an exploding global population threatened to outstrip natural resources and human innovation. Disparities in wealth increased, with developed nations prospering and underdeveloped nations starving. Amid the crumbling of former European colonial empires, Western technology, goods, and culture increasingly enveloped the globe, seeping into, and undermining, non-Western cultures—a process that contributed to a surge of religious fundamentalism and ethno-nationalism in the Middle East, Asia, and Africa. As people became more alike, they also became more aware of their differences. Ethnic and religious rivalries grew in intensity everywhere as the century closed.

The political changes during the twentieth century have been no less profound than the social, economic, and cultural ones. Many of the books in the series focus on political events, broadly defined, but no books are confined to politics alone. Political ideas and events have social effects, just as they spring from a complex interplay of non-political forces in culture, society, and economy. Thus, for example, the modern civil rights and women's rights movements were at once social and political events in cause and consequence. Likewise, the Cold War created the geopolitical framework for dealing with competing ideologies and nations abroad and served as the touchstone for political and cultural identities at home. The books treating political events do so within their social, cultural, and economic contexts.

Several books in the series examine particular wars in depth. Wars are defining moments for people and eras. During the twentieth century war became more widespread and terrible than ever before, encouraging new efforts to end war through strategies and organizations of international cooperation and disarmament while also fueling new ideologies and instruments of mass persuasion that fostered distrust and festered old national rivalries. Two world wars during the century redrew the political map, slaughtered or uprooted two generations of people, and introduced and hastened the development of new technologies and weapons of mass destruction. The First World War spelled the end of the old European order and spurred communist revolution in Russia and fascism in Italy, Germany, and elsewhere. The Second World War killed fascism and inspired the final push for freedom from European colonial rule in Asia and Africa. It also led to the Cold War that suffocated much of the world for almost half a century. Large wars begat small ones, and brutal totalitarian regimes cropped up across the globe. After (and in some ways because of) the fall of communism in eastern Europe and the former Soviet Union, wars of competing cultures, national interests, and political systems persisted in the struggle to make a new world order. Continuing, too, has been the belief that military technology can achieve political ends, whether in the superior American firepower that failed to "win" in Vietnam or in the American "smart bombs" and other military wizardry that "won" in the Persian Gulf.

Another theme evident in the series is that throughout the century nationalism has continued to drive events. Whether in the Balkans in 1914 triggering World War I or in the Balkans in the 1990s threatening the post–Cold War peace—or in many other places—nationalist ambitions and forces would not die. The persistence of nationalism is yet another reminder of the many ways that the past becomes prologue.

We thus offer the series as a modern guide to and interpretation of the historic events of the twentieth century and as an invitation to consider how and why those events have defined not only the past and present but also charted the political, social, intellectual, cultural, and economic routes into the next century.

Randall M. Miller
*Saint Joseph's University, Philadelphia*

# Preface

When did the women's liberation movement begin? Who were its leaders and who made up its rank and file? What were the movement's philosophies, goals, and tactics? Are the terms *women's liberation*, *women's rights*, and *feminism* synonymous? If not, what are the differences? Is the movement in existence today, and if so, how popular is it; or did it die out, and if so, when and why? The answers to these questions depend, not so surprisingly, on context, perspective, and definition.

This study seeks answers to the above questions by placing the women's liberation movement of the 1960s and 1970s within the larger context of the history of feminism across the landscape of twentieth-century America. This interpretation does not negate those of other historians who link the emergence of women's liberation to the historically specific conditions that produced the political and social unrest of the 1960s. Still, this text is predicated on the assumption that earlier examples of feminist agitation laid the groundwork for the critique of American society offered by those who would rediscover feminism during the turbulent decades of the 1960s and 1970s.

Chapter 1 introduces readers to the concepts of women's rights and women's liberation, terms generally associated with the most recent feminist agitation. Then the chapter moves back in time to examine both the flowering of feminism during the Progressive and New Deal eras and the political assaults on the movement during the years following World War I and World War II. Chapters 2 and 3 pick up the story of modern feminism by exploring its stirrings in the early 1960s with the creation of President John

F. Kennedy's President's Commission on the Status of Women and the participation of young, college-age women in the civil rights and student left/antiwar movements. While this new generation of women activists attempted to build upon the feminist legacy bequeathed to them by their grandmothers' generation, they also found it necessary to wrestle with the problem of how to redefine the meaning of equality for their own times. This redefinition led to the formation of two branches of feminism by the late 1960s: the equal rights wing, identified primarily with the newly-formed National Organization for Women, and the women's liberation wing, which was comprised of a multitude of grass-roots organizations such as New York Radical Women, the Women's International Terrorist Conspiracy from Hell, and the Boston Women's Health Book Collective. Included in these two chapters is an analysis of the race, class, and sexual tensions that surfaced within both branches of the movement. Chapter 4 analyzes the key issues that defined the feminist agenda during the decade of the 1970s, noting the gains made in civil rights, employment, education, health care, sexuality, and reproductive freedom. Chapter 5 chronicles the growing backlash against feminism that reached its peak in American life during the 1980s. Orchestrated by a loose alliance of political and religious conservatives, this movement targeted two of the most important items on the feminist agenda: abortion and the Equal Rights Amendment. The Epilogue offers a brief assessment of the impact of the women's liberation movement on American society and a few thoughts on the direction feminism may take in the twenty-first century.

Readers are encouraged to form their own ideas about the significance of feminism in shaping American culture and society. To assist in this endeavor, this text includes the following supporting material: a chronology of events, thirteen biographical sketches of women who shaped the movement, the text of fifteen primary sources, a glossary of selected terms, an annotated bibliography, and a key-word index.

# Acknowledgments

Institutional and individual support facilitated the research and writing of this book, and I am grateful for the generous assistance I received. My home institution, the University of North Carolina at Wilmington, provided financial support and an even more precious commodity, time—in the form of a Summer Initiatives grant for June 1996 and a research reassignment for the Fall 1996 semester. My department also provided much needed support by granting me the Thomas V. Moseley Award, which I used for the production of the photographic essay.

Many individuals too numerous to mention, including students in my women's history courses and "baby boom" women and men with firsthand experience with the women's liberation movement, commented on my ideas and made suggestions for improving portions of the manuscript. To all of them I owe a heartfelt thanks. Three people, however, deserve special recognition: Randall M. Miller, the series editor; Barbara Rader, an executive editor at Greenwood Publishing Group; and Harry Tuchmayer, a librarian by profession and my spouse.

Randall Miller is a superb, meticulous editor who holds his writers to incredibly high standards. He brought a fresh and penetrating perspective to each of the three drafts I submitted to him. I appreciate how gently, but firmly, he asked me to clarify (i.e., provide evidence for) some of my assertions and to adjust my feminist tone in order to create a more balanced portrait of the women's liberation movement. An excellent writer himself, he made numerous suggestions for improving the readability of my prose. For all of these contributions, I thank him.

Barbara Rader had the near impossible task of keeping me to a schedule. I am most grateful that she liked enough of what she read (and heard from Randall) to grant me several extensions when I seemed most desperate and to wave her magic wand in approval of the final manuscript.

For twenty-three years Harry Tuchmayer has been not only my best friend and critic, but also my personal reference librarian and research assistant. For this project, which consumed our lives for the past three years, Harry outdid himself. He ran interference for me on the home front and put up with my endless requests to find and bring home "just one or two more sources." His greatest contribution came at the eleventh hour of this project when, with the final deadline looming and the manuscript still 14,000 words over the press's limit, he read the entire manuscript (again) and penciled in his suggestions for cutting words, sentences, and paragraphs that were (in his words) "extraneous to the text." When the smoke cleared (at this point, I had to defend every word I wanted to retain), the manuscript was 10,000 words lighter and my presentation much stronger. Thanks HT!

Last, but not least, I want to acknowledge the encouragement and gentle teasing demonstrated by our sons Jeremy and David when the family's dinner conversations invariably turned to "mom's book" and the state of feminism today; my mother's generous offers to run errands and cook dinners when deadline pressures threatened to overwhelm me; and the unexpected visits to Wilmington between July 1996 and August 1998 of three powerful female forces of nature: Bertha, Fran, and Bonnie.

# Chronology of Events

1848        The first Woman's Rights Convention, organized by Elizabeth Cady Stanton and Lucretia Mott, is held July 19 in Seneca Falls, New York.

1866        Elizabeth Cady Stanton, Susan B. Anthony, and Lucy Stone found the American Equal Rights Association to promote universal suffrage.

**1868**

July        The Fourteenth Amendment inserts the word "male" into the Constitution for the first time.

**1869**

February        The Fifteenth Amendment is sent to the states for ratification without including any reference to sex as an impermissible ground for denying a citizen the right to vote.

May        The National Woman Suffrage Association replaces the American Equal Rights Association.

November        Lucy Stone and husband Henry Blackwell found a rival suffrage organization, the American Woman Suffrage Association.

**1870**

March        Ratification of the Fifteenth Amendment to the Constitution. The right to vote cannot be denied on "account of race, color, or previous condition of servitude."

**1874**    The Woman's Christian Temperance Union is founded, the largest grass-roots women's organization of the late nineteenth and early twentieth centuries.

**1875**    *Minor v. Happersett*. The Supreme Court rules that the rights guaranteed to citizens under the Constitution do not necessarily include suffrage.

**1880**    The Woman's Christian Temperance Union endorses woman suffrage.

**1890**    The National American Woman Suffrage Association is founded with the merger of rival organizations, the National Woman Suffrage Association and the American Woman Suffrage Association.

**1896**    The National Association of Colored Women is founded.

**1908**    *Muller v. Oregon*. The Supreme Court upholds an Oregon law limiting working hours for women based on the idea that women's frailty requires protection under the law.

**1915**    Woman's Peace Party is founded; reorganized in 1919 as the Women's International League for Peace and Freedom.

**1916**    National Woman's Party is founded by Alice Paul.

**1919**    The National Federation of Business and Professional Women is founded.

**1920**

February    The National League of Women Voters is created.

June        The Women's Bureau is created within the Department of Labor.

August      The Nineteenth Amendment granting women the right to vote is ratified.

**1921**    The Sheppard-Towner Act passes Congress, providing federal grants for six years to states establishing maternal and pediatric health-care clinics.

**1923**    The Equal Rights Amendment (ERA) is introduced in Congress.

**1927**    After a bitter fight, Congress extends the life of the Sheppard-Towner Act until June 30, 1929.

**1935**    National Council of Negro Women is founded by Mary McLeod Bethune.

**1938**    The Fair Labor Standards Act establishes the principle of equal pay, but it did not apply to women's work.

| | |
|---|---|
| **1942** | "Rosie the Riveter" makes her appearance as the symbol of the patriotic, feminine, war worker. |
| **1945** | Thousands of "Rosies" are fired at the end of World War II. |
| **1946** | *Baby and Child Care* by Dr. Benjamin Spock is published, promoting "stay-at-home moms." |
| **1947** | *Modern Women: The Lost Sex* by Marynia Farnham and Ferdinand Lundberg is published, arguing that competition between the sexes not only stripped women of their femininity but also promoted alcoholism in husbands and delinquency in children. |
| **1952** | *The Second Sex* by French author Simone de Beauvoir is translated into English and published in the United States. |
| **1960** | The Student Nonviolent Coordinating Committee is founded. |
| **1961** | The President's Commission on the Status of Women is created by President John F. Kennedy. |
| **1962** | Students for a Democratic Society is founded. |
| **1963** | |
| February | *The Feminine Mystique* by Betty Friedan is published. |
| June | The Equal Pay Act passes Congress. |
| October | The President's Commission on the Status of Women issues its report to President Kennedy. |
| **1964** | |
| July | President Johnson signs the 1964 Civil Rights Act. Title VII prohibits race and sex discrimination in employment. |
| November | Student Nonviolent Coordinating Committee staff retreat at Waveland, Mississippi. An "anonymous" position paper (written by Mary King and Casey Hayden) raises the issue of sex discrimination within the Student Nonviolent Coordinating Committee. |
| **1965** | *Griswold v. Connecticut.* Supreme Court strikes down a state law preventing the use of contraceptives by married couples. |
| **1966** | |
| April | The King-Hayden Student Nonviolent Coordinating Committee position paper on sex discrimination is revised and published in *Liberation*, a New Left magazine. |
| October | The National Organization for Women (NOW) is founded; Betty Friedan is elected president of the equal rights organization. |

**1967**

August        Inaugural issue of *The Phyllis Schlafly Report* is mailed to 3,000 supporters.

August        Conflicts over race and gender disrupt the Chicago convention of the New Left's National Conference for a New Politics.

September     In Chicago, the first women's liberation group (the Westside group) begins meeting to discuss male oppression.

October       President Johnson issues Executive Order 11375 prohibiting sex discrimination in employment by the federal government.

October       New York Radical Women is founded (by Shulamith Firestone and Pam Allen), pioneering in consciousness raising.

November      NOW adopts a "Bill of Rights for 1968," which includes support for the ERA and the repeal of antiabortion laws.

**1968**

March         *Voice of the Women's Liberation Movement,* newsletter of Chicago's radical feminists, is published.

June          *Notes from the First Year,* published by New York Radical Women, promotes radical feminism.

September      New York Radical Women initiates plans for the Miss America Beauty Pageant demonstration.

October       Women's International Terrorist Conspiracy from Hell, a politico-feminist group, is founded by Robin Morgan.

November      Shirley Chisholm is the first black woman elected to Congress.

November      The first National Women's Liberation Conference is held in Chicago.

December      The Women's Equity Action League is founded by Elizabeth Boyer.

**1969**

January       The National Association for the Repeal of Abortion Laws is founded (name is changed after legalization in 1973 to the National Abortion Rights Action League).

February      Redstockings, a radical feminist group founded in New York City, demands the repeal of antiabortion laws before a meeting of the state legislature.

March         *Weeks v. Southern Bell.* Landmark U.S. Court of Appeals decision based on the application of Title VII of the 1964 Civil Rights Act; strikes down weight-lifting restrictions.

| | |
|---|---|
| March | Cornell University offers the nation's first accredited course in women's studies. |
| December | New York Radical Feminists is organized. |

**1970**

| | |
|---|---|
| January | Rita Mae Brown resigns from NOW and joins in founding Radicalesbians. |
| January | The Women's Equity Action League files a sex discrimination class-action lawsuit against the University of Maryland based on Executive Order 11375 guidelines. |
| May | At the second annual Congress to Unite Women, twenty lesbian feminists challenge straight feminists to confront their homophobia. |
| May | The U.S. Senate opens hearings on the ERA. |
| August | Women's Strike for Equality rallies are held nationwide. |
| September | Published: *Sisterhood Is Powerful: An Anthology of Writings from the Women's Liberation Movement,* by Robin Morgan and *Sexual Politics*, by Kate Millett. |

**1971**

| | |
|---|---|
| January | New York Radical Feminists sponsors the nation's first "speak-out" on rape. |
| March | The House of Representatives begins hearings on the ERA. |
| April | New York Radical Feminists organizes the nation's first conference on rape. |
| July | The National Women's Political Caucus is founded by Bella Abzug, Shirley Chisholm, Betty Friedan, and Gloria Steinem. |

**1972**

| | |
|---|---|
| January | Representative Shirley Chisholm declares her intent to seek the Democratic presidential nomination. |
| February | Phyllis Schlafly opens her assault on the ERA in her newsletter. |
| March | The ERA is approved by Congress and sent to the states for ratification. Ratification deadline: March 22, 1979. |
| June | Title IX of the Higher Education Amendments Act passes Congress, prohibiting sex discrimination in all educational programs and activities receiving federal funds. |
| July | *Ms.* magazine begins monthly publication. |

November      Phyllis Schlafly founds STOP ERA.

**1973**

January       *Roe v. Wade* and its companion *Doe v. Bolton*. Landmark Supreme
              Court decision(s) that overturn antiabortion statutes.

May           *Frontiero v. Richardson*. Supreme Court decision overturns armed
              forces regulations denying military women's dependents the same
              benefits to which dependents of military men were entitled (case is
              argued by Ruth Bader Ginsburg).

May           The National Black Feminist Organization is founded.

September      Billie Jean King defeats Bobby Riggs in a tennis match dubbed "the
              battle of the sexes."

**1974**

August        The Women's Educational Equity Act passes Congress, funding
              provided for the development of nonsexist curricula and
              educational programs that promote equity between the sexes.

**1975**      Phyllis Schlafly founds The Eagle Forum as "an alternative to
              women's lib."

**1976**      The Hyde Amendment passes Congress limiting Medicaid funds
              for abortion. A temporary stay is lifted in November after the
              Supreme Court refuses to uphold the injunction in *Califano v.
              McRae*.

**1977**      The National Women's Conference is held in Houston, Texas.
              Delegates endorse a twenty-six-plank "Plan of Action" that
              includes lesbian rights, welfare mothers' rights, and the ERA.

**1978**

February      Arson attack on a Cleveland, Ohio, abortion clinic.

June          Arson attack on an Iowa City, Iowa, abortion clinic.

June-July     With the ERA ratification process stalled since 1975, NOW lobbies
              Congress, organizes a rally (estimated at 100,000) and wins a new
              deadline: June 30, 1982.

October       The Pregnancy Discrimination Act passes Congress.

**1979**

January       Bella Abzug, cochair of the National Advisory Committee for
              Women, is fired by President Jimmy Carter.

February      Arson attack on a Long Island, New York, abortion clinic.

October      The newly formed Women Against Pornography holds a rally (estimated at 5,000) in New York City's "notorious Times Square porn district."

**1980**

March      The first National Hispanic Feminist Conference is organized by Sylvia Gonzales.

June      *Harris v. McRae.* Supreme Court decision upholds the constitutionality of the Hyde Amendment.

**1981**

January      The Human Life Amendment, banning abortion and some forms of birth control, is introduced in Congress by Senator Jesse Helms (R-North Carolina) and Representative Henry Hyde (R-Illinois).

July      Sandra Day O'Connor is nominated to the Supreme Court by President Ronald Reagan.

**1982**      The ERA "dies" after ratification efforts are defeated in Illinois (May), North Carolina (June), and Florida (June).

**1983**

January      The ERA is reintroduced in Congress.

June      *City of Akron v. Akron Center for Reproductive Health.* Supreme Court decision invalidates a 1978 law mandating a twenty-four-hour waiting period (for an abortion) after securing an "informed consent" form from the patient.

November      The reintroduced ERA fails for lack of support in the House of Representatives.

**1984**

February      *Grove City College v. Bell.* Supreme Court decision undermines the intent of Title IX, limiting its scope to specific programs rather than the entire institution.

July      Geraldine Ferraro wins the Democratic nomination for vice president and serves as Walter Mondale's running mate.

November      The ERA fails again in the House of Representatives.

September–      At least six arson attacks on abortion clinics are reported from December      California to Florida.

**1985**

January      The controversial antiabortion documentary *The Silent Scream* is screened in the White House. Arson attacks on abortion clinics are reported throughout the spring.

**1986**

June            *Thornburgh v. The American College of Obstetricians and Gynecologists.* Supreme Court decision invalidates a Pennsylvania law requiring doctors to provide women with specific information on fetal development, medical risks, and alternatives to abortion.

August          The Family and Medical Leave Act is introduced in Congress.

**1987**          After a three year "logjam," Congress approves the Civil Rights Restoration Act, protecting women, minorities, the elderly, and disabled and restoring the original intent of Title IX (see the 1984 *Grove City* decision). Civil Rights Restoration Act is vetoed by President Reagan.

**1988**          The Civil Rights Restoration Act becomes law when Congress overrides the president's veto.

**1989**          *Webster v. Reproductive Health Services.* Supreme Court decision upholds a Missouri law banning public funds and public facilities to perform abortions; also mandates medically unnecessary fetal viability testing at twenty weeks and supports the controversial position that life begins at conception.

**1990**

June            *Hodgson v. Minnesota* and *Ohio v. Akron Center for Reproductive Health.* Supreme Court decisions uphold state laws requiring parental consent or judicial approval before a minor can obtain an abortion.

**1991**

July            President George Bush nominates Judge Clarence Thomas, an African American, to replace retiring justice Thurgood Marshall.

October         Senate Judiciary hearings on the confirmation of Clarence Thomas are reopened and televised amid accusations that Thomas sexually harassed Anita Hill (an African American law professor) when she worked for Thomas a decade ago. Thomas is confirmed, and many women voters are outraged.

October         *Backlash: The Undeclared War against American Women,* by Susan Faludi, is published.

**1992**

June            *Planned Parenthood of Southeastern Pennsylvania v. Casey.* Supreme Court decision confirms the Court's position in *Roe v. Wade* regarding a woman's right to an abortion prior to the point of fetal viability (while questioning *Roe*'s trimester framework) and lets stand several restrictive provisions.

November | The "Year of the Woman." Women dramatically increase their presence in Congress (forty-seven in the House and six in the Senate) with several Democratic candidates capitalizing on the feminist anger that surfaced following the Thomas hearings. Carol Moseley-Braun (D-Illinois) becomes the first African American woman elected to the Senate.

November | The Democrats recapture the White House as "soccer moms" (suburban, white, middle-class women) and black women turn out in overwhelming numbers to vote for Bill Clinton.

**1993** | President Clinton's cabinet includes Janet Reno, Attorney General; Donna Shalala, Secretary of Health and Human Services; Carol Browner, Director of the Environmental Protection Agency; and Hazel O'Leary, Secretary of Energy. Madeline Albright is appointed Ambassador to the United Nations (named Secretary of State in 1996).

January | President Clinton lifts the ban on importing the French "abortion pill" RU-486 and ends the "gag" rule preventing doctors at federally funded clinics from providing abortion information to their patients.

February | President Clinton signs the Family and Medical Leave Act.

June | President Clinton nominates Ruth Bader Ginsburg to replace retiring Supreme Court Justice Byron White.

November | *Harris v. Forklift Systems Inc.* Supreme Court ruling on sexual harassment in the workplace establishes a "reasonable person's standard" in defining harassment.

**1995**

September | Senator Robert Packwood (R-Oregon) resigns following the Senate Ethics Committee's recommendation of expulsion for alleged sexual harassment and influence peddling.

**1996**

November | California voters pass Proposition 209 (54% to 46%), banning affirmative action in hiring, contracts, and higher education.

**1997**

April | Ninth U.S. Circuit Court of Appeals overturns an injunction blocking implementation of Proposition 209.

**1998**

January | Bombing of an abortion clinic in Birmingham, Alabama. Under oath and before the media, President Clinton denies allegations of a sexual relationship with former White House intern Monica Lewinsky.

August    President Clinton admits to an "inappropriate relationship" with Monica Lewinsky.

September White House Special Prosecutor Kenneth Starr releases his report documenting President Clinton's affair.

October   The House Judiciary Committee votes to open impeachment hearings on President Clinton.

October   Dr. Barnett Slepian (a Buffalo, New York, abortion provider) is murdered at home by sniper fire, the seventh victim of antiabortion violence since 1993.

November  Washington voters pass Measure 200 (59% to 41%), banning affirmative action in hiring, contracts, and higher education.

December  President Clinton is impeached for committing perjury before a federal grand jury and for obstructing justice. Both charges stem from the president's efforts to conceal his affair with Monica Lewinsky.

**1999**

January   Senate impeachment trial of President Clinton begins.

February  President Clinton is acquitted of both charges.

# THE WOMEN'S
# LIBERATION MOVEMENT
# EXPLAINED

# 1

# Women's Liberation: The View from the Past

## BRA-BURNING WOMEN: FORM OVER SUBSTANCE IN POPULAR MEMORY

The term women's liberation conjures up vivid images of "bra-burning women" that originated from the press's creative retelling of a single event that occurred on September 7, 1968. On that date the fledgling women's liberation movement caught the attention of the American public when members of New York Radical Women, a liberation group founded the previous year, organized a day-long demonstration on the boardwalk in Atlantic City, New Jersey. The group's target was the Miss America Beauty Pageant.[1] The organizers of this "counter-pageant" issued a position paper listing their opposition to the beauty contest, which they believed promoted a view of American women as sex objects enslaved by a narrow image of beauty perpetuated by the fashion and cosmetics industries. The protesters also criticized the pageant promoters' support for the controversial war being waged in Vietnam by the United States. In particular, they objected to the 1967 Miss America's tour of military bases in Vietnam. Although the demonstrators engaged in such traditional political behavior as picketing, lobbying, and leafleting, these actions were overshadowed by two staged "street-theater" events that came to define and subsequently trivialize the women's liberation movement. Gathering before a "freedom trash can" the women protesters tossed, *but did not burn,* several symbols of their oppression. Included among the many discarded items were "bras, girdles, curlers, false eyelashes, wigs, and representative issues of *Cosmopolitan, Ladies'*

*Home Journal* [and] *Family Circle*."[2] The day's events ended with a satirical performance led by a handful of the organizers. As midnight approached and the newest representation of American beauty stepped forward to receive the "Miss America" title, symbolized by the requisite tiara, the protesters held an alternative ceremony outside the convention center where they solemnly crowned a live sheep.

It is ironic that the image of the women's liberation movement that survives in popular memory stems from a fictitious "bra-burning" incident. The women's political message, which offered up a substantive critique of American culture and institutions, hardly captured public attention and as yet lies buried deep within historical memory. The irony exists, too, not only in what is remembered and forgotten but also in how an event, even a false one, is represented over time.

By the last decade of the twentieth century, the idea that women once burned their bras in the name of liberation seemed not only funny but, more importantly, unthreatening to American society. This is precisely the view presented by Chance Browne, the creator of "Hi and Lois," a nationally syndicated daily cartoon strip depicting a white, middle-class suburban couple and their four children: Chip, the teenage son; Dot and Ditto, preadolescent, fraternal twins; and Trixie, the baby.[3] In the first of a two-panel sketch drawn in 1996, Dot and her girlfriend are talking while sitting on a porch step. The friend announces that her mom was a participant in the women's movement of the 1970s. "So was **MY** mom!" retorts Dot (Browne's emphasis). In the second panel Dot is in the kitchen addressing her mother, Lois, who turns away from the stove with a quizzical expression on her face when Dot asks, "Did you ever burn your bra?"[4]

Funny? Yes, but the strip reveals much about the fleeting, superficial impact that women's liberation supposedly had on American culture and society. Two decades have passed since Browne's cartoon figure presumably participated in a movement symbolized by its most radical, well-known mythic event. Lois's youthful discomfort with her prescribed "place" in society, which may have led her to "burn her bra," resulted in neither a rejection of family nor a fundamental reordering of gender roles within the two-parent household—two feared outcomes of feminism that many contemporary critics rashly predicted. The second panel of the sketch, after all, places mother Lois in the kitchen, stirring a pot on the stove. Readers familiar with the cartoon strip are left to wonder if Lois's earlier activism is as anachronistic to her present domesticated life as husband Hi's occasional efforts to recapture his "radical" youth by donning his old, too tight bell-bottoms, tie dye shirt, peace symbol, and "hippie" beads.

Chance Browne's benign, nostalgic view of activists in the women's movement of a bygone era is cultural revisionism at its best. Thirty years earlier, popular culture labeled these women *libbers* (a derisive term) and portrayed them as young, white, angry, and radical. Radical women, by the controversial issues they raised and the positions they took, frequently were accused of harboring antimale attitudes and promoting antifamily values.

The 1970s supposedly marked the heyday of women's liberation. During that decade, movement members focused the public's attention on such social problems as rape, incest, and domestic violence by calling for changes in the treatment of the victims and the punishment of the perpetrators. Women activists combined old-fashioned political lobbying with direct action demonstrations as they worked for the repeal of antiabortion laws, the ratification of the Equal Rights Amendment (ERA), a national child-care bill, a displaced homemakers bill, and lesbian rights. While many activists worked for inclusion and power-sharing in the male-dominated fields of politics, business, education, medicine, and the law, others argued for separatism and the creation of alternative institutions.

The women's liberation movement suffered a direct hit in 1980 with the election of the popular, conservative Ronald Reagan to the White House. In part, Reagan was swept into office on a rising tide of antifeminism, a movement that began gathering strength midway through the decade associated with women's liberation. For the first time since the 1940s, the Republican party backed away from its support for the ERA. The 1980 party platform also furthered the cause of antifeminism by endorsing a call for a constitutional amendment banning abortion (a medical procedure legalized in this country by the 1973 Supreme Court decision *Roe v. Wade*) and advocating the appointment of pro-life judges to the federal courts.[5] Two years later, when the ERA's ratification bid ended in defeat, many contemporary observers of modern American life predicted the imminent demise of the women's liberation movement.

This volume tells a different story of the women's liberation movement in America. It does so by situating the women's liberation movement of the 1960s and 1970s within the context of a larger, more complex history of feminism that has ebbed and flowed over the course of twentieth-century American life. This analysis is not at odds with one that relates the emergence of the women's liberation movement of the late 1960s to the historically specific political, social, economic, and cultural conditions of that era. Nonetheless, it is shortsighted to assume that the philosophy, issues, goals, and strategies of the women's liberation movement bore no relationship to earlier flowerings of feminist agitation. Each generation, though unique, does not invent anew its problems or its resolutions; nor, unfortunately, do complex problems such as sexism or racism disappear from American society within the life span of a single generation. Viewed from this perspective, the story of the women's liberation movement of the 1960s and 1970s unfolds as one of many chapters that comprise the still ongoing history of American feminism.

## A UNITED SISTERHOOD? FEMINISM AND THE RIDDLE OF RACE, CLASS, AND GENDER

The term "feminism" was coined in France by a women's rights activist in the latter part of the nineteenth century but did not come into common usage in the United States until the second decade of the twentieth century. When it did, according to historian Nancy F. Cott, early twentieth-century feminists understood the concept to encompass much more than a single issue or organization.[6] Indeed, by the time Americans became familiar with feminism, a number of women's organizations, some with overlapping constituencies, already were hard at work advocating for the rights and protection of women and children.

The Woman's Christian Temperance Union, which sought to outlaw alcohol, ranked among the largest of the grass-roots organizations in the late nineteenth and early twentieth centuries.[7] Other prominent women's voluntary associations included the Young Women's Christian Association, the National American Woman Suffrage Association, the National Consumers' League, the National Association of Colored Women, the Women's Trade Union League, the Woman's Peace Party, the National Woman's Party, and the American Birth Control League. Some of these organizations represented the outlook of predominantly white, middle-class women (the Woman's Christian Temperance Union, the National American Woman Suffrage Association, the National Woman's Party, the American Birth Control League); others promoted cross-class alliances (the Young Women's Christian Association, the National Consumer's League, the Women's Trade Union League). Cross-race and gender alliances were virtually nonexistent at the turn of the century. White women's organizations were hesitant (some might say unwilling) to support challenges to racist laws and customs, whereas racial justice organizations led by black men tended to downplay problems that were unique to black women because of the interplay between racism and sexism. Thus, African American women discovered the necessity of creating a separate organization to advance their twin concerns.

In common, all feminists believed that their "sex" lacked political, economic, and social power and that the American legal system contrived to hold women to that subordinate status. Their advocacy of that shared conviction, however, took many different forms—alcohol prohibition, higher national standards for age-of-consent laws, the abolition of prostitution, child labor reform, the establishment of minimum wage and maximum hour requirements for working women, legalization of birth control, social welfare issues, passage of antilynching laws and other forms of racial justice, and voting rights for women. Tactics employed by feminists also differed. Some women preferred to work solely through their autonomous organizations; others sought alliances with powerful men's organizations. Some women were more comfortable with behind-the-scenes lobbying efforts; others engaged in direct action marches, parades, and demonstrations that bordered on civil disobedience. Some women eschewed partisan politics, others did not; and some women supported the passage of state and federal laws that "protected" women from harsh conditions, primarily within the area of work.[8]

Feminism's umbrella stretched wide enough to cover a range of organizations, issues, and tactics by the eve of America's entry into World War I. Contributing even further to the appearance of consensus within the movement was the widespread support by the various organizations for securing passage of the suffrage amendment. In part, this short-lived unanimity stemmed from a belief among the different feminist groups that the same goal—suffrage—could serve different purposes. Black women leaders thought that the suffrage amendment would prove a useful tool in defeating interracial marriage laws, raising the status of black women, and outlawing the practice of lynching in the South; Woman's Christian Temperence Union women believed that the vote could be an effective weapon in their war to eradicate alcohol from American society; and working- and middle-class advocates of protective legislation for women believed that the potential power of the women's vote would influence male legislators to support women's reform initiatives.[9]

Consensus on suffrage masked stark differences among early twentieth-century feminists. Distinctions among feminists were shaped by their varied regional cultures, political ideologies, and social characteristics (race, class, ethnicity, and gender). Once the suffrage amendment was ratified in 1920 and the National American Woman Suffrage Association disbanded, feminism lost its unifying cause and its institutional anchor. Differences among feminists reasserted themselves and conflicts emerged as the various women's organizations attempted to put the ballot to work for their respective causes. Feminism did not wither in the aftermath of the woman suffrage amendment, but it was transformed.

One attempt to maintain the feminist momentum inspired by the suffrage coalition occurred in 1920 when Maud Wood Park, head of the newly created nonpartisan National League of Women Voters, laid the groundwork for the creation of a women's legislative lobby. Several prominent women's organizations heeded Park's call. By 1922, according to both popular women's magazines and professional journals, the Women's Joint Congressional Committee already had become "the most powerful and highly organized lobby in Washington."[10] The Women's Joint Congressional Committee's initial legislative agenda included maternal and infant health care, prohibition, protective labor legislation, the creation of a Department of Education, and international disarmament.

By far, the Women's Joint Congressional Commitee's single most important accomplishment was the passage of the Sheppard-Towner Act of 1921. Three years in the making, this controversial bill provided an annual budget of over 1 million to aid states (on a matching funds basis) in the establishment of education centers and nursing services for poor women and their babies. The impetus behind this legislation came from the Children's Bureau's 1918 study documenting the shockingly high infant and maternal mortality rates among the nation's poorest families who lacked consistent pre- and postnatal care. The American Medical Association opposed the bill on the grounds that it would introduce "socialized medicine" to this country; other organizations attacked the bill and its feminist supporters as "communist dupes." Historians agree that the bill's passage was the result of male legislators' fears about the potential power of a collective "woman's vote." Still, to get support for the bill, the Women's Joint Congressional Committee had to agree to a six-year limit on appropriations. When the bill came up for renewal in June 1927, pronounced divisions within the feminist movement and the failure of the "woman's vote" to materialize as a bloc created a political climate ripe for defeat. Given a two-year extension, the legislation lapsed the year the Great Depression began (1929); not until 1935, under provisions established by the Social Security Act, would the federal government once again concern itself with the health of poor women and children.[11]

The feminist lobby met with only limited success with the remainder of its 1921 agenda. Following the 1927 defeat of the Sheppard-Towner Act, the Women's Joint Congressional Committee's ability to influence public policy in Washington declined precipitously. Support among its initial core organizations also evaporated; by the mid-1930s two key mainstream women's groups, the Woman's Christian Temperence Union and the General Federation of Women's Clubs, had left the fold. During that same period, efforts were made to revive the flagging feminist coalition through the creation of the Women's Charter. The Women's Charter was a dismal failure, its policy issues ignored by the federal government. Worse still, the charter's endorsement of protective labor legislation as a means for securing equity for women, a tactic favored by many Women's Joint Congressional Committee affiliates, put it at odds with an alternative feminist agenda: the Equal Rights Amendment (ERA).[12]

Individually and collectively African American women and their organizations were noticeably absent from white feminists' attempts at coalition building during the 1920s and 1930s. Black women's aloofness had little to do with a disinterest in the feminist issues advanced by the white women's organizations and everything to do with undercurrents of racism that persisted within feminism. Toleration, not acceptance, had defined the shaky alliance between white and black feminists during the suffrage campaign. Prior to the passage of the suffrage amendment many southern white suffragists had tried to sidestep the inherent contradiction between their advocacy of "votes for women" and their tacit support for white supremacy (in theory, the federal amendment extended the vote to all women without regard for their race or color). Caught between the strong, public support for the vote by black women and the nefarious use made of this support by southern white antisuffragists, southern white suffragists struggled to contain the race issue.[13] Once the vote was won, however, there was no hiding the oppressive monster of white supremacy as black women made every effort to secure the vote for themselves.

In Virginia, North Carolina, Georgia, Alabama, Texas, and Florida, black women's organizations prepared instructions to help members pass their states' mandatory literacy tests. They also devised clever strategies they hoped would ensure success when the voter registration books opened in advance of the fall 1920 election. To blunt the influence of potential black women voters, who were predisposed to support the Republican party, many southern white suffragists planned counterregistration drives. Joined by a number of white male politicians, the registration efforts targeted reluctant white women, urging them to join the Democratic party. In Jacksonville, Florida, for example, the local woman suffrage league reorganized as the Duval County League of Democratic Women Voters and dedicated themselves to registering white women voters in a blatant attempt to preserve white supremacy.[14]

Black women's suspicions were confirmed by the actions of southern white feminists, but racism's presence was not confined solely to the southern wing of the feminist movement. Prior to ratification, white feminist leaders at the highest levels of the National American Woman Suffrage Association and the National Woman's Party often acted capriciously toward black feminists. Sometimes white feminists attempted to allay black concerns about an indifferent white-dominated movement; such was the case in 1917 when Congresswoman Jeannette Rankin (R-Montana) spoke before an audience of black female students from Howard University. On other occasions, however, white feminists tried to put some distance between themselves and black feminists. In 1919 nervous (and insensitive) white feminists asked the president of the Northeastern Federation of Colored Women's Clubs to withdraw her organization's request for membership in the National American Woman Suffrage Association because of the national suffrage association's pressing need to win converts among southern whites (Tennessee put ratification over the top). In a meaningless gesture by white feminists, the black women's organization was welcomed to reapply once the vote was obtained.[15] Once the need to placate southern whites had disappeared, black feminists might have expected more support in their struggle from their white allies. In this assumption they were sadly mistaken. In 1921 the leaders of the National Woman's Party rejected black feminists' request for a show of support in fighting black disenfranchisement in the South. In the eyes of the National Woman's Party, the inability of black women to exercise their right to vote in the South was a "race issue" not a "woman's issue."[16]

Black women were not the only members of the feminist coalition alienated by the National Woman's Party's increasingly narrow feminist stance during the 1920s. At the 1921 convention called to consider the organization's postsuffrage agenda, Alice Paul, founder of the National Woman's Party, and her lieutenants successfully fended off several resolutions, from safeguarding black civil rights to seeking world peace through global disarmament, and won approval for a more focused purpose. For Alice Paul and her constituents, securing the ballot was but the first step toward the feminist revolution; the second and final maneuver focused on eliminating all laws that discriminated solely against women. Between 1921 and 1923, when the National Woman's Party unveiled its proposal for an Equal Rights Amendment, the organization's single-minded focus on obtaining equal rights for women before the law widened the rift within the feminist movement. Philosophical differences about the meaning of equality (and how to achieve it), competing class interests, and rival political affiliations marred all efforts to create a feminist consensus around the issue of "equal rights."[17] So divisive was the ERA that not until the mid-1970s would a broad array of feminists representing different political and social philosophies, classes, and ethnic identities come together in support of the amendment's passage.

Once considered the most radical organization associated with the feminist movement because of its direct action tactics and its inclusion of socialists and other representatives from the political left, the National Woman's Party's single-issue focus after 1923 created a stumbling block to a united feminist front that would endure for the next half-century. Whereas the suffrage issue had temporarily united disparate elements within the greater feminist movement, the ERA did not. Instead, this amendment, which is often considered the centerpiece of the modern feminist movement, widened the fault line dividing protectionist-based social feminists from equal rights-oriented political feminists and exacerbated class and race tensions.

Central to the conflict over the ERA was the issue of protective legislation for women. By the time the National Woman's Party was busy promoting the ERA as the solution to achieving equality with men, social feminists promoting labor reform had worked for over two decades to secure passage of special legislation that defined women as a separate, special class in need of protection from onerous working conditions. In essence, social feminists like Florence Kelly of the National Consumers' League and Margaret Dreier Robins and Mary Anderson of the Women's Trade Union League championed sex-based protective labor legislation because they believed that the inherent biological differences between men and women put women at a disadvantage in the workplace. "Men," Kelly noted, "do not bear children [and] are freed from the burdens of maternity."[18] Long hours and a hazardous working environment did not have the same adverse effect on men's and women's health (overworked mothers, for example, suffered miscarriages and stillbirths).

These feminists insisted that society's interests were best served by the government stepping in to protect the "mothers of the race." However convoluted the argument appeared, social feminists reasoned that equal treatment for working women "required laws different from those needed by men."[19] In 1908, social feminists had won support for their position when the U.S. Supreme Court, in *Muller v. Oregon*, upheld a maximum working hours law for women. The Court's positive response to the protectionist argument encouraged a spate of sex-based labor legislation, with social feminists lobbying in many states for prohibitions on night work, minimum wage laws, mandated rest periods, and lunch breaks. Social feminists also sought federal protection. They appeared to have the upper hand in influencing the direction of federal legislation after Mary Anderson of the Women's Trade Union League was appointed in 1920 to serve as the first director of the Women's Bureau, an agency located within the Department of Labor.

In 1923, social feminists were brought up short when a newly constituted and more conservative Supreme Court struck down a minimum wage law in *Adkins v. Children's Hospital*. Apparently, the Court's majority was able to distinguish between its continued support for maximum hour limitations in order to safeguard maternal and infant health and its rejection of minimum wage laws. The Court observed that "the ancient inequality of the sexes, otherwise than physical has continued [but] with diminishing intensity because of the Nineteenth Amendment." According to historian Joan Hoff, the Court's opinion in *Adkins* "asserted that suffrage had so completely ended women's civil inferiority that they no longer needed special protection in the workplace that would infringe on their 'liberty of contract.' "[20] Prior to the *Adkins* decision, over two dozen states and the District of Columbia had passed minimum wage laws; in the aftermath of *Adkins*, only one state statute remained. Given the Court's reading of equal protection in light of the Nineteenth Amendment, social feminists reasoned that the Court likely would move to strike down sex-based protective legislation rather than extending such legislation to men if the ERA became law.

Little wonder then that feminists associated with the National Consumers' League, the Women's Trade Union League, and the Women's Bureau opposed the National Woman's Party's proposal for a federal amendment that promoted equal rights for women before the law, but offered no compromise for retaining existing protective labor legislation. Initially, the National Woman's Party was willing to entertain such a proposal; and in fact, when Wisconsin passed the first state-level equal rights bill in 1921, it contained such a clause. By the time the National Woman's Party had decided that a piecemeal state-by-state strategy for achieving equal rights was ineffectual, support within the organization for the coexistence of equal rights and sex-based legislation was waning. Business and professional women, women interested in breaking into male-dominated occupations (printing and bookbinding, for example), and women interested in running for political office objected to legislation that emphasized their inherent difference from men. Instead, they stressed the commonality between men and women that rested in their essential "human" condition. Protective legislation, reasoned these political feminists, not only perpetuated stereotypes about the fragile, weaker sex, but also created legal barriers that blocked the "advancement of women in business and industry."[21]

By the onset of the Great Depression, support for the ERA came from political feminists associated primarily with the National Woman's Party, an organization with a membership that was simultaneously declining and becoming more elitist. By the middle of the depression decade, the upper-class profile of the pro-ERA feminist became even more pronounced when the National Federation of Business and Professional Women, the National Association of Women Lawyers, and the American Medical Women's Association joined the National Woman's Party's lobbying efforts on behalf of the amendment. Meanwhile, social feminists remained committed to cross-class alliances and used their organizations both within and outside of the government to lobby against the proposed amendment. By the mid-1940s the two leading black women's organizations had also divided over the issue of supporting the ERA. Largely on the basis of its preeminent spokeswoman, Mary Church Terrell, the National Association of Colored Women (the older of the two organizations) supported the ERA. Mary McLeod Bethune's National Council of Negro Women opposed the amendment.

Political splits also developed within feminism mirroring the class divisions that had begun to distinguish social feminists from political feminists. During the late 1920s and on into the 1930s, social feminists, who considered Eleanor Roosevelt one of their own, gravitated toward the Democratic party. When Franklin Roosevelt assumed the Presidency in the spring of 1933, the social feminists' agenda became the social welfare policy of the New Dealers; and for the first time, thanks to the influence of Eleanor Roosevelt and Molly Dewson (leader of the Women's Division of the Democratic party), significant numbers of social feminists filled the federal offices of the expanding social welfare agencies. Not to be outdone, political feminists working primarily through the National Woman's Party sought alliances with the Republican party and won a formal endorsement of the amendment in 1940.

Feminism entered a quieter period during the 1940s and 1950s as World War II and the Cold War refocused Americans' attention and energies. Understandably, social reform took a backseat to waging war against Japan, Germany, and Italy. In the years following the Allied victory in World War II, however, equity issues for women and people of color did not reclaim the sympathies of the American people or the interest of the country's political leaders. Instead, the politics of the Cold War abroad and at home rendered social reform and social justice movements "suspect."

Following World War II, the term "feminism" fell out of favor even among long-standing feminist organizations. In 1946 the National League of Women Voters explicitly renounced its affiliation with the feminist movement and within a few years had severed its ties with the Women's Joint Congressional Committee. In 1947, under the management of director Frieda Miller, the Women's Bureau sought to separate its agenda for working women from any activity that smacked of "women's rights."[22] The rush to distance oneself from the feminist label also included Margaret Chase Smith (R-Maine) and Helen Gahagan Douglas (D-California), leading women members of Congress from both sides of the political aisle. Women politicians (whose numbers had remained fairly steady in Congress since the 1930s, ranging between eight and eleven members) may have spurned the term, but they did not completely turn their backs on the issue of equity for women. According to historian Susan Hartmann, "every congress-woman sponsored at least one piece of legislation designed to remove discriminations against women or to advance their opportunities."[23] Still, no new feminist issue surfaced with the potential for encouraging coalition-building. The ERA remained a highly partisan issue among the female congressional delegation; a brief attempt in 1947 to rally support for the "Status Bill," which aimed at eliminating sex discrimination in the law without nullifying protective labor legislation, failed.[24]

Female members of Congress may have hoped that by disavowing the feminist label, they could shield themselves and their careers from the anticommunist hysteria sweeping the nation in the 1950s. If such was the case, they had miscalculated the extent to which this fixation gripped America's political culture. The Red Scare claimed many political innocents among elected and appointed officials.

Red-baiting, false accusations of communist sympathies, was so divisive that it created internal divisions within feminism. Although several women's organizations came under the scrutiny of the House Committee on Un-American Activities (which investigated suspected communist subversion), some individuals within these associations were not above using anticommunism to win support for their cause. According to historian Leila Rupp and sociologist Verta Taylor, the National Woman's Party made use of this strategy by exploiting the American Communist Party's and the American Labor Movement's opposition to the ERA in order to win support for the amendment among conservative legislators.[25]

The taint of anticommunism also seeped into the ranks of black women activists. Mary McLeod Bethune survived an encounter with the House Committee on Un-American Activities in the early 1940s; following her brush with this congressional committee, Bethune became more protective of her organization, the National Council of Negro Women. When a House Committee on Un-American Activities report linked one of the organization's former officers and lifetime members, Charlotte Hawkins Brown, to two "subversive" groups, Bethune took Brown to task for endangering the National Council of Negro Women's reputation. Bethune not only reminded Brown that it was the policy of the National Council of Negro Women "to avoid direct or indirect association or affiliation with Communist front groups or subversive activities" but also requested a statement outlining Brown's relationship with the suspect group.[26]

Still, students need to treat the historical record with some care lest they overemphasize the constraints that the politically conservative postwar era had on feminism. Feminist activity may not have taken center stage during the decade and a half following World War II, but neither was its run cancelled. With little support from political leaders and disseminators of popular culture, diverse groups of women continued working on behalf of what they defined as "women's issues": peace, labor, social justice, women's rights. Feminism (like other movements for social change) was not very "popular" during the 1940s and 1950s. Its presence in American life during this period may have been ignored, dismissed, or discounted, but it endured.

To paraphrase historian Susan Ware's observations, historians have documented a pattern of intense feminist activity amid more generalized eras of social change in America; conversely, historians also have noted that feminist agitation appears to lessen as the reform climate weakens.[27] Thus, during the first half of the twentieth century, feminism was at its strongest during the Progressive era (1900–1920) and the New Deal (1933–1938) and at its weakest during the waning of the reform spirit that characterized the years following the conclusion of World War I (1918–1933) and World War II (1945–1960).

The conservatism, constraints, and consensus that marked the 1950s proved to be not only short-lived but also erroneous. Between 1954 and 1957 the stirrings of the civil rights movement and President Eisenhower's decision to support the newly established anticommunist government in South Vietnam planted seeds of change that would bear fruit in the next decade. On January 20, 1961, that very call for change echoed across America. Observing that "the torch has been passed to a new generation of Americans," the youthful, energetic, and optimistic John F. Kennedy used the occasion of his inaugural address to issue a challenge to the American people: "Ask not what your country can do for you, ask what you can do for your country." The nation listened; among those responding were black Americans, college students, and women. The moment for *Liberation* had arrived.

## NOTES

1. Judith Hole and Ellen Levine, *Rebirth of Feminism* (New York: Quadrangle Books, Inc., 1971), p. 123.

2. Robin Morgan, ed., *Sisterhood Is Powerful: An Anthology of Writings from the Women's Liberation Movement* (New York: Random House, 1970), pp. 520–24.

3. In keeping with the reality of work and family life among the "baby boom generation" (1946–1963), Lois works outside the home selling real estate (a "woman's job" by the 1980s) and Hi occasionally cooks dinner for the family when Lois works late. Chance Browne is careful not to stretch gender boundaries too far. When Hi cooks dinner, he wears a frilly apron and sometimes burns the food. Naturally, the children hate dad's cooking and long for mom's return to the kitchen.

4. Chance Brown, "Hi & Lois" King Features Syndicate, November 14, 1996.

5. Cynthia Harrison, *On Account of Sex: The Politics of Women's Issues, 1945–1968* (Berkeley: University of California Press, 1988), p. 19 and Susan M. Hartmann, *From Margin to Mainstream: American Women and Politics since 1960* (Philadelphia: Temple University Press, 1989), p. 154.

6. Nancy F. Cott, *The Grounding of Modern Feminism* (New Haven: Yale University Press, 1987), pp. 3–4, 13–15.

7. Ruth Bordin, *Woman and Temperance: The Quest for Power and Liberty, 1873–1900* (Philadelphia: Temple University Press, 1981).

8. Estelle Freedman, "Separatism as Strategy: Female Institution Building and American Feminism, 1870–1930," *Feminist Studies* V (1979): 512–29 and Kathryn Kish Sklar, "Hull House in the 1890s: A Community of Women Reformers," *Signs* X (1985): 657–77.

9. Cott, *Modern Feminism*, pp. 29–34; Glenda Gilmore, *Gender and Jim Crow: Women and the Politics of White Supremacy in North Carolina, 1896–1920* (Chapel Hill: University of North Carolina Press, 1996); and Dorothy M. Brown, *Setting a Course: American Women in the 1920s* (Boston: Twayne Publishers, 1987), pp. 49–52.

10. Brown, *Setting a Course*, p. 52. Brown gives 1919 as the founding date of the National League of Women Voters (LWV). Nancy Cott cites a 1920 date.

11. Brown, *Setting a Course*, pp. 52–54; Cott, *Modern Feminism*, p. 98. According to a survey of twenty of the most industrialized nations in the world conducted by the Children's Bureau in 1918, the United States ranked eighteenth in maternal mortality rates and eleventh in infant mortality rates. Between 1921 and 1929 U.S. rates in both areas dropped only to rise again when the Sheppard-Towner Act was not renewed. See Cott's analysis of the mystique surrounding the "woman's vote" during the 1920s in *Modern Feminism*, pp. 99–114.

12. Susan Ware, *Holding Their Own: American Women in the 1930s* (Boston: Twayne Publishers, 1982), pp. 98, 105–7.

13. Marjorie Spruill Wheeler, *New Women of the New South: The Leaders of the Woman Suffrage Movement in the Southern States* (Oxford: Oxford University Press, 1993).

14. Rosalyn Terborg-Penn, "Discontented Black Feminists: Prelude and Postscript to the Passage of the Nineteenth Amendment," in Lois Scharf and Joan M. Jensen, eds., *Decades of Discontent: The Women's Movement, 1920–1940* (Boston: Northeastern University Press, 1987), pp. 265–67.

15. Terborg-Penn, "Discontented Black Feminists," pp. 263–64 and Paula Giddings, *When and Where I Enter: The Impact of Black Women on Race and Sex in America* (New York: William Morrow and Company, 1984), pp. 161–62.

16. Cott, *Modern Feminism*, pp. 69–71.

17. Ibid., pp. 70 and ch. 4, "Equal Rights and Economic Roles," pp. 117–42.

18. "Florence Kelly Explains Her Opposition to Full Legal Equality, 1922," in Mary Beth Norton and Ruth Alexander, eds., *Major Problems in American Women's History,* 2nd edition (Lexington: D.C. Heath and Company, 1996), p. 327.

19. Ibid, p. 327.

20. Joan Hoff, *Law, Gender, and Injustice: A Legal History of U.S. Women* (New York: New York University Press, 1991), p. 204.

21. Cott, *Modern Feminism*, pp. 124–26.

22. Lelia J. Rupp and Verta Taylor, *Survival in the Doldrums: The American Women's Rights Movement, 1945 to the 1960s* (Columbus: Ohio State University Press, 1990), pp. 48–49.

23. Susan M. Hartmann noted a significant difference between the women elected to national office prior to and after the start of World War II. Before 1940, "more than one-third of the women were appointed to or elected to serve the unexpired terms of their husbands." After 1940, more and more women were "winning election or reelection on their own." See Hartmann, *The Home Front and Beyond: American Women in the 1940s* (Boston: Twayne Publishers, 1982), pp. 149–52.

24. Harrison, *On Account of Sex*, pp. 26–30 and Hartmann, *The Home Front and Beyond*, p. 152.

25. Rupp and Taylor, *Survival in the Doldrums,* pp. 136–44.

26. Giddings, *When and Where I Enter*, pp. 249–50 and Letter From Mary McLeod Bethune to Arabella Denniston, April 5, 1946, in the Records of the National Council of Negro Women, Series 5, Box 4, Bethune Museum and Archives, Washington, D.C. (hereafter NCNW Records) and Mary McLeod Bethune to Charlotte Hawkins Brown, October 23, 1949, Series 5, Box 5, Folder 83, NCNW Records. Brown had attended a Win the Peace Conference held in Washington, D.C., in 1946 and was a member of the Congress of American Women, an affiliate of the Women's International Democratic Federation.

27. Ware, *Holding Their Own*, p. 88.

# 2

# Equal Rights, NOW!

If the moment for liberation had arrived with the election of John F. Kennedy to the White House in 1960, it soon became apparent to the president's women supporters that the "feminist moment" would be delayed. Kennedy was neither a friend nor foe of feminism; instead, he appeared indifferent. The president's benign neglect, which angered many loyal women Democrats and feminist activists, was reflected in the dearth of women appointed to anything but minor positions in the new administration and the apparent absence of a coherent policy on women's issues. Indeed, critics noted that in many ways Kennedy's record on women's appointments was worse than that of his four immediate predecessors.

Despite Kennedy's catchy rhetoric that emphasized change, his dealing with women seemed decidedly old-fashioned. This was precisely the point made by journalist Doris Fleeson in her *New York Post* column of December 20, 1960. Responding to the announcement of Kennedy's cabinet appointments, she quipped: "At this stage, it appears that for women the New Frontiers are the old frontiers."[1] Subsequent White House releases of administrative appointees, meant to pacify women activists, had the opposite effect when the lists reconfirmed Kennedy's poor record.[2]

Still, despite the evidence pointing to tokenism, the abortive Kennedy years defy easy analysis when it comes to evaluating actual gains made on behalf of women. Even as scholars acknowledge Kennedy's shortcomings, his administration also earns high marks. After all, how could a president credited with establishing the President's Commission on the Status of Women and supporting passage of the Equal Pay Act (1963) be labeled indifferent to feminist issues? All well and good, note feminist critics. If, however, the president was sensitive to feminists' demands for equity before the law, why then did he deliberately ignore the problem of sex discrimination when he urged Congress to consider "sweeping new civil rights legislation in June 1963"?[3] A paradox? Perhaps.

When it came to supporting feminist issues, President Lyndon Baines Johnson also appeared to drag his feet, especially during the early years of his administration. In the wake of the Kennedy assassination in 1963, Johnson pledged support for the civil rights measure that remained bottled up in a reluctant Congress, but he too, like his predecessor, remained cold toward including any provision supporting women's rights. Johnson's hesitancy in linking the advancement of blacks with women's rights was not without historical precedent. In the aftermath of the American Civil War, Republicans charged with drafting the Fourteenth and Fifteenth Amendments (granting civil and voting rights to black Americans) also had turned a "deaf ear" to feminists' pleas for inclusion.

According to many a popular and scholarly retelling, when the famous amendment prohibiting sex discrimination in employment was added to Title VII of the 1964 Civil Rights Act, it was included as a "joke" by a conservative southern congressman in an effort to derail the entire bill (just as Johnson had feared).[4] Much to the dismay of those who hoped to scuttle the legislation, however, the bill passed intact, and feminists were euphoric. By the end of the decade, Title VII would become one of the most important legal weapons in women's battle for economic equality, but not before the initial optimism generated by the bill's passage had turned into disappointment and frustration. A section of the legislation had called for the creation of a federal agency, the Equal Employment Opportunity Commission (EEOC), charged with investigating complaints about possible violations of Title VII and enforcing compliance with the new law. In a delicious example of political irony fraught with far-reaching implications for feminism, the EEOC's willful indifference to pursuing sex discrimination cases became a critical factor in the 1966 resurgence of a mass feminist movement similar to that which existed at the height of the Progressive era (1900–1920).

By the end of the decade, this revitalization produced two distinct ideological strains within the larger feminist movement: liberal feminism and radical feminism. Liberal feminism's pragmatic focus on "equal rights before the law" provided the foundation for such centralized organizations as the National Organization for Women (NOW) and the Women's Equity Action League. In stark contrast stood radical feminism's espousal of "liberation ideology," which became the raison d'être for the formation of grass-roots organizations such as The Feminists, New York Radical Women, Women's International Terrorist Conspiracy from Hell, and Bread and Roses. Unlike NOW or the Women's Equity Action League, these localized "radical" feminist groups were not known for their staying power, and by the early 1980s, most of them either had disappeared or been transformed.

## OLD ISSUES, NEW SOLUTIONS?: THE PRESIDENT'S COMMISSION ON THE STATUS OF WOMEN AND THE EQUAL PAY ACT

When John Kennedy issued Executive Order 10980 on December 14, 1961, establishing the President's Commission on the Status of Women, the concept of women's liberation was far removed from the minds of the fifteen women and eleven men appointed to the commission. Indeed, Kennedy's charge to the commission contained contradictory statements about the position of women in American society. Noting that "prejudices and outmoded customs act as barriers to the full realization of women's basic rights," the president called on the commission to develop "recommendations for overcoming discriminations in government and private employment on the basis of sex."[5] At the same time, however, Kennedy's statement reaffirmed traditional cultural values upholding the primacy of wifehood and motherhood when he requested that the commission develop "recommendations for services which will enable women to continue their role as wives and mothers."[6]

The driving force behind the President's Commission on the Status of Women was Esther Peterson, the highest ranking woman in the Kennedy Administration. Peterson served not only as the Director of the Women's Bureau but also as the Assistant Secretary of Labor. Peterson was a longtime labor organizer and lobbyist, an ardent Democrat and member of Kennedy's presidential campaign staff, and a social feminist. She was instrumental in persuading Kennedy to create the commission, and she and her boss, Secretary of Labor Arthur J. Goldberg, handpicked its membership. The commission included five cabinet members, the chairman of the Civil Service Commission, women members of Congress, college presidents, labor leaders, and representatives from some of the leading women's voluntary organizations.[7] Former First Lady and Ambassador to the United Nations Eleanor Roosevelt chaired the commission until her death in October 1962, but her position was largely ceremonial. Instead, Peterson, who served as the commission's executive vice chair, did the bulk of the work in guiding the commission.

The commission's actual work occurred within seven committees: Civil and Political Rights, Education, Federal Employment, Home and Community, Private Employment, Protective Labor Legislation, and Social Insurance and Taxes (the most politically sensitive committee was Civil and Political Rights largely because its agenda included the proposed Equal Rights Amendment [ERA]). Each committee had at least two commission members assigned to it with one serving as the chair. Additional committee members (all told approximately eighty-nine individuals served) were drawn from fields similar to those of the commission members: education, labor, the professions, public service (state and federal), and women's voluntary organizations. The commission also sponsored four "consultations" at which the following issues were discussed and summaries produced: New Patterns in Volunteer Work, Private Employment Opportunities, Portrayal of Women by the Mass Media, and Problems of Negro Women.[8]

According to her memoir, Esther Peterson was determined to derail the pro-ERA campaign, a strategy that was central to her lobbying efforts on behalf of establishing the commission. She did so because she firmly believed that a conservative Supreme Court (one hostile to labor concerns) would use the ERA to strike down protective labor legislation for women. Thus, it became necessary to foil any effort by political feminists, who were pro-ERA, to secure the Kennedy administration's support for the amendment. Peterson claimed that she "bent over backwards to keep the commission politically and geographically balanced," but it also was apparent that she stacked the commission with individuals whose views on the ERA closely mirrored her own. Indeed, the only openly pro-ERA advocate selected for the commission was Marguerite Rawalt, an attorney and past president of two pro-ERA women's organizations. Outmaneuvered by Peterson, representatives from women's organizations favoring the ERA were miffed, and some tried without success to secure a seat on the commission.[9]

The Committee on Civil and Political Rights, chaired by Congresswoman Edith Green (D-Oregon), took up the issue of "equality of rights under the law" and focused its attention on "the existence of laws and practices that discriminate against women" in such areas as jury selection, personal and property rights, and legal residence. Asserting the right of the federal and state government to "classify persons for the purposes of legislation," the committee insisted that this classification be based on "reasonable ground." In its deliberations, the committee took up several proposals for alleviating sex discrimination: legislative action at the state level, litigation aimed at overturning discriminatory laws that would be reviewed by the Supreme Court, and an equal rights amendment to the Constitution. The committee's summary dutifully reported on the controversy some of these proposals engendered. "Divergent viewpoints on these methods, particularly among national women's organizations and labor union groups were made known in documents lodged with the Commission and in oral presentations in two hearings."[10]

Compromise between pro- and anti-ERA forces appeared in the unlikely form of African American lawyer and civil rights activist, Pauli Murray. In essence, Murray argued that key elements of the Fourteenth Amendment protected individuals from arbitrary sex discrimination and that a test case should be sought to validate this principle by the Supreme Court.[11] Murray hoped for a ruling that would distinguish between laws that were appropriate when applied to women (those that "protected family and maternal functions") and laws that prohibited women from "participating fully in public life" (prohibitions on jury duty). The question arose among committee members as to what the next step would be if the Supreme Court "refused to rule favorably in a test case."[12] Some members argued that the committee might recommend supporting the ERA at some time in the future. Others vehemently dissented because they believed that such a statement was tantamount to supporting the ERA. In the end, the committee's decision read: "Since the Commission is convinced that the U.S. Constitution now embodies equality of rights for men and women, we conclude that a constitutional amendment need not now be sought in order to establish this principle. But judicial clarification is imperative in order that remaining ambiguities with respect to the constitutional protection of women's rights be eliminated."[13]

With this compromise, the President's Commission on the Status of Women closed the gap between old-line social and political feminists. Both sides agreed that the Constitution implicitly guaranteed women equal rights under the law, and both sides were willing to pursue the route of looking for a suitable test to make that point. Before such a case could be made, however, other events conspired to render obsolete social feminists' concerns about safeguarding protective labor legislation. Labor leaders, Democrats, and social feminists, including Esther Peterson, eventually withdrew their opposition to the ERA "after Title VII of the 1964 Civil Rights Act outlawed discrimination based on 'sex' and [subsequent] court cases disallowed protective labor legislation."[14]

The President's Commission on the Status of Women issued its report to President Kennedy on October 11, 1963, the birthday of its recently deceased chairwoman, Eleanor Roosevelt. In keeping with the Cold War mentality, the report represented a careful balancing act between documenting discrimination against women and recording their "progress in a free, democratic society."[15] The commission's conclusions reflected this ambiguity. Its recommendations ranged from limited initiatives to some that were, potentially, far-reaching.

The commission's findings did little to alter the long-standing cultural assumption that a woman's "biology" determined her social destiny. A woman's primary obiligation was to care for her husband and children; any desire for furthering educational or career goals automatically took a backseat to the needs of her family. Indeed, so strongly did the commission hold to the cultural imperative that "a woman's place was in the home" that it found it "regrettable" when mothers with young children sought work outside the home. The committee, however, did part company with tradition by recognizing that mothers who had to work outside the home needed adequate child-care services. Still, the Committee on Home and Community stopped short of endorsing federally funded child care.

The other six committees of the President's Commission on the Status of Women weighed in with their recommendations: expansion of skilled homemaking services; education for the mature woman and homemaker; standardizing states' labor legislation and expansion of protective labor legislation (minimum wage and maximum hours requirements); changes in the social security system and in tax laws that would increase benefits for widows and dependents of single-headed (female) working households; mandating federal civil service hiring practices based solely on merit; a request for an executive order affirming equal opportunity for women in private industry in the areas of hiring, training, and promotion; and an endorsement of a long-standing objective of the Women's Bureau, equal pay for comparable work legislation. On this last point, the commission's recommendation actually became law four months before transmitting its final report to the president. Unfortunately for women workers, the new law was far more restrictive than the commission had intended.

On June 10, 1963, the Equal Pay Act reached President Kennedy's desk ready for his signature. The concept of equal pay for equal work was not new in the 1960s. In its first appearance in 1945, the bill was quite modest, calling for a prohibition on wage discrimination in interstate commerce. The fight for passage was led by the Women's Bureau with the full support, initially, of the labor movement whose leaders hoped that the bill's passage would forestall employers from substituting the cheaper labor of women for men. Once, however, the postwar labor market returned to its "prewar stratification by sex, the threat of women undercutting wages and taking men's jobs diminished" and organized labor stopped testifying before Congress on behalf of the bill, although its leadership continued paying lip service to the idea.[16] The Women's Bureau maintained its campaign for an equal pay measure throughout the 1950s and even won support for the concept from the Eisenhower administration, but the bill never got out of the congressional committee to which it was assigned.

A new president and a more sympathetic congressional committee chairman gave the Women's Bureau and the President's Commission on the Status of Women renewed hope, but the bill signed by Kennedy was much more limited in scope than that which the Women's Bureau and the commission had envisioned. In its final form the bill did more to raise expectations among women activists than it did in redressing discriminatory wage practices. The bill approved by Congress in 1963 excluded women workers at both ends of the pay scale (agricultural, domestic, executive, administrative, and professional workers), exempted employers with less than twenty-five employees, eliminated an independent enforcement agency, made no reference to discriminatory hiring practices, and substituted the clause "equal pay for equal work" for the original language of the measure which called for "equal pay for comparable work."[17]

During the period in which the Equal Pay Act was making its way through the legislative process, approximately 24 million women (representing one-third of all American women) worked for wages. Three-quarters of all women workers were "clustered in 57 occupations: 30 white-collar, 14 service and 13 blue-collar or farm. Women made up over 90 percent of workers in 17 of these occupations and at least 75 percent in the remaining 31."[18] As late as 1970, six out of every ten women workers still labored in occupations in which they constituted an 80 percent majority. In 1963 when the largest concentration of women workers could be found in clerical and service occupations, they were significantly underrepresented in business, the professions, government service, and industry.[19]

The employment situation for black women was far worse, suffering as they did from "double discrimination." The vast majority of black women were employed in domestic and service occupations with clerical, sales, and many skilled jobs closed to them. At the opposite end of the occupational scale, because of the unique interplay between racism and sexism, more black women than black men found professional positions (albeit in segregated offices and institutions).[20] According to evidence gathered by the President's Commission on the Status of Women, labor force stratification by sex and race accounted for the fact that in 1961, full-time women workers earned sixty cents for every dollar men earned, and black women earned only seventy percent of what white women earned.[21] In 1963 "equal pay for equal work" had a limited effect on all women workers as occupational stratification persisted; by 1965 women's wages had slipped to fifty-eight cents for every dollar men earned.[22]

Although the Kennedy administration's two crowning achievements for women resulted in few immediate gains, the groundwork was being laid at the federal and state levels for the reemergence of a powerful, multifaceted feminist movement. Shortly before his death, Kennedy issued an executive order formalizing two of the President's Commission on the Status of Women's final recommendations: the creation of a cabinet-level Inter-Departmental Committee on the Status of Women and the establishment of a Citizens' Advisory Council on the Status of Women. The former was staffed by the heads of several federal agencies and reported to a member of the president's cabinet, and the latter initially included former members of the recently disbanded President's Commission on the Status of Women. These agencies were charged with moving forward with the agenda set by the commission and with formulating new proposals.[23]

The organizational infrastructure and leadership provided at the federal level by the Inter-Departmental Committee on the Status of Women and the Citizens' Advisory Council were matched at the state level. Even before the President's Commission on the Status of Women had completed its work, local chapters of several national women's organizations were urging governors to create parallel state organizations. By August 1963 over two dozen states had approved the establishment of such commissions, and by 1967 a network of State Commissions on the Status of Women stretched across all fifty states. In 1964 the Inter-Departmental Committee on the Status of Women brought representatives from these state commissions together in the nation's capital. This meeting, which became an annual event, inadvertently contributed to a revitalized feminist movement. Each June women activists from across the country would meet in Washington, D.C., to compare notes on the status of women in their respective states, share strategies for promoting change, and renew friendships.

Unbeknownst to these women, they were also laying the foundation for a national feminist organization. All that the feminist movement lacked was an emotional reference point, an easily identifiable leader, and a frustration born of unmet rising expectations. Between 1964 and 1966 these conditions coalesced with the publication of Betty Friedan's best-seller, *The Feminine Mystique*, the hard-fought battle to bring women under the protection of the 1964 Civil Rights Act, and the Johnson administration's failure to invoke Title VII of that act in cases pertaining to sex discrimination.[24] Betty Friedan's presence in Washington, D.C., at the June 1966 meeting of the State Commissions on the Status of Women was hardly an accident. The time was ripe for NOW.

## INCIPIENT FEMINISM AND "THE PROBLEM THAT HAS NO NAME"

By 1966 *The Feminine Mystique* was a staple item in many a suburban household, and its author, Betty Friedan, a familiar figure among the small band of feminist activists living and working in the nation's capital. An overnight sensation, *The Feminine Mystique* was based on the almost two hundred responses to a questionnaire Friedan had mailed to her Smith College classmates (Class of 1942) in preparation for their fifteenth class reunion. The book identified and popularized "the problem that has no name" that afflicted not only Friedan's Smith classmates but also hundreds of thousands of educated, white, middle-class suburban women who had exchanged their diploma for a marriage license. That "problem" was a growing sense of disquietude with an ideology that encouraged middle-class white women to "seek fulfillment [solely] as wives and mothers."[25]

Why did millions of white American women succumb to this "feminine mystique?" Since the end of World War II, books and articles written by "experts" (male and female), advertisements for consumer products, the mass media, and political speeches touted the ranch-style home in the suburbs as the natural domain of white women. Black women were excluded from these messages because "positioned on the fulcrum of race and sex, they were expected to perform different roles." Indeed, many a white suburban household employed a black woman domestic.[26]

According to Friedan, postwar American culture urged white women "to pity the neurotic, unfeminine, unhappy women who wanted to be poets or physicists or presidents." Instead of following the siren song of "careers, higher education, and political rights," white women were encouraged to dream of being "perfect wives and mothers with five children and a beautiful house." "The problem" was one that each suburban housewife struggled with alone, until Friedan named it, collectivized it, and popularized it. "As she made the beds, shopped for groceries, matched slipcover materials, ate peanut butter sandwiches with her children, chauffeured Cub Scouts and Brownies, [and] lay beside her husband at night, she was afraid to ask the silent question—Is this all? What kind of woman was she if she did not feel this mysterious fulfillment waxing the kitchen floor?"[27]

By the mid-1960s, "the problem" confronting middle-class, married, white women was far more complex than that of a stifling cultural message. This cohort of women had married earlier than their mothers' generation (Friedan's study put the average age of marriage for a woman at twenty) and had begun and finished their child-bearing responsibilities sooner than their mothers' generation.[28] Once their children reached school age, many of these women deviated from the pattern of their mothers' lives in yet another way: they went (back) to work. In the years following World War II, acquiring and maintaining a middle-class life style—a home, a car, a television, and a nest egg for the children's college education—increasingly depended on a two-income family.[29] By 1960, 30 percent of married women worked for wages, "39% of all mothers with school-age children were in the labor force," and among middle-class families earning $10,000 a year, two-thirds depended on a working wife.[30] By 1962 a popular women's magazine had identified this trend in women's employment as "crypto-feminism."[31]

The cost of juggling two divergent expectations, one based on economic "necessity" and the other on cultural assumptions, was too high for some women. Drug and alcohol consumption soared in the suburbs. Tranquilizers became especially popular among the drugs' targeted population: women. According to one study, tranquilizers were "nonexistent in 1955," but by the end of the decade, physicians were treating "the problem that has no name" with 1.15 million pounds of drugs with such trademark names as Valium.[32] That some women felt stifled by the cultural constraints of wifehood and motherhood was born out by their response to a contest sponsored by a woman's magazine in 1960. When the September 1960 issue of *Redbook* urged mothers to respond (for $500) to the article "Why Young Mothers Feel Trapped," the editors received over 24,000 letters.[33]

## MALE BUNNIES AND HOUSE MOTHERS?: TITLE VII, FEMINIST ANGER, AND NOW

Title VII of the 1964 Civil Rights Act could not rescue women trapped in suburban homes by the feminine mystique, but it did hold out the promise of an escape route out of the pink-collar ghetto. Traditional cultural assumptions about womanhood probably contributed to men's refusal to hire women in "nontraditional" jobs in the 1950s and 1960s, but institutionalized job discrimination prevented women from applying for these positions. Until Title VII made the practice illegal, newspapers' classified job advertisements (the "want ads") maintained separate postings for "male" and "female" jobs. While the men's section listed positions in the better paying, high-status professions (engineering, dentistry, and the law), in business management and accounting, and in commission sales of durable goods, the women's section offered job seekers opportunities in domestic work, in clerical and noncommission sales positions, and in the poorer paid "helping" professions (nursing, social work, elementary school teachers, librarians). Title VII defined this as well as other employment practices as discriminatory and therefore illegal, but until the five-person EEOC took its charge of enforcement seriously, the 4,000 cases of sex discrimination filed by women workers between 1964 and 1966 were treated as frivolous complaints.

Making light of women's concerns was hardly a new national pastime. Even as mass media publications were busy printing articles similar to the one that appeared in the 1960 *Redbook* issue, their stories trivialized women's concerns by offering superficial explanations of "the problem." Moreover, this tendency toward ridicule was not confined to the popular press. Indeed, the male political establishment had responded in a similar manner when Congressman Howard W. Smith, the eighty-one-year-old Democrat from Virginia, sought to amend Title VII of the 1964 Civil Rights act by adding the word "sex" during congressional debates in February 1964.

By all accounts, including Smith's own, his effort was intended not only as a joke but also as a serious attempt to doom the civil rights legislation. Smith, an ardent segregationist, had hoped that his amendment to Title VII (which in its original form prohibited job discrimination based on race, color, religion, or national origin) would trivialize the bill's importance and garner enough opposition to defeat the bill. Smith got the response he had sought—laughter; but the result of his action was not what he had intended. Congresswoman Martha Griffiths (D-Michigan), a former member of the National Woman's Party, whose leaders actually had approached Smith with the request that he make the "sex amendment" proposal, had anticipated this action and prepared for it. Her timely and clever response—"I presume that if there had been any necessity to have pointed out that women were a second-class sex, the laughter would have proved it"—and her adroit questioning of the opposition resulted in the improbable.[34] In the House, the amendment to Title VII passed by a vote of 168–133, and the entire bill passed by a margin of 160 votes (290–130). Opposition to the legislation surfaced in the Senate, including some last minute attempts by southern Democrats to derail the bill by adding the word "sex" to several other provisions, but all attempts proved futile, and President Johnson signed the bill into law on July 2, 1964.

Women's inclusion in the 1964 Civil Rights legislation did not mean acceptance of gender equality before the law by either the American people or their elected officials. Instead, the small band of feminists within the government grew increasingly frustrated by the EEOC's willful neglect and "virulent hostility" toward sex discrimination.[35] Title VII contained a clause, the *bona fide occupational qualification* (*bfoq*), that exempted employers from hiring women for positions that "required" a man (for example, an attendant in a men's bathroom). This loophole, continuing pressure from unions and the Department of Labor to maintain protective labor legislation for women, and a lingering belief by some EEOC members that the sex amendment had passed as a joke made compliance in sex discrimination cases moot. Commission members, newspapers, and participants at a 1965 White House conference on the ramifications of Title VII made the sex provision the butt of their jokes. Were men "entitled" to women secretaries? Would Playboy Clubs be forced to hire "male bunnies?" Would sorority houses be forced to hire "male house mothers?" Following the White House conference, the press actually dubbed Title VII "the bunny law." Then, in a 3–2 decision in 1966, the EEOC delivered a coup de grâce to feminists' hopes for equal opportunity in employment: Employers and newspapers could continue segregating job postings by sex, but not by race.[36] The two votes favoring the ban on sex-segregated "want ads" were cast by Aileen Hernandez, the lone woman on the commission, and Richard Graham.

By June 1966 Congresswoman Martha Griffiths' anger toward the jocular sentiments of the press and government officials toward sex discrimination in employment had reached its boiling point, and her timing was perfect. Betty Friedan was in Washington, D.C., gathering research for a book on sex discrimination and Title VII; Richard Graham's term on the EEOC was up and feminists wanted him retained; and the third annual meeting of the State Commissions on the Status of Women was about to get underway. On June 20, Griffiths rose from her seat in the House of Representatives and in an hour-long address denounced the EEOC for "its arbitrary arrogance, disregard of the law and hostility to the human rights of women."[37]

When the annual meeting of the State Commissions on the Status of Women convened on June 28, participants were handed copies of Griffiths' speech. On the second night of the conference, fifteen women crowded into Betty Friedan's hotel room. Discussion centered on two resolutions, one urging Richard Graham's reappointment to the EEOC and the other calling for enforcement of Title VII, and the pros and cons of founding a feminist action group independent of the state commissions. After heated debate, the women decided to hold off on forming an organization but agreed to introduce the two resolutions for a vote on the final day of the conference.[38]

The next day, in a sudden reversal of the decisions arrived at the night before, NOW was born when Esther Peterson and two other members of President Johnson's administration blocked the introduction of the two resolutions. Commandeering two tables at the luncheon, each woman anted up $5.00 for dues for the new organization, and Betty Friedan proposed its name. Before scattering to make their plane connections, the women agreed on their purpose—"to take the actions needed to bring women into the mainstream of American society, now, full equality for women, in fully equal partnership with men"— and named Kathryn Clarenbach, head of the Wisconsin Commission on Women, interim chair.[39] Before departing the nation's capital, the twenty-eight founding mothers initiated two actions: Each EEOC commissioner received a telegram calling for the rescinding of sex-segregated job postings, and President Johnson received a telegram urging the reappointment of Richard Graham. June 1966 was a turning point in that decade's feminist revival. With the formation of NOW, control over the feminist agenda shifted from the federal government to an independent organization; and whereas the government had moved slowly to institute change, the National Organization for Women believed in action, *now*.

The twenty-eight original members of NOW moved quickly. Within four months, thirty women prepared to descend on Washington, D.C., carrying with them the names of 300 charter members. At the national press conference called for October 29, 1966, Betty Friedan was named president of the new feminist organization. From the beginning, NOW's membership and early leadership included men. This policy reflected the integration model of more moderate civil rights groups, like the National Association for the Advancement of Colored People (NAACP), with whom NOW has been compared. From its inception, NOW also sought to attract prominent black women to its membership; but although Pauli Murray and Aileen Hernandez were charter members, the organization was dominated by and reflected the interests of middle-class white women.

NOW's initial agenda followed closely that set by the President's Commission on the Status of Women. Task forces were created to gather evidence of discrimination and propose solutions in education, employment, the family, the media, politics and the law, and religion. Despite its middle-class orientation, NOW also demonstrated a concern for poor women by creating a task force to explore their special problems. Similar to the structure of the commission, NOW's founders expected policies to be hammered out at the annual meetings with the bulk of the actual work being carried out by the officers, board of directors, and task force leaders. NOW's leaders anticipated the formation of local chapters across the country, and expected that these chapters would choose to work on one of the seven task force issues that best reflected their local interests.

Even as NOW followed the President's Commission on the Status of Women's agenda, the feminist organization was breaking new ground in its analysis of women's "place" in American society. The commission's report had upheld traditional cultural assumptions that linked women's biological (reproductive) differences with men to women's unique social role: motherhood. NOW unequivocally rejected this "biology is destiny" argument. In its statement of purpose, NOW repudiated the "difference argument" long touted by old-line social feminists in favor of a theory of sameness based on the human condition of women and men.

## SUCCESS AND DIVISION: NOW, THE WOMEN'S EQUITY ACTION LEAGUE, AND THE FEMINISTS

By the end of its first year, NOW had worked diligently to gain national exposure and had increased its membership rolls to approximately 1,200 individuals. Recognition and growth came because the organization did not shy away from confrontational situations and because it got results. President Johnson had promised to appoint fifty women to significant posts in his administration. He had yet to deliver fully on that promise by 1966. Even before the ink had dried on the organization's charter, NOW's leaders visited several cabinet members to remind them of Johnson's verbal commitment. NOW also signaled its break with social feminists, labor leaders, and the Women's Bureau when its legal committee assigned Marguerite Rawalt (formerly with the President's Commission on the Status of Women) to handle two appeals stemming from an EEOC decision upholding protective legislation. NOW's opposition to protective labor legislation stemmed from a belief that this type of legislation, based on an assumption of "difference," actually did more harm than good for women workers. By 1968, when the EEOC agreed to explore this issue on a case-by-case review rather than by adopting a uniform policy, more and more women's groups (especially the State Commissions on the Status of Women) had begun to support NOW's position.

In that first year, NOW's leadership also weighed in on the side of a sex-based job discrimination complaint first brought before the EEOC by airline stewardesses in 1965 (and not resolved favorably until 1968). The case centered on a policy supported by all airlines that forced a stewardess to retire either when she married or when she reached age thirty-two, whereas no similar policy existed for stewards. In December 1966, NOW petitioned the EEOC to hold public hearings on sex-segregated "want ads," which the committee did five months later. When the EEOC continued to equivocate on this issue, NOW, in a surprise move, adopted the political tactic of direct action favored by some of the more militant civil rights groups like the Student Nonviolent Coordinating Committee. On August 30, 1967, NOW's New York chapter began picketing the office of the *New York Times* to protest the newspaper's sex-segregated jobs section. This single act was followed four months later with NOW organizing a National Day of Demonstration Against the EEOC. On December 14, local NOW chapters set up picket lines in at least a half a dozen cities with EEOC offices. Adverse publicity and continued pressure from New York NOW had their desired effect on the *New York Times*; the paper and several others in the New York area voluntarily ended sex-segregated "want ads." The EEOC finally ruled in favor of integrated ads in August 1968, but many papers continued segregating job postings until the Supreme Court ruled against this policy on June 21, 1973, in the *Pittsburgh Press Company v. the Human Relations Commission*.[40]

Still in its first year, NOW also claimed victory in persuading President Johnson to amend an executive order (EO 11246) issued in 1965 prohibiting discrimination based on race in federal employment and in companies receiving federal contracts. Soon after Johnson had issued this order, he was pressured by Esther Peterson and representatives from such old and venerable women's organizations as the National Federation of Business and Professional Women's Club, to bring his order under full compliance with Title VII. On October 13, 1967, President Johnson signed Executive Order 11375 prohibiting sex discrimination in federal employment and in companies receiving federal contracts.

Dissension soon surfaced within NOW's ranks from both ends of the political spectrum, and within two years of NOW's founding, new groups with more conservative and more radical leanings were formed. Conservative members were the first to break away from NOW; the impetus for their departure was the adoption, at the second annual conference held in November 1967, of NOW's Bill of Rights for 1968. At that meeting, six of the eight rights passed with little opposition; apparently all shades of feminism could support a ban on sex discrimination in employment, maternity leave rights in employment and social security benefits, tax deductions for home and child-care expenses for working parents, child-care centers, equal and unsegregated education, and equal job-training opportunities and allowances for poor women. Two rights passed only after bitter and protracted debates, and their passage led to a number of departures from NOW. The first one called for the United States Congress to recommend ratification of the ERA. The last right, which insisted that women have complete control over their bodies, called for repealing antiabortion and anticontraceptive laws.

By 1967 the majority of NOW's union women were in favor of the ERA. Title VII of the 1964 Civil Rights Act and NOW's subsequent pressure on the EEOC to overturn protective labor legislation had made opposition to the ERA a moot point. Still, as the labor women argued, although they favored the ERA, their unions did not support this position, yet. Many labor women, including NOW's secretary/treasurer Caroline Davis of the United Auto Workers were lobbying their unions to drop their anti-ERA stance, but until the unions capitulated on this issue, as one woman warned, union women might have to resign or take a "back seat" if NOW supported the amendment. That prediction proved true, and in the months that followed the second annual conference, the national structure was thrown into turmoil. Some union women did leave NOW; others retained their membership but became much less active. Caroline Davis fell into the latter category, but her withdrawal from "active duty" was disastrous for NOW. As secretary/treasurer, Davis had run NOW's correspondence out of her United Auto Workers' office (meaning that the union subsidized NOW's printing and mailing expenses). That perk ended with NOW's support for the ERA, a costly decision that left the national office scrambling for months for an alternate source of support. The irony is that by 1970, the United Auto Workers became the first union to endorse the ERA; and as union opposition to the ERA diminished, union women returned to active duty just in time for the legislative fight of their feminist lives: the ten-year ratification battle for the ERA.[41]

The last right, reproductive freedom, proved even more contentious than the conflict over ERA. When NOW voted to support an abortion plank, a number of women not only left the organization but also founded another feminist organization, the Women's Equity Action League. NOW's leaders took a big risk in 1967 when the organization came out in favor of repealing abortion laws. A more moderate position might have been to advocate for reforming abortion laws. Abortion reform had begun to gain some support by 1967, but repeal was still considered too radical. Reform laws regulated abortion, making the procedure more accessible to middle- and upper-class women, whereas repeal implied that all women had the right to make decisions about their reproductive life without interference from either the medical establishment or the state.

When Elizabeth Boyer, a lawyer from Ohio, left NOW's second annual conference in November 1967, she was determined to found an organization for women like herself, a professional woman from the American heartland. Organizing began in the spring of 1968, and by December the Women's Equity Action League was incorporated in Cleveland, Ohio, for the purpose of challenging sex discrimination in education, employment, and taxes. The league's philosophy was down-to-earth and pragmatic. "Give a woman a decent education, a decent paycheck and don't clobber her with unfair taxes, and she can survive pretty well," Boyer stated in a 1970 interview.[42] Within three years, The Women's Equity Action League had chapters in over forty states and, more so than NOW, represented the interests of elite, professional women. The league's contributions to feminism were significant. The organization played a critical role in orchestrating the public and backstage pressure needed to get the ERA out of the House Judiciary Committee in 1970 and made its most lasting imprint on feminism in gains made for women in higher education.

The exodus of radical women from NOW began at the third annual conference. On October 17, 1968, nine members of NOW's New York chapter left the organization to found "The October 17th Movement," later called The Feminists. Ti-Grace Atkinson, president of the New York chapter, precipitated the walkout when her proposal to decentralize NOW's organizational structure failed. Atkinson's proposal called for replacing NOW's hierarchical leadership—president, vice president, secretary, treasurer, board of directors—with a more egalitarian model in which "decision making would be chosen by lot and rotated frequently."[43] Not surprisingly, Atkinson lost this vote. According to several written accounts, Atkinson and her group had a second reason for their departure from NOW. Apparently, radical feminists believed that despite NOW's stance on abortion repeal, the organization's unwillingness to confront the churches' opposition to abortion, especially the Catholic church, was indicative of NOW's "reformist" tendencies, which radical women were beginning to reject.

The band of nine radical feminists who departed from NOW in 1968 represented something new and different from the liberal, equality feminism of NOW or the Women's Equity Action League. Moreover, the defectors from NOW who began the "October 17th Movement" were hardly unique, even in 1968. The previous year, a group of young women disenchanted with the male-dominated structure of the "Student Left" had formed a radical feminist group in Chicago and another one in New York. The latter, known as the New York Radical Women, had recently staged the 1968 Miss America Beauty Pageant demonstration. In addition to these newly formed groups, another group soon catapulted itself into the public limelight. On October 31, 1968, members of the Women's International Terrorist Conspiracy From Hell dressed themselves as witches and descended on Wall Street delivering hexes. What was happening? *Women's Liberation*, rooted in a political tradition far different from the political origins of liberal feminism, was making its appearance on the American (feminist) scene. At the same time, the proliferation of, and divisions among, the various women's rights organizations suggested that there was no single route to achieving women's liberation.

## NOTES

1. Cynthia Harrison, *On Account of Sex: The Politics of Women's Issues, 1945–1968* (Berkeley: University of California Press, 1988), p. 76.

2. Ibid., pp. 76–77.

3. Carl M. Brauer, "Women Activists, Southern Conservatives, and the Prohibition of Sex Discrimination in Title VII of the 1964 Civil Rights Act," *The Journal of Southern History* 49 (1983), p. 39.

4. Ibid., p. 45.

5. *American Women: Report on the President's Commission on the Status of Women, 1963* (Washington, D.C.: U.S. Government Printing Office, 1963), pp. 76, 85.

6. Ibid., p. 76

7. Ibid., p. 85.

8. Ibid., pp. 77–83.

9. Esther Peterson, with Winifred Conkling, *Restless: The Memoirs of Labor and Consumer Activist Esther Peterson* (Washington, D.C.: Caring Publishing, 1995), pp. 106–7.

10. *American Women,* pp. 44–45, 77.

11. Pauli Murray, *Song in a Weary Throat: An American Pilgrimage* (New York: Harper and Row Publishers, 1987), pp. 349–51; and *American Women*, pp. 44–45, 77.

12. Harrison, *On Account of Sex*, pp. 130–32.

13. *American Women*, p. 45.

14. Blanche Linden-Ward and Carol Hurd Green, *Changing the Future: American Women in the 1960s* (New York: Twayne Publishers, 1993), p. 7.

15. *American Women*, p. iv. Linden-Ward and Green, *Changing the Future*, pp. 5–6 make the point about reading this document within the framework of Cold War politics.

16. Susan M. Hartmann, *The Home Front and Beyond: American Women in the 1940s* (Boston: Twayne Publishers, 1982), pp. 134–35.

17. Critics of "equal pay for comparable work" argued that it would be impossible to come up with a fair pay scale, whereas supporters of this concept (the Women's Bureau and the President's Commission on the Status of Women) insisted that such a scale could be devised through formal job analysis and the cooperation of labor and management. See Harrison, *On Account of Sex,* pp. 95-105; and Linden-Ward and Green, *Changing the Future*, pp. 9–10.

18. Ibid., p. 93; and Steven D. McLaughlin et al., *The Changing Lives of American Women* (Chapel Hill: University of North Carolina Press, 1988), pp. 101–2.

19. Barbara Sinclair Deckard, *The Women's Movement: Political, Socioeconomic, and Psychological Issues*, 3rd edition (New York: Harper and Row Publishers, 1983), p. 117; and *American Women*, pp. 27–28.

20. Paula Giddings, *When and Where I Enter: The Impact of Black Women on Race and Sex in America* (New York: William Morrow and Company, 1984), pp. 245–46.

21. Ibid., p. 28; and Linden-Ward and Green, *Changing the Future,* p. 94. In 1967 (based on full-time employment), white men averaged an annual income of

$7,164; non-white men, $4,528; white women, $4,152; and non-white women, $2,949. Eight years later, the median income of full-time workers was as follows: white men, $15,230; black men, $10,618; white women, $8,787; and black women, $8,217. See Deckard, *The Women's Movement,* p. 89.

22. Alice Kessler-Harris, *Out to Work: A History of Wage Earning Women in the United States* (New York: Oxford University Press, 1982), p. 311.

23. Flora Davis, *Moving the Mountain: The Women's Movement in America since 1960* (New York: Simon & Schuster, 1991), p. 38; and *American Women*, p. 54.

24. Betty Friedan, *The Feminine Mystique* (New York: W.W. Norton, 1963).

25. Ibid., p. 11.

26. Giddings, *When and Where I Enter,* pp. 246, 299.

27. Friedan, The *Feminine Mystique,* pp. 13–15.

28. McLaughlin et al., *The Changing Lives of American Women,* pp. 123, 126–27, 135.

29. By 1960, roughly 70 percent of American families owned their own homes (with the help of a bank mortgage), 75 percent owned a car, and 87 percent owned a television. In the mid-1950s an income that ranged between $3,000 and $10,000 per year put a family into the middle class. By 1963, 20 percent of American families earned over $10,000 per year. See Stephanie Coontz, *The Way We Never Were: American Families and the Nostalgia Trap* (New York: Basic Books, 1992), pp. 24–25.

30. Susan M. Hartmann, "Women's Employment and the Domestic Ideal in the Early Cold War Years," in Joanne Meyerowitz, ed., *Not June Cleaver: Women and Gender in Postwar America, 1945–1960* (Philadelphia: Temple University Press, 1994), p. 86.

31. Linden-Ward and Green, *Changing the Future*, p. xii.

32. Coontz, *The Way We Never Were*, p. 36.

33. Friedan, *The Feminine Mystique*, p. 59.

34. Brauer, "Women Activists, Southern Conservatives," p. 49.

35. Harrison, *On Account of Sex*, p. 187.

36. Linden-Ward and Green, *Changing the Future*, pp. 10–11; and Davis, *Moving the Mountain,* p. 46.

37. Harrison, *On Account of Sex*, p. 191.

38. Betty Friedan, *It Changed My Life: Writings on the Women's Movement* (New York: Random House, 1976), p. 82.

39. Ibid., p. 83.

40. Judith Hole and Ellen Levine, *Rebirth of Feminism* (New York: Quadrangle Books Inc., 1971), pp. 86–87, 404–7; Friedan, *It Changed My Life,* pp. 92–95; and *Pittsburgh Press Company v. the Human Relations Commission*, 413 U.S. 376 (1973).

41. Friedan, *It Changed My Life,* pp. 104–6.

42. Hole and Levine, *Rebirth of Feminism,* pp. 95–96.

43. Ibid., p. 90; and Friedan, *It Changed My Life*, p. 109.

# 3

## Liberation, Not Equality, Is Our Goal: The Women's Liberation Movement, 1967–1977

EQUALITY: To have the same rights, privileges, status
LIBERATION: To set free as from oppression[1]

Robin Morgan opens her *Sisterhood Is Powerful* (1970), the first anthology of writings on the cutting edge of the women's liberation movement produced for a commercial publishing house, with the following call to arms:

This book is an action. It was conceived, written, edited, copy-edited, proofread, designed, and illustrated by women. . . . During the year that it took to collectively create this anthology, we women involved had to face specific and very concrete examples of our oppression. . . . Speaking from my own experience . . . I twice survived the almost-dissolution of my marriage, was fired from my job (for trying to organize a union and for being in women's liberation), gave birth to a child, worked on a women's newspaper . . . was arrested on a militant women's liberation action, spent some time in jail, stopped wearing makeup and shaving my legs, started learning Karate, and changed my politics completely. That is, I became . . . a "feminist" committed to a Women's Revolution.[2]

1970 proved a banner year for feminist texts, indeed.

Morgan was not alone in attracting the attention of a mainstream press. Shulamith Firestone's "fiery" polemic, *The Dialectic of Sex: The Case for a Feminist Revolution,* was published by William Morrow, and Columbia University professor Kate Millett's *Sexual Politics* appeared under the Doubleday imprint. These three books were widely read, often quoted, and soon recognized as feminist literary classics.

By the time Morgan wrote her introduction in 1970, the term women's liberation was a familiar one to the American public. The movement's goals, however, were less-well-understood. What did liberated women want? What exactly did Morgan mean when she wrote about her commitment to a "Women's Revolution"? Was women's liberation a utopian search for freedom from male-dominated values and institutions, or was there a more pragmatic bent to the movement? Did liberated women want a gender-blind society? If so, then were the goals of the women's liberation movement that different from those espoused by the equal rights movement? To answer these questions, one must search for the roots of the women's liberation branch of second-wave feminism.

## SOCIAL UNREST AND RADICAL ROOTS: 1964–1967

Since the early 1960s, reform-minded college-age white students, male and female, had spent their summers in the South working on a variety of direct action projects sponsored primarily by the Student Nonviolent Coordinating Committee, an organization founded in 1960 by southern black college students. Through participation in sit-ins, freedom rides, and voter registration campaigns, these students aimed to overturn segregation and win political rights for black southerners. These intense campaigns brought together individuals from diverse backgrounds and experiences; and the mix of class, race, gender, ethnic, and regional values and styles proved volatile. What white women, in particular, discovered as they joined in the struggle to eradicate racism was that they were the victims of sexism.

Black men and (to a much lesser extent) white men held the more powerful (and dangerous) jobs within these summer projects: writing position papers, meeting with community leaders, canvassing for voter registration. White women often found themselves confined to the offices where they typed, answered phones, mimeographed position papers, and arranged the community meetings. Moreover, back in the communal freedom homes where the workers lived, white women not only found themselves assigned to housekeeping tasks but also pressured to engage in sex (especially interracial sex) as a test of their "commitment to black and white equality."[3]

Black women occupied a unique position in the racial/sexual hierarchy being played out in the Student Nonviolent Coordinating Committee. Many of them held positions of power, running their own projects without the assistance of male staffers. Sometimes they worked alongside black men, but they did not share power equally; and on rare occasions, black and white men bonded at the expense of black and white women. White women viewed strong black women as role models, but black women frequently kept their distance from white women. Many black women viewed black men's sexual interest in white women as a rejection of their sexuality; and they blamed white women, not black men, for the sexual competition. Black women also tried to distance themselves from sexual encounters with white men because this paradigm served as a symbolic reminder of white men's appropriation of black women's bodies during slavery.

Although these tensions had simmered for years, they reached a boiling point during the Freedom Summer of 1964. That summer, the Student Nonviolent Coordinating Committee's emphasis was on voter registration in Mississippi, and with approximately 300 white women descending on the state, disparities between the experiences of men and women, black and white, reached a new high. At the conclusion of the summer project, the volunteers returned to their schools and homes, and the permanent staff members prepared for a retreat to be held in November at Waveland, Mississippi.

The primary purpose of the retreat was to evaluate the Student Nonviolent Coordinating Committee's organizational structure, to discuss future projects, and to examine the position of whites in the movement. In 1964 the concept of integration was losing favor among a small but steadily increasing group of black activists who favored separatism. Among the many papers presented at Waveland was one, written anonymously, on the position of women. Although the authorship has been attributed incorrectly to Ruby Doris Smith Robinson, a black woman elected to the position of executive secretary of the committee in 1966, the document was drafted by two white women staffers, Mary King (the primary author) and Casey Hayden.

In her autobiography, *Freedom Song,* King recalls her intense feelings as she began her draft: "My heart was palpitating and I was shaking as I typed it. My fear of a joking response was making me unsteady in my resolve." In addition to her concern about being taken seriously by her comrades, King also worried about *how* to "write about some of my concerns involving women because—within the framework of the civil rights movement women's rights had no meaning and indeed did not exist." Lacking a theoretical construct, King adapted the language of black oppression to describe the status of women in the movement:

The average white person finds it difficult to understand why the Negro resents being called "boy," or being thought of as "musical" or "athletic," because the average white person doesn't realize that *he assumes he is superior* [emphasis in original]. And naturally he doesn't understand the problem of paternalism. So too the average SNCC worker finds it difficult to discuss the woman problem because of the assumption of male superiority. Assumptions of male superiority are as widespread and deep-rooted and every much as crippling to the woman as the assumptions of white supremacy are to the Negro.[4]

As the women feared, their position paper was roundly criticized during its formal presentation and became the butt of a joke by Stokely Carmichael, who would rise to prominence within the Student Nonviolent Coordinating Committee as its executive chairman in 1966 (Carmichael's leadership years are synonymous with the committee's shift to Black Power). "What is the position of women in SNCC," he asked. To which he answered, "The position of women in SNCC is prone!"[5]

Despite the ridicule King and Hayden encountered (King claims that those present at Waveland knew who wrote the paper) and the lack of interest on the part of movement activists in pursuing the issues raised about gender discrimination, they persisted. One year later King and Hayden revised their memo, claimed authorship of it, and decided to broaden their appeal by mailing the manifesto to forty women activists connected to the era's major peace and freedom movements: Students for a Democratic Society (Hayden's spouse, Tom Hayden, was a founding member of this group and the author of its 1962 manifesto, the Port Huron Statement), the National Student Association, the Northern Student Movement, and the Student Peace Union. The two women had few illusions about the response to their memo:

We had no hope that a [women's] movement would develop. We wanted the support of other women who were politically involved with civil rights and antiwar issues, women who were risk takers and who shared a commitment to fostering social change. We hoped that a [women's] network would evolve.[6]

Instead, the immediate and electrifying response from white women activists exceeded King's and Hayden's wildest expectations. Recipients of the manifesto read it and reread it until as one woman recalled, "it became creased and dirtied. Finally I could hardly read it anymore but by then I knew it by heart."[7] They shared it with other women; but more importantly, they acted on it. In December 1965 at a Students for a Democratic Society convention, women staged a walkout from the general meeting and organized a separate "Women's Caucus" to discuss sex-role stereotyping within the New Left. The following spring, the King-Hayden piece was given wide circulation within the New Left movement when it appeared in the April 1966 issue of *Liberation*, a leftist periodical.

Black women activists who received the King-Hayden missive also responded, but with a telling silence. In part, their response reflected their ambiguity toward challenging the sexism of black men (for fear of appearing disloyal) and their conviction that "discrimination against women was of secondary importance to the subjection of all blacks and the inequitable distribution of power in society."[8] Their response also reflected the rift that had developed recently between black and white women. Last but not the least important, their response was symbolic of black women's historic sense of unease with feminism and represented a strong desire to distance themselves from the concerns of white women. That division along the color line never completely disappeared, even at the height of second-wave feminism.

The walkout staged by radical white women at the 1965 Students for a Democratic Society convention was precipitated by the men's verbal taunts at a workshop on women's roles within Students for a Democratic Society. That radical men were hostile to the women's question is borne out by their response to a request for a "women's liberation plank" at the 1966 Students for a Democratic Society convention. The women making the request were "pelted with tomatoes and thrown out of the convention."[9]

Over the next year, leftist women made a few stabs at getting leftist men to confront their chauvinism; but at every turn, the women's position was criticized, shouted down, and belittled. In an eerie replay of the sexual exploitation some white women experienced in the Student Nonviolent Coordinating Committee, radical women also discovered that their bodies were appropriated by men for political purposes. Radical men burned their draft cards to protest the war in Vietnam and encouraged other men to do the same, and women were supposed to reward and support draft protesters with their bodies: "'Girls Say Yes to Guys Who Say No!' was a widespread slogan of the movement."[10]

Then came the National Conference for a New Politics, the first attempt at bringing together representatives from almost every major and minor organization associated with the New Left. In late August 1967, Chicago found itself playing host to some 2,000 delegates representing close to 200 leftist organizations. Although one purpose of the convention was to foster unity among a fragmenting Left, the conference fell short of this goal. Instead, factionalism (white versus black and male versus female) contributed the spark that ignited an independent women's liberation movement.

Over fifty women had attended a women's workshop sponsored by the conference out of which a general resolution calling for civil rights for women was produced. Rebuffed on their first attempt to get the resolution accepted for discussion (a much softer, more innocuous resolution calling for women to continue their activism within the peace movement was accepted for discussion instead), Jo Freeman and Shulamith Firestone took matters into their own hands. Late into the night they worked on yet another resolution. More strongly worded than the first one, it called for the convention "to condemn the media for stereotyping women as sex objects, to endorse the revamping of marriage, divorce, and property laws, to support the dissemination of birth control information to all women and the removal of all prohibitions against abortion."[11] If that was not enough, Freeman and Firestone decided to take a page from the position of the black caucus that had demanded 50 percent black representation on all conference committees. Because women constituted 51 percent of the population, Freeman and Firestone reasoned that women deserved that proportional representation.

On their return trip to meet with the resolutions' chairman, the women had little success with their lobbying until they threatened to disrupt the convention with procedural motions. When, however, it came time to introduce the women's resolution, the chair, William Pepper, substituted the "peace proposal" for the Freeman-Firestone resolution and quickly brought it to a vote. According to Jo Freeman's recollection, when the women protested "William Pepper patted Shulie [Shulamith Firestone] on the head and said, 'Move on little girl; we have more important issues to talk about here than women's liberation.' That was the genesis [of the first autonomous women's liberation group]. We had a meeting the next week with women in Chicago."[12]

Almost from the beginning, the women who joined liberation groups could not agree on either the root cause of their oppression—capitalism or male supremacy—or on a single strategy for achieving liberation—direct action or consciousness-raising. The former depended on demonstrations staged for the media, such as the 1968 Miss America Beauty Pageant protest; the latter involved small group discussions in which the participants (women only) shared personal experiences in order to understand better how their lives were shaped by "patriarchy" and its "male chauvinist" value system. Women favoring a capitalist explanation of their oppression supported action over discussion and believed that the solution to the women's problem lay in left-wing politics. Those who viewed patriarchy as the enemy used consciousness-raising techniques to make women aware of their oppression (consciousness-raising emphasized that the "personal was political") and insisted that women were an exploited class (a concept leftist women found counterrevolutionary). Although most members of the feminist faction preferred discussion over action, a few feminist groups (the Redstockings and the Feminists) were committed to militant, protest actions.

Although the liberation wing of the women's movement developed within the context of 1960s political radicalism, radical feminists' definition of liberation varied considerably from the beginning of its autonomous existence and changed over the course of the movement's rise and fall in American society. Robin Morgan's story is a case in point. Though her experiences were at once personal and individual, they also were emblematic of many women's experiences in the early years of radical feminism.

## FROM LEFTIST TO FEMINIST: ROBIN MORGAN'S EPIPHANY

Robin Morgan was hardly a newcomer to radicalism or the women's liberation movement at the time she wrote her introduction to *Sisterhood Is Powerful*. An early member of New York Radical Women, Morgan had taken a leading role in orchestrating the group's protest of the Miss America Beauty Pageant in September 1968. Several months later, however, Morgan left New York Radical Women declaring it neither radical nor political enough and became a cofounder of the "zap-action" leftist group—the Women's International Terrorist Conspiracy from Hell—that descended on Wall Street delivering hexes.[13] No doubt about it, Morgan envisioned herself a committed revolutionary. Something happened to Morgan during the year she spent working on *Sisterhood Is Powerful*. While sharing and discussing the information she and her collaborators collected about the condition of women, she discovered within herself a wellspring of anger toward all men, radical and establishment alike. That "five-thousand-year-buried anger" led her to join in the January takeover of the male-dominated, New Left underground newspaper, the *Rat*.[14] Indeed, her contribution to the women's issue of the *Rat* ("Farewell to All That") has been described as the "shot heard round the Left" for its revolutionary, feminist fervor.[15]

Thus, although Robin Morgan's revolutionary stance was not new in 1970, her feminist awakening certainly was. Moreover, Morgan's feminist declaration symbolized something larger and more significant than the culmination of her personal odyssey toward feminism. It represented one of several critical turning points in a movement that, despite its two and a half years of existence, continued to defy an easy definition and was in a constant state of flux.

When Robin Morgan joined New York Radical Women, one of only a handful of women's liberation groups in existence by early 1968, she considered herself "a radical woman who regarded the Women's Liberation Movement as an important 'wing' of the Left."[16] Like a majority of the group's earliest members, Morgan was a veteran of the student left/antiwar movement. Despite the overt hostility radical women experienced within this movement, they continued to support the Left's view that "women's oppression derived from capitalism," and they were willing to subordinate "women's issues" (however defined) "to the larger struggle for socialist change."[17] Whereas many radical women truly believed in this position, others only accepted this view because they dreaded being labeled counter-revolutionaries if they articulated too strong a feminist position. Still, this socialist perspective, and the women who embraced it, formed the dominant ideology of the women's liberation movement during its early years (1967–1969).

There was, however, a well-established minority position within the fledgling women's liberation movement. New York Radical Women co-founder Pam Allen and member Kathie Amatniek (who would soon renounce her "patriarchal surname" in favor of "Sarachild" as a way of identifying with her mother's lineage) had acquired their radical education from a different source within the Left, the student-led wing of the civil rights movement. Their involvement with the struggle to overcome racism had "raised their consciousness" and had sensitized them to a view of oppression neither limited to class struggle nor defined solely by capitalism. Although the parallel between white supremacy and male supremacy was becoming all too obvious to these radical women, in early 1968 they still lacked "a language or theory with which to distinguish themselves and their ideas from other radical women."[18] That void would be filled over the next two years as writers and theorists like Shulamith Firestone revised the old image of the feminist as a "granite-faced spinster obsessed with the vote" and reclaimed feminism from its "reformist [and] bourgeois" image.[19]

## WOMEN'S LIB AND THE MEDIA: A MARRIAGE OF (IN)CONVENIENCE?

Between 1968 and 1970 several well-publicized actions, including the Miss America Beauty Pageant protest, the Halloween hexing of Wall Street, and demonstrations at public agencies where couples applied for marriage licenses, had catapulted women's liberation onto the pages of every major newspaper and magazine in the country. Although these and other actions were planned to entice media attention, the results often were mixed. Women activists garnered the publicity they sought, but media coverage frequently focused on the image of the messengers at the expense of their message and frequently distorted both with unflattering descriptions of the former and trivializations of the latter. One might have expected condescension or hostility from the mainstream press, which reflected the traditional power hierarchy by hiring women for only the lowest positions, but even the alternative press was not immune to bouts of sexism.[20]

In the months preceding the publication of Firestone's, Millett's, and Morgan's books, feminists—liberals and radicals alike—targeted the media. In January 1970 at the instigation of Robin Morgan's friend Jane Alpert, radical women seized control of the *Rat* and put together a special issue on women's liberation as their protest of the male-dominated staff's belittling of "women's issues." Then on March 16, 1970, the very day that

*Newsweek*'s cover story on feminism appeared, forty-six women staffers "held a press conference to announce that they had filed sex discrimination charges against the magazine"; women staffers at *Time* and NBC would file similar charges soon after the *Newsweek* incident.[21] Three days later, over one hundred women representing a coalition of liberal and radical women's groups staged a sit-in at the editorial office of the *Ladies' Home Journal*.

The decision to target the *Journal*, the quintessential magazine of the "American housewife" with a readership of 14 million, was a political statement in and of itself. As the demonstrators anticipated, their action netted media attention; once reporters and camera crews were in place, a statement was handed out that indicted the *Journal* for "dealing superficially, unrealistically, or not at all with the real problems of today's women: job opportunity, day care, abortion."[22] After a protracted standoff, a settlement was reached in which the women were given the opportunity to produce an eight-page supplement to be included in a future issue. When the supplement appeared in the August 1970 issue, it contained information on women and work, how to start consciousness-raising groups, a contact list of women's liberation groups, a proposal for a housewife's bill of rights, and a tongue-in-cheek critique of marriage (a parody of the *Journal*'s feature column "Can This Marriage Be Saved?") entitled "Should This Marriage Be Saved?"[23]

There is no doubt that radical women bore some responsibility for the media's misrepresentation of women's liberation and the public's confusion with its philosophy, goals, and tactics. Whereas the mainstream, liberal feminists of the National Organization for Women (NOW) used their organizational structure and annual conventions to hammer out a feminist agenda that the majority of the membership could support and work toward, the grass-roots, antihierarchical position of groups identified with women's liberation created a unique environment that encouraged a wide-ranging level of participation and expression. Women with more flamboyant personalities and styles had little difficulty in capturing and playing to the media's attention; and for these women, the more outrageous and radical their stance or action, the easier it became to popularize their political message.

## GROWTH AND DIVISION WITHIN THE WOMEN'S LIBERATION MOVEMENT

By 1970, when the mainstream publishing world was discovering that women's liberation was profitable, the movement had expanded from its original handful of groups in Chicago, New York, Washington, D.C., and Boston to hundreds of groups in well over forty American cities (with a parallel movement underway in Canada, too). East-Coast feminism had spread not only to the West Coast but also to smaller cities in the American heartland. Communities that had grown familiar if not comfortable with the liberal version of feminism espoused by NOW and the Women's Equity Action League suddenly discovered radical feminism. In addition to those who eagerly joined the liberation groups that seemed to spring up almost overnight, the movement's growth also could be measured by the increase in the number of newsletters such as *Real Women* (St. Louis, Missouri) and *Scarlet Letter* (Madison, Wisconsin) produced at the grass roots and their ever-expanding readership.

According to a study of the women's liberation movement commissioned by the Russell Sage Foundation in 1974, "only two such periodicals were produced in 1968, ten in 1969, thirty in 1970 and sixty in 1971."[24] Moreover, the influence of such newsletters far outweighed the number of active participants in liberation groups. In most of the cities studied, the ratio between reader and active member was three to one, and in a few of the larger metropolitan areas the ratio reached four to one. In San Francisco, which by the close of 1970 had thirty-five distinct women's liberation groups with over several hundred participants, subscriptions to the cooperative newsletter, the *San Francisco Women's Newsletter*, reached a readership of 1,200.[25] Little wonder then that Morgan's, Millett's, and Firestone's books were so well received in 1970 or that by 1972 women's liberation would be considered mainstream enough that Warner Communications was willing to chance investing approximately $1 million in a new magazine, to be called *Ms.*, for the liberated woman.

During the same period in which public awareness of and participation in the women's liberation movement was on the increase, the movement was also marked by factionalism. The first conflict to surface was one that had been there from the beginning: the rift between the politicos and the feminists. Some members of the early liberation groups remained committed politicos clinging to the belief that "feminism expanded rather than contradicted a left analysis." These activists continued to insist that "women's oppression could be ended only through a socialist revolution."[26] Not all such women remained committed to the Left at the expense of feminism. Some, like Robin Morgan, became so disenchanted with the chauvinist behavior of radical men that they severed their ties with socialism in favor of feminism.

Many of the older liberation groups dating back to the late 1967–early 1968 period succumbed to this ideological strife between politicos and feminists. In the New York movement, New York Radical Women dissolved by 1969 as its members spun off in two opposing directions: the politico-oriented Women's International Terrorist Conspiracy from Hell (founded in October 1968) and the feminist-oriented Redstockings (founded in February 1969). The Redstockings lasted only a year; and when this group folded, two members founded another group, The Class Workshop (1970), which also survived for only a year. The New York experience was far from unique and would be replicated in scores of communities across the country.

Ideological hairsplitting was not confined solely to differences between politicos and feminists. As it turns out, not all politicos agreed with each other, and neither could members of the feminist faction reach an accord among themselves. Some politicos, while remaining committed to a left-analysis, were influenced enough by the feminists' focus on gender that they began articulating a new brand of politico feminism—socialist-feminist—which allowed them to "organize simultaneously around the issues of gender and class."[27] Socialist-feminists expanded the orthodox socialist view of work by including women's unpaid work within the home. Because childbearing as well as childrearing were considered unpaid labor, this interpretation allowed socialist-feminists to join in the struggle for abortion rights. In Chicago, the socialist-feminist group, the Chicago Women's Liberation Union, operated an underground abortion clinic where approximately 11,000 abortions were performed during the four years preceding the 1973 Supreme Court's decision, *Roe v. Wade*, legalizing abortion.[28]

Among those women who considered themselves feminists, factionalism grew out of competing theories as to how male supremacy worked and the extent to which women were implicated in the maintenance of male supremacy. The Redstockings, for example, developed a pro-woman line in order to explain women's apparent acquiescence to male oppression. According to this interpretation, women were not "brainwashed" into submission, neither were they "stupid" nor "sick." Instead, it was the "continual, daily pressure from men" that led women to submit to their "oppressors." According to the pro-woman line, institutions such as marriage were not corrupt, but they were the "tools of the oppressor." To identify men as oppressors, however, was not the same thing as being antimale. The Redstockings believed that men were redeemable. All men had to do was give up their "male privileges and support women's liberation" for the greater good of all humanity.[29]

Members of Cell 16, the Boston feminist group that began in 1968, provided a very different perspective on male supremacy. Although Cell 16 members joined the Redstockings in believing that men oppressed women, that was the extent of their common ground. In direct opposition to the Redstockings, Cell 16 members argued that women were conditioned into accepting male domination and that women colluded in their oppression. The key to "unconditioning" themselves was for women to avoid men. Thus, Cell 16 called for its members to embrace separatism, and in order to "achieve a degree of self-sufficiency and control over their lives," members were encouraged to adopt the practice of celibacy and take up karate.[30]

Ideological rigidity contributed to the rise of a phenomenon called *trashing*, a practice in which a woman was verbally attacked by other members of her collective. The most likely target of a trashing was a woman who was perceived by others as putting herself above the group or a woman whose motives or commitment to radical feminism was suspect. Within some feminist circles the offenses ranged from the trivial—wearing makeup—to the absurd—having a dominant (which meant male) personality and using that personality to control a meeting or direct an action.

Lesbianism, which first surfaced as an issue within the feminist movement in 1970, quickly became a subject for trashing. Some straight feminists worried that a society fearful of or hostile to homosexuality would use the "lavender menace" to discredit the feminist movement. They counseled lesbians to maintain a discreet silence about their sexuality. Among gay feminists, however, lesbianism was as much a political issue as it was a question of sexual preference and personal choice. This point was made quite forcefully in 1970 with the distribution of a position paper, "The Woman-Identified Woman," by the recently formed lesbian collective, Radicalesbians.

Once lesbianism was redefined as a political issue, some straight women felt pressured to declare (falsely) that they were lesbians, while others hid their relationships with men. Lesbian-feminists quickly responded to this defensive posturing by insinuating that this tactic demonstrated not only intolerance on the part of straight feminists but also (and far more importantly) their lack of commitment to the cause of liberation. Both straight and gay feminists could claim the mantle of oppression; thus, both sides responded by trashing.

## THE COLOR OF FEMINISM: RACIAL TENSIONS WITHIN THE MOVEMENT

Tensions between women of color and white women did not reach the same level of animosity as did the conflicts between politicos and feminists or straights and gays; nonetheless, there was a distinct sense of discomfort about race within the women's liberation movement. White feminists were uneasy about their whiteness and felt guilty about their middle-class origins. They also worried that women of color, especially radical black women, would ridicule their claims of oppression. As one radical white feminist stated when the question was raised about including radical black women's groups in a planning conference scheduled for August 1968 at Sandy Springs, Maryland: "I don't want to go to a conference and hear a militant black woman tell me she is more oppressed and what am I going to do about it."[31] White women did not imagine this response on the part of black women; instead they were told so unequivocally: "It is time that definitions be made clear," a black woman reported in an interview with the *Black Scholar*. "Blacks are oppressed. White women are suppressed and there is a difference."[32]

Why did black women want to keep their distance from the women's liberation movement? White women's emphasis on the oppressive institutions of marriage and the family as well as their preoccupation with sexuality led black women to conclude that women's liberation was "basically a family quarrel between White women and White men."[33] Even when black women conceded that they supported some of the goals of the movement (like equal pay), they hesitated in joining with white women. Their reluctance had deep historical roots, as Toni Morrison suggested in an article written for the *New York Times Magazine* in August 1971. "Too many movements and organizations," she wrote, "have made deliberate overtures to enroll blacks and have ended up rolling over them." According to Morrison, the very "whiteness" of the women's liberation movement engendered a deep sense of mistrust in black women: "They [black women] look at White women and see the enemy—for racism is not confined to the White man."[34]

Divided loyalties also inhibited black women from joining the women's liberation movement in any significant numbers. Although black women activists recognized the existence of sexism, they viewed the struggle against racism as more critical. Black women were reluctant to call attention to the sexism of black men, even as they acknowledged its existence. They worried that their participation in the women's liberation movement would be interpreted as an indictment of black men when they preferred to place the blame for black sexism squarely on the shoulders of the ultimate oppressor: white men.

Even as Morrison condemned the women's liberation movement for its emphasis on issues trivial to the concerns of black women, she held out the possibility that white and black women could find common ground through the formation of a women's political movement. It's ironic that the organization that gave Morrison hope was not the creation of radical feminists but the brainchild of liberal feminists. For some time, equal rights feminists "while not disputing the need to change public attitudes and put pressure on policymakers" had decided that it was time for feminists to make rather than shape public policy.[35]

Thus was born the National Women's Political Caucus, a bipartisan group that set its sights on increasing the power of women within the two major political parties and electing women to office (local, state, and national). Morrison noted with a great deal of satisfaction the presence of three politically diverse, powerful black women at the July 1971 organizing conference for the National Women's Political Caucus: Shirley Chisholm, the first black woman to serve in the U.S. Congress (1969–1983); Fannie Lou Hamer, a civil rights activist and founder of the Mississippi Freedom Democratic Party; and Beulah Sanders, chairwoman of the New York City Coordinating Committee on Welfare Groups. For Morrison, the presence of these and other women of color (LaDonna Harris, a Native American activist; and Lupe Anguiano, a Chicana activist) as well as the caucus's commitment to combating "sexism, racism, institutional violence, and poverty" signaled a new beginning.[36]

## BRIDGING THE GAP BETWEEN EQUALITY AND LIBERATION FEMINISTS

As confusing and contradictory as it sounds, the revolutionary image of second-wave feminism is both accurate and misleading. Like almost all social movements, the feminist movement of the 1960s and 1970s was multifaceted. Feminists differed according to ideology, strategy, goals, and style. Unfortunately however, the more liberationists pushed the radical button, the easier it became for the media and the public to assume incorrectly that there was a fixed and unalterable division between mainstream, liberal equality feminism (which emphasized political and legal reform) and avant-garde, radical, liberation feminism (which stressed revolutionary socioeconomic and cultural changes). To deny that differences existed between NOW, Women's Equity Action League, Women's International Terrorist Conspiracy from Hell, and Redstockings is, of course, an exercise in futility; but to presume that these differences either precluded liberal and radical women from promoting many of the same issues or prevented them from supporting agreed-upon actions is also inaccurate.

Betty Friedan, president of NOW until 1970, had recognized the political importance of building bridges between the two branches of feminism and had urged her organization to reach out to younger, radical feminists. Her successor, Aileen Hernandez (a black woman), would travel even further down the road toward mutuality when she addressed the NOW membership on the touchy subject of lesbianism. In response to concerns by conservative members of NOW who feared that support for lesbians' rights would adversely affect the organization by making it appear too radical, Hernandez stated, "If the issue of lesbianism were put on the basis of a legal right to sexual privacy, I think even conservative NOW members would work for the repeal of laws that denied people that right."[37]

NOW's success at "bridging the generation gap" between the under-thirty feminists, who tended to join liberation groups, and the over-thirty-five equal rights feminists was mixed prior to 1972. In part, the blame rests with Betty Friedan's contradictory and sometimes confrontational style. Although she recognized the importance of reaching out to liberationists, her characterization of them as man-hating and anti-motherhood did little to encourage radical feminists to reach out to equality feminists. At the same time, some of the radical women also contributed to the feminist divide by making clear their disdain for the "bourgeois feminists" of NOW. For a significant number of white women activists, however, the chasm between liberal and radical feminism was bridgeable; indeed, to many it was an artificial divide. Many women saw no ideological inconsistency between joining their local NOW chapter and participating in grass-roots liberation groups.

As the feminist movement matured between 1972 and 1977, tactical distinctions between the two branches of feminism became less pronounced. Although equality feminists continued to believe that change came through reforming the system, they were not above borrowing the direct action, protest tactics of radical feminists in order to secure the attention of legislators. By 1972, the Women's Equity Action League, which had considered NOW too radical on the abortion issue in 1968 not only favored abortion rights but also claimed a page from the texts of liberationists by "declaring itself in favor of 'responsible rebellion.' "[38] Meanwhile, radical feminists may not have softened their critique of capitalism and patriarchy, but many recognized that ideological posturing and protests brought few long-lasting results. Eventually, pragmatism won out. Those members of liberation groups who believed that the split between liberals and radicals was never very significant "began to seek reform of laws and established institutions" through participation in politics.[39]

In part, ideological and tactical differences diminished as the two branches of feminism sought common ground in defining "feminist" issues. On the subjects of abortion repeal and child care, liberal and radical feminists reached an early accord; on issues such as rape, domestic violence, and welfare mothers' rights, radical feminists led the way with liberal feminists eventually lending their support; on the issue of securing passage of the Equal Rights Amendment (ERA), liberal feminists directed the campaign until the mid to late 1970s when they picked up the support of radical feminists; and on the "hot button" issue of lesbianism, a surprisingly wide range of opinions could be found among both liberal and radical feminists.

Symbolic of the blurring of the differences between liberal and radical feminists was the consensus achieved at a national women's conference held over four days in November 1977 in Houston, Texas. The Houston Conference was heralded by feminists and the media alike for hammering out an ambitious and socially progressive agenda for change. One paper reported that "the women's movement is now a truly national, unified engine of change which could conceivably become the cutting edge of the most important human issues America faces in the next decade."[40]

At the top of the feminist agenda was passage of the ERA, but participants also pledged to work on issues of concern to minority women, domestic violence, rape, reproductive freedom, sexual preference, child care, and a displaced homemakers' bill. Though the Houston Conference denoted the high-water mark of second-wave feminism, it also represented a turning point in the social and political fabric of American life. Even as liberal and radical feminists celebrated their newfound unity, a "Pro-Family Rally" with its anti-ERA, antiabortion, antigay and lesbian rights agenda was underway across town. Perhaps it was deliberate, but neither the participants at the feminist conference nor the reporters covering this event took much notice of the other "women's conference." Maybe they should have, because the feminist backlash had begun. Instead, participants left the Houston Conference with a higher commitment to the feminist cause and, as it turns out, a naive belief that passage of the ERA lay just around the corner.

## NOTES

1. *American Heritage Illustrated Encyclopedic Dictionary* (Boston: Houghton Mifflin Company, 1987), pp. 596, 973.

2. Robin Morgan, ed., *Sisterhood Is Powerful: An Anthology of Writings from the Women's Liberation Movement* (New York: Random House, 1970), pp. xiii–xiv.

3. Mary Aickin Rothschild, "White Women Volunteers in the Freedom Summers: Their Life and Work in a Movement for Social Change," *Feminist Studies* 5 (Fall 1979), pp. 481–83.

4. Mary King, *Freedom Song: A Personal Story of the 1960s Civil Rights Movement* (New York: William Morrow and Company, 1987), pp. 445, 443, 568.

5. Ibid., p. 452

6. Ibid., pp. 458, 571–74.

7. Ibid., p. 466.

8. Anne Standley, "The Role of Black Women in the Civil Rights Movement," in Vicki L. Crawford, Jacqueline Anne Rouse, and Barbara Woods, eds., *Women in the Civil Rights Movement: Trailblazers and Torchbearers, 1941–1965* (Brooklyn, NY: Carlson Publishing, Inc., 1990), p. 200.

9. Morgan, *Sisterhood Is Powerful*, p. xxi.

10. Sara Evans, *Personal Politics: The Roots of Women's Liberation in the Civil Rights Movement and the New Left* (New York: Vintage Books, 1980), p. 179.

11. Alice Echols, *Daring to Be Bad: Radical Feminism in America, 1967–1975* (Minneapolis: University of Minnesota Press, 1989), p. 48.

12. Evans, *Personal Politics,* pp. 198–99.

13. Echols, *Daring to Be Bad,* pp. 76, 96–98.

14. Morgan, *Sisterhood Is Powerful,* pp. xv–xvi.

15. Winifred D. Wandersee, *On the Move: American Women in the 1970s* (Boston: Twayne Publishers, 1988), p. 1.

16. Morgan, *Sisterhood Is Powerful*, p. xiv.

17. Judith Hole and Ellen Levine, *Rebirth of Feminism* (New York: Quadrangle Books, Inc., 1971), p. 108.

18. Ibid., p. 116.

19. Echols, *Daring to Be Bad*, p. 54 and Connie Brown and Jane Seitz, "'You've Come a Long Way, Baby': Historical Perspectives," in Morgan, *Sisterhood Is Powerful*, pp. 3–28.

20. Lucy Komisar's report on "Women in the Media," which she presented to the April 1970 Professional Women's Conference, documents the rampant sex discrimination within "all areas of the media—television, radio, wire services, newspapers, magazines, advertising, and publishing." In radio and television, for example, women held only 10 percent of the managerial positions; in the newspaper business, women accounted for less than 5 percent. In the speciality area of "women's magazines," women claimed 55 percent of the editorial posts, but men controlled the "top jobs." See Hole and Levine, *The Rebirth of Feminism*, pp. 252–54.

21. Flora Davis, *Moving the Mountain: The Women's Movement in America since 1960* (New York: Simon & Schuster, 1991), p. 110.

22. Ibid., p. 112

23. Ibid., pp. 111–13.

24. Maren Lockwood Carden, *The New Feminist Movement* (New York: Russell Sage Foundation, 1974) p. 65.

25. Ibid.

26. Echols, *Daring to Be Bad*, pp. xiv, 135.

27. Ibid., p. 136.

28. Davis, *Moving the Mountain*, p. 167.

29. Morgan, *Sisterhood Is Powerful*, pp. 533–36.

30. Echols, *Daring to Be Bad;* p. 160.

31. Ibid., p. 105.

32. This statement, by Linda J. M. LaRue, first appeared in "Black Liberation and Women's Liberation," *Trans-Action* (November–December 1970), p. 61 and is reprinted in Paula Giddings, *When and Where I Enter: The Impact of Black Women on Race and Sex in America* (New York: William Morrow and Company, 1984), p. 308.

33. Ibid., p. 309.

34. Toni Morrison, "What the Black Woman Thinks about Women's Lib," *New York Times Magazine,* Sunday, August 22, 1971, p. 15.

35. Susan M. Hartmann, *From Margin to Mainstream: American Women and Politics since 1960* (Philadelphia: Temple University Press, 1989), p. 74.

36. Ibid., p. 76

37. Hole and Levine, *Rebirth of Feminism,* p. 94.

38. Hartmann, *From Margin to Mainstream,* p. 65.

39. Ibid.

40. Ibid., p. 176.

# 4

# The Feminist Agenda, 1970–1980: Two Steps Forward and One Step Back

August 26, 1970, marked the fiftieth anniversary of the woman suffrage amendment, and second-wave feminists were determined that the day would not pass unnoticed. Months earlier, Betty Friedan, the soon-to-be outgoing president of the National Organization for Women (NOW), had proposed celebrating the day with a "twenty-four-hour general strike, a resistance both passive and active, of all women in America against the concrete conditions of their oppression."[1] As Friedan's idea took hold, strike committees composed of liberal and radical feminists were formed in towns and cities across America, and marches, teach-ins, and street-theatre skits were planned. Building on the optimism generated by the recent success of several lawsuits challenging sex discrimination in the workplace (lawsuits that tested the power of the 1964 Civil Rights Act's Title VII to overturn state-level protective labor legislation), organizers of the Women's Strike for Equality Day decided to highlight three issues critical to the emerging feminist agenda: abortion repeal, equal opportunities in jobs and education, and child care.

As the largest mass demonstration in support of women's rights at the time, and one that received extensive media coverage, feminists believed that the Women's Strike for Equality Day was an unqualified success. Some members of the press disagreed, however, calling the turnout "disappointing." Still, tens of thousands of women and men took to the streets, and millions of Americans previously unaware of the women's movement awoke to the potential political power of a unified "sisterhood." Although no single event can be credited with ushering in the feminist era (1970–1980), the symbolic importance of this event cannot be overlooked. For a brief moment, liberal and radical feminists managed to put aside their differences and work together on a project. Even though this coalition proved fragile in the short run, the potential for compromise and cooperation between the two branches existed; and within a few years, the ideological and tactical differences between liberals and radicals would become less pronounced as a clearly defined feminist agenda emerged.

Liberal feminism experienced the most positive bounce from the August 26 demonstration of sisterhood's growing strength. Membership in the two mainstream organizations—NOW and the Women's Equity Action League—increased dramatically, and spin-off organizations were founded. As gains were made in the areas of employment, education, and reproductive rights, liberal feminists concentrated on securing passage of the Equal Rights Amendment (ERA). Continuing pressure from the political Left also encouraged them to join with their more radical sisters in expanding the feminist agenda to include more controversial issues relating to family life, sexuality, violence, and health.

NOW's membership rolls increased from approximately 4,000 in 1970 to over 20,000 by 1973 (by the end of the decade NOW claimed a membership of 125,000). Although precise figures remain unavailable for the Women's Equity Action League, this organization expanded to forty state chapters by 1973 (with a minimum of twenty-five members to a chapter). Though the league's membership was much smaller than NOW's, the former wielded considerable influence in defining public policy issues pertaining to women. After the league relocated its headquarters from Cleveland to Washington, D.C., late in 1972, the organization's political clout became even more apparent, especially in continuing the fight against sex discrimination in higher education. One year later, NOW followed the league's example and shifted the site of its national office; by the close of the decade, dozens of women's groups had established headquarters in the nation's capital for the express purpose of lobbying.[2]

During the early 1970s when the two mainstream organizations focused on legal tactics to secure gains for women, NOW (in 1971) and the Women's Equity Action League (in 1972) incorporated their legal defense committees. Members of NOW and the Women's Equity Action League also created spin-off organizations such as the Women's Legal Defense Fund (1971), which had a similar bent toward litigation. A year later, the American Civil Liberties Union developed the Women's Rights Project under the direction of Ruth Bader Ginsberg (later to be appointed to the U.S. Supreme Court), who argued many cases before the Supreme Court including the 1973 decision, *Frontiero v. Richardson*.

At the heart of the *Frontiero* case was the issue of "establishing sex as a suspect basis for classification under the Fourteenth Amendment" (this definition already existed in discrimination cases based on race, religion, and national origin). Women's rights advocates achieved a narrow but important victory in this case when the Court ruled that the armed service regulations could no longer deny women the same dependents' rights as men. On the constitutional issue of "strict scrutiny in cases of sex discrimination," only a plurality of the justices concurred (William Brennan, William Douglass, Thurgood Marshall, and Byron White). According to legal scholar Joan Hoff, one of the justices (Potter Stewart) wrote a separate decision expressing his support for the position put forth by the plurality, but in 1973 he "preferred that this issue be addressed by the passage of the then-pending Twenty-seventh Amendment (the ERA) which he was convinced would soon be ratified."[3] In 1973 Justice Stewart had every reason to believe that the ERA was on the fast track toward ratification and that the constitutional issue raised in the *Frontiero* case would soon be resolved. As it turned out, Justice Stewart surmised incorrectly; over the next few years, an anti-ERA movement would gather enough strength not only to derail passage of the ERA, but also to threaten many feminist gains.

## TITLE VII VICTORIES BRING AN END TO PROTECTIVE LEGISLATION

Liberal feminists represented by NOW achieved one of their original goals in August 1969 when the Equal Employment Opportunity Commission (EEOC) ruled that federal antidiscrimination laws took precedence over, and indeed negated, state protective labor legislation. This decision, which reversed the commission's February 1968 ruling favoring a case-by-case approach, followed an appellate court ruling in March 1969 in the case known as *Weeks v. Southern Bell Telephone and Telegraph Company*. The Court's finding in favor of *Weeks* created the legal precedent needed for ending the *bona fide occupational qualification* (*bfoq*) provision in Title VII. This legal loophole had permitted the EEOC to uphold state protective legislation (weight and height requirements, overtime, night work) that could be invoked to deny jobs and/or promotions to women.

For almost four years, NOW had engaged in a series of legal battles to get the commission to rule definitively against the states' protective labor laws. NOW's legal committee had thousands of cases from which to choose and had pursued hundreds. Though many of these cases were resolved in favor of the female plaintiffs, none was considered definitive until the *Weeks* case, which began in 1967 when Lorena Weeks took Southern Bell to court in

Georgia after the company refused to hire her for a high-paying switch-man's position. Although Weeks had demonstrated that she could perform this job, which required lifting heavy equipment, she lost out on a perma-nent position to a man with less seniority because company policy sup-ported Georgia laws "protecting" women from lifting heavy equipment (defined in excess of thirty pounds).

Weeks had been through one round of appeals and lost when NOW took the case. When the state legislature repealed the weight-limit law prior to NOW's intervention in the second appeal process, Southern Bell was forced to argue that the company's policy limiting weights met the bfoq provision under Title VII. This time the Court thought otherwise, stating that "the em-ployer has the burden of proving that he has reasonable cause to believe that all women would be unable to perform safely and efficiently the duties of the job involved." In finding against Southern Bell, the Court's language boldly interpreted the intent of Title VII for America's working women.

Title VII rejects this type of romantic paternalism as unduly Victorian and instead vests individual women with the power to decide whether or not to take on unro-mantic tasks. Men have always had the right to determine whether the increase in remuneration for strenuous, dangerous, obnoxious, boring or unromantic tasks is worth the candle. The promise of Title VII is that women are now to be on equal footing.

Southern Bell did not accept the Court's decision in the Weeks case with grace. Ordered to promote Lorena Weeks and make restitution, the com-pany complied only after NOW organized a series of well-publicized rallies in the spring of 1971.[4]

Bell Telephone companies across the country had much to lose by the *Weeks* decision. American Telephone and Telegraph, the parent company, was the largest single employer of women at the time and was among the worst offenders in job discrimination. As late as 1970, women were "system-atically excluded from both higher-level management jobs and from the bet-ter craft jobs." A year after the *Weeks* decision, women still comprised only 1 percent of all craft workers and 99 percent of all telephone operators.[5] Change would be slow, but the Court's intent was clear: Title VII would be in-terpreted broadly in order to equalize opportunities for working women.

Similar favorable decisions for working women, in such cases as *Rosen-feld v. Southern Pacific Company* and *Bowe et al. v. Colgate-Palmolive Company*, not only rendered the policy of protective legislation obsolete but also had important implications for the ERA drive. The United Auto Work-ers union had been among the first members of organized labor to recognize that Title VII could and would be used to invalidate state protective legislation, and had actually filed an amicus brief in support of the *Bowe* case. The successful adjudication of this case (as well as others) removed organized labor's primary opposition to the ERA. With great foresight, the United Auto Workers took the opportunity at its 1970 annual convention to became the first labor union to declare its support for the ERA. In early May, when the U.S. Senate opened hearings on the ERA for the first time since the mid-1950s, Olga Madar, a vice president from the international order, was among those speaking in favor of the amendment's passage.[6]

## REVISIONING FAMILY RESPONSIBILITIES: THE DEMAND FOR CHILD CARE

One of the three demands made by organizers of the 1970 Women's Strike for Equality Day was child care—an issue that drew widespread support from liberal and radical feminists alike as well as from women who had not considered themselves feminists. Child care's emerging importance to the feminist agenda, and its popularity with women in general, was linked to changes taking place within the American family as more and more mothers entered the labor force during the 1970s.

When NOW called for the establishment of state-supported child-care centers and for tax deductions for child-care expenses for working parents in its 1968 Bill of Rights, the feminist organization touched on an issue of economic concern to American families that reached back to the World War II era. When the unprecedented demand for labor during that war required reaching out to married women with children, the federal government responded by passing the Lanham Act in 1941, which called for the establishment of federally funded child-care centers. By mid-1944, approximately 3,100 child-care centers were in existence, servicing approximately 130,000 children. Once the war ended, however, and the federal government no longer considered women workers (especially mothers) "essential" to the well-being of the American economy, federal funds were withdrawn and the centers folded.[7]

The withdrawal of federal funds for child-care centers was a potent symbol of postwar America's growing fascination with domesticity and the primacy of the "stay-at-home" mother. Unfortunately for a significant portion of American families, the economic reality of postwar life frequently collided with this cultural emphasis; for many families struggling to become part of the great middle class, a second income was a necessity. Even at the height of the baby boom (1946–1964), working wives' contribution to the family economy was substantial, ranging between 23 to 28 percent (an amount that would change little between 1950 and 1980).[8]

Radical feminist groups were quick to respond to the need for child care by founding private child-care centers, many of which were managed cooperatively and featured a sliding-scale fee arrangement. These centers also offered a "nonsexist" approach to child-rearing with books, toys, and "educational centers" emphasizing nontraditional social roles for girls and boys. New York's feminist community is credited with opening the first such progressive child-care center in 1967; over the next four years another forty to sixty similar institutions would appear in cities across the country. During this same period, demands for on-site child-care centers at colleges and universities also become a staple of the feminist agenda pushed by women faculty, staff, and students.[9]

Liberal feminists recognized early on that small, private child-care centers could not keep up with the demand. State intervention from the municipal level to the national level was essential if the needs of working mothers were to be met. At the 1970 White House Conference on Children (held every decade since the Progressive era), NOW called for legislation supporting the funding of a national child-care network. In December 1971 when the Comprehensive Child Development Act was introduced in Congress as part of a larger Office of Economic Opportunity Bill, the emerging coalition of child-care advocates was elated, but not for long. In a surprising defeat for the feminist agenda, President Richard Nixon vetoed the bill. Even worse for the feminist agenda was Congress's inability to override the president's veto on this matter. What had happened?

According to several accounts, feminists paid too little attention in the fall of 1971 (when they also were working to get the ERA out of Congress) to the political forces marshaling a concerted drive to derail the child-care legislation. Two groups in particular were very interested in defeating the child-care initiative. The staunchly anticommunist John Birch Society likened the Mondale-Brademas bill to the Soviet's child-care system, and an emerging coalition of fundamentalist Christian churches trumpeted the dangers of state intervention in private family matters. Despite the widespread need for child care and its continued popularity among voting women, later attempts to pass child-care legislation (in 1975 and 1979) were brought down by an increasingly well-organized and powerful conservative minority.[10]

## A RIGHT TO CONTROL ONE'S BODY: HEALTH, SEXUALITY, AND ABORTION

The right to control one's body was at the heart of the feminist health movement and was interpreted by feminists to mean possessing knowledge about how their bodies functioned, having the power to make informed decisions about their bodies, and being treated with dignity and respect by the medical establishment. Education and self-help were key components of the early phase of the feminist health movement, but soon feminist concerns about the relationship between sexuality and reproduction would require activists to lobby for concrete changes in medical practices and the passage of new public policy initiatives.

The 1970 publication of *Women and Their Bodies* (soon to be retitled *Our Bodies, Ourselves*) gave the women's health movement its proverbial shot in the arm. This project, conceived and written by a small, radical feminist collective from Boston, grew out of a women's liberation conference held in the city during the spring of 1969. Following the success of the conference, a dozen women conducted a free course on women's health issues for individuals and community groups; so popular was this course that the women, who eventually incorporated themselves as the Boston Women's Health Book Collective, decided to publish their research on women's health issues. The book became a runaway best-seller with over 200,000 copies sold by 1973 and over 2 million by the end of the decade. Much of the book's focus, like the women's health movement in general, centered on such topics as sexuality (heterosexuality and homosexuality), reproduction (from menstruation to menopause), abortion, violence against women, and lessons in self-defense. The authors' growing awareness of the politics of health care also led them to include a critique of the American health-care system.

Boston feminists were not alone in their determination to educate women about their bodies. In Los Angeles a consciousness-raising group moved from talk to action in the early 1970s. At first, the group limited itself to providing free pregnancy tests and instructions in self-examination (for the treatment of common yeast infections and early detection of venereal diseases). Soon, however, the women added an abortion referral service (abortions were legal in California after 1967, but services were restrictive and expensive), and by 1973, a full-fledged, female-operated clinic offered a full range of gynecological services.

Within a few years the concept of founding women's health centers/clinics had caught fire; and by mid-decade there were over forty such institutions in operation around the United States (the movement also had spread to Canada and Great Britain). Although the feminist health movement remained community-oriented, the mid-1970s witnessed the start of a series of national conferences (the first of which was held at Harvard Medical School and was organized by the Boston Women's Health Book Collective) and the formation of the National Women's Health Network. African

Americans, Hispanics, and Native Americans joined the mainstream women's health movement, but they also created separate, spin-off organizations that focused specifically on women's health problems that, they argued, were exacerbated by racism (teen pregnancy, high infant-mortality rates, forced sterilization, fetal alcohol syndrome, and pesticide-related infections and diseases). In 1981 Byllye Avery began the National Black Women's Health Project; in 1986 Luz Alvarez Martinez started the National Latina Health Organization; and in 1988 Charon Asetoyer opened the Native American Women's Health and Education Resource Center.[11]

Feminist health advocates frequently tangled with the male-dominated medical establishment. They questioned the wisdom of doctors who prescribed antidepressant drugs or recommended hysterectomies as routine "cures" for women's ailments (both physical and mental), and they parted company with those in the profession who insisted that pregnancy was a disease that needed treatment. Feminists were especially insistent that physicians inform them about the changes taking place in their bodies (during pregnancy) and in fetal development so that they could make informed decisions about the birthing process. They also advocated for the introduction of "natural childbirth" techniques by pushing hospitals to open labor and delivery rooms to coaches (usually, but not always the father) and by refusing drugs that rendered them unconscious (and therefore passive) during childbirth. Finally, feminist health advocates insisted that women had the right to control their fertility and to enjoy their sexuality without suffering the consequences of an unplanned pregnancy. This assertion led to the demand for safe and effective methods of birth control and for unrestricted access to abortion procedures.

Abortion had never been completely outlawed in the United States; instead, for almost a century, this medical procedure was controlled by the state and the medical community. In the years following World War II, this alliance had grown increasingly uneasy from the perspective of the medical profession's more liberal members, many of whom were beginning to question the state's "right" to intervene in a doctor's professional decision. At issue was the definition of acceptable (meaning legal and medical) guidelines for performing a "therapeutic" abortion. The long-accepted legal position held that "therapeutic abortions were performed for physical indications only [after] a thorough hospital review procedure and only in hospitals." By the 1950s, some physicians were applying a more liberal interpretation to the law and were willing to accept "social, economic, and psychiatric indications for therapeutic abortions."[12]

Doctors desirous of securing legal protection for a broader interpretation of the penal code welcomed Planned Parenthood Federation of America's role in organizing a 1955 conference to discuss reforming abortion laws. By the late 1950s, the liberal wing of the legal profession, represented by the American Law Institute, appeared ready to join with the reform wing of the medical profession. In 1959 the American Law Institute took the bold step of drafting a "model abortion law" that would allow "licensed physicians to perform abortions for physical and mental health reasons, fetal defects, or when pregnancy was the result of rape or incest."[13] On the eve of feminism's reemergence as a potent political force, abortion reform advocates remained more concerned with protecting the rights of doctors (including the right to be free from prosecution) than they were with protecting the rights of pregnant women. Still, the model law's existence was a positive and progressive step; over the next several years state medical and legal organizations used the model law to lobby for changes in their local legislatures.

Once feminists joined the debate over abortion, women's physical and mental health and the well-being of the fetus took center stage. Therapeutic abortions had always existed as an option, and in the wake of two tragic and well-publicized incidents in the early 1960s, grounds for performing them slowly became more liberal (between 1962 and 1964 the nation was made aware of the dangers of thalidomide, a tranquilizer routinely prescribed for pregnant women, which caused hideous birth defects, and the serious threat posed to fetal development when women in the early stages of pregnancy were exposed to rubella or "German measles"). Still, this costly procedure remained under the control of the male-dominated medical community. Thus, whereas many (but certainly not all) middle- and upper-class married women were able to secure a therapeutic abortion, poor women, unmarried women, and women in rural areas were never as fortunate. As feminists pointed out, a woman's inability to obtain a safe, legal abortion did not always act as a deterrent. Instead many women (from all classes, races, and ethnic groups) took their chances with illegal abortions; many women suffered severe complications from these illegal procedures, and many women died. By the early 1960s, the medical staff of Chicago's Cook County Hospital, "reported caring annually for nearly five thousand women with abortion-related complications." A decade earlier, Los Angeles County Hospital reported two thousand cases per year, and hospital records in New York City indicated that between 1951 and 1962 "the absolute number of abortion deaths nearly doubled from twenty-seven in the early 1950s to fifty-one per year in the early 1960s."[14]

A few forward-thinking groups took up the issue of abortion repeal prior to NOW entering the debate. In 1961 the California-based Society for Humane Abortion began by lobbying the state legislature to repeal its antiabortion measure. Within a few years, the group moved from lobbying to direct action by operating an abortion referral service (women were directed to clinics where safe but illegal abortions were performed). By the mid- to late 1960s, such covert "counseling" services, like the one begun by Chicago feminists operating under the name of "Jane," existed in several of the country's large urban areas.

These and other acts of civil disobedience, like the Redstockings' 1969 "speak-out" on abortion (which coincided with a hearing on abortion conducted by the New York state legislature), helped to redefine the terms of the abortion debate. Abortion referral providers viewed their actions as political statements, not criminal acts; speak-outs were public events designed to remove the feelings of shame, humiliation, and illegitimacy associated with abortion. Thus, abortion became a legitimate political issue for the public to debate and to resolve through the political process.

Between 1967 and 1971 the repeal wing of the abortion movement gained momentum. In 1967 California, Colorado, and North Carolina became the "first" states in the nation to pass abortion reform legislation. By the end of the decade, twelve more states had passed similar measures, and reform adovocates were confident that more states would follow this trend toward liberalization. In 1969 a national conference on abortion in Chicago produced a new lobbying organization, the National Association for the Repeal of Abortion Laws (Betty Friedan represented NOW at National Association for the Repeal of Abortion Laws inaugural meeting), and a Harris Poll found that almost two-thirds of those interviewed agreed that abortion was a private matter.

In 1971 the Supreme Court entered the debate over abortion by agreeing to hear two cases, one that examined the constitutionality of a restrictive, nineteenth century abortion law—the *Roe v. Wade* case from Texas—and the other that challenged the constitutionality of the more recent abortion reform legislation—the *Doe v. Bolton* case from Georgia. Almost eighteen months later, on January 22, 1973, the Court issued its historic ruling, but one that fell short of unqualified support for the feminist position, which sought constitutional guarantees for abortion under the equal protection clause as well as under the right to privacy.

While the *Doe* decision is usually ignored in the relevant literature, the *Roe* decision is frequently presented as supporting a woman's right to an unrestricted abortion ("abortion on demand" as described by *Roe* critics). In actuality, these cases and their rulings pertained not only to the rights of women (as patients) but also to the rights of physicians to practice medicine. In the *Roe* case, the majority opinion did not support the position that "a woman's right is absolute and that she is entitled to terminate her pregnancy as she chooses." Even as the Court acknowledged that a woman's "right of personal privacy includes the abortion decision," it insisted that her right was "not absolute" and that her right had to be weighed against the "State ['s] interests in safeguarding health, maintaining medical standards, and in protecting potential life." Thus, the Court introduced the concept of fetal viability (an issue of medical technology) and opted for a truncated, trimester approach to abortion rights. In *Doe*, the case was drawn more narrowly and focused on the power of hospital committees (composed of several physicians) to restrict abortions to those that met the "therapeutic" guidelines. In striking down this reform measure, the Court found that the intervention of a third party (the hospital committee) violated "the right of women to health care and of physicians to [freely] practice" their craft.[15]

With these two decisions, abortion became a legal medical procedure. It also became a decision that women were entitled to make with some degree of constitutional protection; and for that reason, feminists celebrated the Supreme Court's companion rulings. According to numerous scholars, however, the *Roe* and *Doe* decisions "broke no new constitutional ground; but instead, left the door open for statutory restrictions on abortion even though the medical procedure was declared legal."[16] The surprise for feminists would be the speed with which the opposition would march through that door.

## A RIGHT TO BE FREE OF FEAR: ANTIVIOLENCE CAMPAIGNS

Radical women were among the first to take the feminist assertion of a woman's right to control and protect her body one step further by challenging prevailing assumptions about rape. In particular, radical feminists' insistence that rape was a crime of violence, not sex, called into question the "blame the victim" syndrome that had provided the underlying rationale for federal rules of evidence in rape cases and states' rape statutes. Radical feminists also politicized rape by arguing that it was a weapon men used to maintain their dominance over women. "Men do not rape for sexual pleasure. They rape to assert power and dominance," wrote Carole Sheffield, a feminist activist and women's studies professor.[17] Women's autonomy, their physical movements, their access to public spaces (especially at night), were limited by the often-legitimate fear of rape. "I have never been free of the fear of rape. Rape is a kind of terrorism which severely limits the freedom of women and makes them dependent on men," wrote Susan Griffin, a feminist writer/activist whose literary contributions shaped the direction of the antirape and antipornography movements.[18] These perspectives became one of the driving forces behind the "Take Back the Night" march, an event first organized in 1978 by feminist groups across the country, and one that remains an annual event in many communities, especially those with college campuses.

New York Radical Feminists became the first group to address women's concerns about sexual violence when it organized a "speak-out" on rape in January 1971. Hundreds of women from all walks of life shared their horror stories as rape victims. Three months later, New York Radical Feminists held a conference that highlighted the problem of rape from a more academic perspective (one that provided information on crime statistics, the legal system, and research). Rape soon became part of a wider, public discourse after *Ramparts* published "Rape: The All-American Crime" by Susan Griffin in September 1971. Four years later, Susan Brownmiller wrote the first published history of rape, *Against Our Will: Men, Women, and Rape* (1975).

Although highly praised, Brownmiller's study did not lack for critics even within the feminist community. Black feminists were incensed by the white radical feminist's myopic and racist analysis of interracial rape. While she dismissed the rape of slave women by their white masters, Brownmiller's retelling of the 1955 Emmet Till murder in Mississippi perpetuated long-standing racist assumptions about black men's sexual interest in the "forbidden fruit": white women. (Till was a black teenager who supposedly violated the white South's cultural code by "wolf-whistling" at a white woman; for that he was murdered. The white men responsible for the crime were acquitted by an all white, all-male jury).[19] Although Brownmiller was hardly sympathetic to the racist crime, she insinuated that Till's whistle made him partly responsible for the provocations against him. Brownmiller's rendering of this case infuriated black feminists and furthered the divide between whites and blacks.

The racial blind spots shared by some white feminists should not obscure the contributions they made in reshaping cultural assumptions about rape and in challenging the legal system's handling of rape cases. In the aftermath of its 1971 conference on rape, New York Radical Feminists focused public attention on and demanded changes in the state's restrictive laws. Like most states, New York law required independent corroboration of the rape victim's testimony on three specific points: identification (of the rapist), penetration, and lack of consent. Given such stringent rules of evidence and the fact that few rapes occurred in the presence of a third-party witness, conviction rates were low. According to statistics compiled in 1971 by New York Radical Feminists, New York City's conviction rate was under 1 percent, not so different from conviction rates in other parts of the country. In

Chicago, for example, of the 3,562 rapes reported for 1972, the police made 833 arrests; and of the 23 guilty pleas, only 8 served jail time.[20]

Liberal feminists eventually joined with their radical sisters in confronting the sex bias present in the prosecution of rape cases. In 1973 NOW established a separate Task Force on Rape in order to lobby for changes in federal legislation and for funds to support rape projects in local communities. In particular, the Task Force worked for changes in the Federal Rules of Evidence that would prohibit defense attorneys from introducing a victim's sexual history and style of dress as evidence ("provocative dress" was routinely described as an invitation to rape). By the end of the decade, state NOW chapters were pressuring their legislatures to drop the marital exemption clause from rape statutes (Oregon became the first state to allow prosecution for marital rape in 1977). As the following incident suggests, this change struck at the roots of deep-seated cultural assumptions about a husband's conjugal rights. Speaking to a group of feminist lobbyists in 1980, a California state senator quipped: "If you can't rape your wife, who can you rape?"[21] As late as 1991, four states still had not struck down their marital exemption clause, and five states had not amended this clause to include rape in cases of cohabitation.[22]

Radical feminists also led the way in exposing the public to the existence of wife beating, with liberal feminists eventually joining forces to combat this social problem (other terms used to describe this type of abuse are battering and domestic violence). Together, they succeeded in "transforming [wife beating] from a subject of private shame and misery to an object of public concern" that demanded the attention of local, state, and national agencies.[23] Until feminists brought this problem to light by exposing its prevalence across race, class, ethnic, and religious lines, most Americans assumed that wife abuse (one of the most underreported crimes according to the law enforcement community) rarely occurred and when it did, it was limited to poor, working-class families.

At its 1975 annual convention, NOW formed a National Task Force on Battered Women and Household Violence for the express purpose of raising public awareness of the problem, promoting the further establishment of shelters (the first independent shelter opened in Phoenix, Arizona, in 1973), working for legislation, and encouraging research on family violence as a preventative measure. By 1978 the number of shelters nationwide had grown to approximately 300. Feminists were not solely responsible for the growing number of shelters founded in the United States. Indeed, according to a survey conducted in 1981, less than half of the shelters in existence in the late 1970s were begun by feminist groups. Nonetheless, feminists made significant contributions in raising the public's awareness of domestic violence, and to that extent they deserve credit for the existence of all shelters for victims of domestic battering.[24]

Funding problems were (and remain) a constant worry for shelters, and liberal feminists used their considerable expertise at lobbying to get institutional support for shelters. In addition to seeking public funds to maintain shelters and victims' programs (programs that ranged from counseling to job retraining), they also lobbied for legislative reforms. Feminists pressured state lawmakers for changes that would ease restrictions on obtaining restraining orders and filing charges and increase criminal penalties for battering. By the late 1970s "more than a dozen states had passed such laws" (a few years later the number had increased to over forty states), and several states had begun "imposing special surcharges on marriage licenses to raise funds for shelters" (California, Pennsylvania, Florida, Montana, and Ohio were among the first to impose such levies).[25]

Pornography proved to be one of the most divisive of the antiviolence issues feminists addressed. Although the dividing line was not always so neatly drawn, the antipornography movement tended to pit radical feminists against liberal feminists. The problem with pornography was not one of definition, per se. Feminists from opposite ends of the ideological spectrum agreed with *Ms.* magazine's editor Gloria Steinem that pornography was not about sex, but about "violence, dominance, and conquest." Problems arose, however, when feminists sought to distinguish between "positive" expressions of sexuality—erotica—and "negative" expressions—pornography. Steinem tried to clarify this point, too. Erotic sex, she insisted, was "a mutually pleasurable, sexual expression between people who have enough power to be there by positive choice," whereas pornographic sex is "used to reinforce some inequality or to tell us that pain and humiliation are really the same as pleasure."[26] Steinem's attempt at clarity only served to muddy feminists' views on sexuality. As one noted feminist scholar pointed out, it did not "seem so obvious that certain sexual expressions are intrinsically liberated and others intrinsically degraded."[27] After all, the line between pain, humiliation, and pleasure in sexual expression is a subjective one.

Though feminists appeared united in their condemnation of pornography, disagreements arose over the causal relationship between pornography and male violence and how to combat the vice. For many radical feminists, the link between pornography and "sexual terrorism" was fairly direct. "Pornography," Robin Morgan wrote in *Going Too Far: The Personal Chronicle of a Feminist* (1977), "is the theory and rape the practice."[28] Marshaling their own evidence, radical feminists refuted the findings of the 1970 study by the President's Commission on Obscenity and Pornography.

In essence, the commission gave pornography a "clean bill of health" by describing it as "harmless," by which the commission meant that no direct link existed between sexually explicit material and sexually violent criminal acts.[29]

As the "politics of pornography" changed in the early 1980s, liberal feminists grew more concerned. They had no qualms with Women Against Violence in Pornography and the Media (founded in 1976) organizing "Take Back the Night" marches or Women Against Pornography (founded in 1979) leading tours through New York's "notorious Time Square porn district." When radical feminists called for a legislative solution to pornography, however, many liberal feminists, who considered themselves free-speech advocates, disagreed. This "pro-censorship" strain within the feminist movement reached a critical point in 1983 when the city of Indianapolis requested the services of writer and Women Against Pornography activist Andrea Dworkin and law professor Catharine MacKinnon in drafting a law banning pornography. Adopted by the city the following year, the Dworkin-MacKinnon ordinance became a model for other cities.

Some radical feminists also broke ranks with the pro-censorship, Women Against Pornography faction. When Cambridge, Massachusetts, considered adopting the Dworkin-MacKinnon law in 1985, the Boston Women's Health Book Collective objected to the impending ordinance for fear that the frank text of *Our Bodies, Ourselves* could be construed as pornographic. By the mid-1980s as lesbian sexuality became a more open topic for exploration in art, literature, and academe, a few lesbian-feminists joined the hue and cry against an increasingly narrow and rigid sexual moralism within radical feminism. Initially, the antipornography movement had attracted a number of well-known political activists, writers, and poets within the lesbian feminist community: Charlotte Bunch, Audre Lorde, and Adrienne Rich. Fed up with the porn industry's use of lesbian sex to sell magazines and films, lesbian feminists had wholeheartedly supported the protests and demonstrations of the two leading antipornography organizatons. Now, however, lesbian writers and activists worried that the antipornography movement would be used to condemn, indeed, outlaw a whole range of sexual behavior from butch-femme roles to sado-masochism. No doubt, this radical "break-away" faction breathed a sigh of relief as the federal courts during the mid- to late 1980s sided with the liberal position by striking down antipornography ordinances as unconstitutional. According to many activists and scholars within the feminist movement, debates over pornography were proving to be every bit as "divisive and debilitating" to second-wave feminism as the "fifty-year debate over protective legislation and the ERA."[30]

## KNOWLEDGE IS POWER: THE FEMINIST
## REVOLUTION IN EDUCATION

Liberal feminists represented by NOW and the Women's Equity Action League had long recognized the relationship between equality of opportunity in education and equality of opportunity in the job market. Beginning in 1970, these two organizations put their considerable legal and lobbying talents to work in an attempt to transform an educational domain that seemed impervious to federal anti–sex discrimination legislation. Exemptions to the Equal Pay Act of 1963 in the administrative, professional, and executive fields had left educators of all ranks unprotected from discriminatory wage structures. Thus, women educators could earn less than men (even when they performed the same job) simply because they were women. In 1970, for example, even in a job in which women predominated—elementary education—male teachers' wages were 7 percent higher than the median income reported for all male workers, while female teachers' earnings were 14 percent below the median male income. At the other end of the educational scale, female college and university professors earned 55 percent less than their male colleagues in 1970.[31]

NOW may have made great strides in the late 1960s in strengthening Title VII enforcement, but because public and private educational institutions were excluded from its provisions, sex discrimination continued unchecked. Women found it difficult to climb the occupational ladder at all educational levels. In 1970, women constituted 66 percent of the nation's public school teachers but claimed only 13 percent of the principalships; as late as 1978, women made up less than 10 percent of full professors but over 50 percent of instructors at the nation's colleges and universities.[32] Although Title VII of the 1964 Civil Rights Act banned discrimination in all federally assisted programs and activities (inclusive of educational institutions), sex was not recognized as one of the prohibitive zones. This sex bias applied across the board in admissions (the professional schools—medicine, law, engineering—were notorious for establishing quotas that limited female enrollment) and among college students seeking support (such as in financial assistance). By far, the most easily demonstrated sex bias was in the area of college athletics. In 1972, for example, women's collegiate sports programs received less than 2 percent of the funding reserved for men's programs with athletic scholarships for women totaling less than $100,000.[33]

Nineteen seventy-two was a banner year for members of NOW and the Women's Equity Action League with feminist gains recorded in education and the equal rights campaign. On the educational front, Congress approved legislation on March 24 amending Title VII of the 1964 Civil Rights Act to include educational institutions and allowing the EEOC to sue employers in the federal courts for noncompliance. On June 23, the 1972 Higher Education Act cleared Congress with the addition of the Title IX amendment banning sex discrimination in all schools receiving federal funds. Title IX also closed the loophole in the Equal Pay Act by ending the administrative, professional, and executive exemptions, but intense lobbying from such prestigious institutions as Harvard, Yale, and Princeton (all of which maintained quotas for women) kept the admission policies of private undergraduate schools beyond the purview of the federal government.

Two members of the Women's Equity Action League deserve the bulk of the credit for these feminist victories, Dr. Bernice Sandler and Congresswoman Edith Green (D-Oregon). Sandler was the first person to bring attention to the issue of sex discrimination in higher education after being turned down for several academic appointments. When Sandler discovered that existing federal legislation offered no solution to her dilemma, she determined to do something about the situation. Putting her academic training to good use, Sandler began researching federal antidiscrimination legislation and discovered an ingenious legal loophole of her own. Although Title VII may have exempted educational institutions from engaging in sex discrimination, Executive Order 11375 aimed at strengthening EEOC guidelines did not.

On January 31, 1970, with Bernice Sandler putting together the statistical evidence, the Women's Equity Action League filed a class-action lawsuit against the University of Maryland for noncompliance with Executive Order 11375. NOW followed suit less than two months later with a similar complaint filed on March 25 against Harvard University, which stood to lose approximately $3 million for noncompliance. Over the next few years between the efforts of the Women's Equity Action League, NOW, and other women's organizations, over 300 colleges and universities and all of the nation's medical and law schools were targeted for sex discrimination complaints. On June 9, 1970, the Department of Labor, responding in part to the publicity surrounding the lawsuits, issued guidelines for ending sex discrimination in jobs determined by federal contracts, but the order did not include provisions for setting goals or issuing a timetable. Angered by these lapses, feminist groups kept up the pressure, and on December 4, 1971, the Department of Labor issued a revised order making these corrections.[34]

Congresswoman Edith Green was instrumental in securing the Title IX amendment to the 1972 education bill. Although Green applauded Sandler's tactics, the congresswoman wanted to secure equal protection for women under the law, and she knew that it was easier to overturn an executive order than it was to overturn congressional legislation. Green, who chaired a House subcommittee on education, used her power to hold hearings during the last week of June 1970 on sex discrimination in education. By the time the hearings concluded, the subcommittee had accumulated over 1,250 pages of evidence, which were used to prepare a two-volume report. Green adroitly guided an amended education bill through the legislative process, and with only one exemption (covering the admission policies of private, undergraduate colleges), Title IX slipped through Congress with little opposition.

Passing Title IX turned out to be the first and easiest step toward ending sex discrimination in education. Feminists found it much more difficult to get written guidelines established for Title IX and to secure its enforcement. In a situation reminiscent of feminist battles with the federal government over Title VII, it would take almost two years of sustained lobbying by women's groups before the government produced such guidelines in June 1974; another twelve-month period would pass before those regulations went into effect in July 1975.

Exposure to radical feminism's focus on oppression rather than discrimination eventually led liberal feminists to recognize that the country's educational system not only denied women equal opportunity, but it also perpetuated sexist assumptions about woman's nature and her proper (and very traditional) social functions. From required courses at junior and senior high schools in home economics to career and/or college counseling, young women were encouraged to link their job training and/or education to the roles of wife and mother. Reading books for elementary school children and textbooks designed for all educational levels either reinforced what amounted to stereotypic assumptions about women or ignored their contributions to humanity in fields ranging from art to zoology.

The entire educational system was a ripe target for feminist scholars. Even as Bernice Sandler began her research into institutionalized sex discrimination on college and university campuses, a grass-roots movement was underway. Professional and academic women looking at their institutions and professional associations were struck by the dearth of attention and respect paid to their scholarly efforts at professional conferences, the lack of women officers in professional associations, and the absence of women's issues from the undergraduate curricula. Buoyed by the rising tide of organized feminism, these activists and scholars were determined to shake up the academy.

Feminist scholars challenged the very foundations of higher education by introducing individual women's studies courses into the college curriculum that became the nucleus for women's studies programs (many such programs eventually met the requirements for granting an undergraduate degree). In the spring of 1969 Cornell University introduced the first women's course for which students could earn academic credit. By 1973 over 500 colleges and universities offered approximately 2,000 courses in women's studies (or related topics such as a women's history course) and 78 institutions had established programs in women's studies. After 1974, these programs received money from the Women's Educational Equity Act Program, which was designed for the express purpose of providing federal dollars for programs and materials that challenged sexism. Incorporated into a much more extensive educational bill, the program (like Title IX) moved through Congress with little fanfare. In 1977 the National Women's Studies Association was formed, and by the end of the decade the number of women's studies courses had increased to 30,000 and the number of programs exceeded 300.[35]

That the feminist revolution in higher education had an effect on young women is born out by several surveys conducted between the mid-1970s and the early 1980s. In a 1975 survey that compared the career aspirations of college women in 1969 and 1973, the researcher discovered that a majority of college women in 1969 not only viewed family life as incompatible with a career but also expected to put their careers on hold by remaining at home until they had raised their children. By 1973, however, only a plurality of college women surveyed adhered to a belief system that saw family life and a career as an either/or decision. In another study conducted on women's educational goals, 23 percent of the women students surveyed in 1971 believed that the main purpose of their college education was career development, whereas 18 percent believed that "preparation for marriage and family was the most important reason for attending college." In the 1980 survey only 1 percent of women students stated that the primary purpose of a college education was "family preparation," whereas 40 percent viewed "career preparation as the major purpose of higher education."[36]

## THE ERA: THE CENTERPIECE OF THE FEMINIST AGENDA

In addition to the landmark gains made in education during 1972, the presidential election year marked a watershed moment for liberal feminists for another reason. At last, after a two-year intensive lobbying effort, what liberal feminists came to regard as the centerpiece of the feminist agenda—the ERA—was voted out of Congress and sent to the states for ratification. Until May 1970, Congress had not bothered to hold hearings on the ERA for almost a quarter of a century (the previous hearings occurred in

1956). Had it not been for the daring act of "civil disobedience" in February 1970 by a handful of NOW members who disrupted a Senate subcommittee meeting on constitutional amendments (called to consider lowering the voting age to eighteen), it is anyone's guess when the chairman would have agreed to consider the ERA. When the subcommittee voted to send the amendment to the full committee (Judiciary), feminists went to work trying to get the amendment process jump-started in the House.

Trouble soon presented itself in the form of Representative Emanuel Celler (D-New York), chair of the House Judiciary Committee and a formidable and longtime ERA opponent. Although Celler was one of the most savvy and powerful men on the Hill, he soon found himself outmaneuvered by Martha Griffiths (D-Michigan), who as a member of the Ways and Means Committee and the Committee on Committees, was a powerful figure in her own right. To circumvent Celler's committee, Griffiths relied on a seldom used tactic—a discharge petition—that required the signatures of two-thirds of the House's membership to bring a petition (in this case the ERA) to the floor for a vote, even though the Judiciary Committee had not approved the measure. Once the motion was filed, a strong lobbying campaign by mainstream, liberal feminist organizations and considerable arm-twisting by Griffiths succeeded in getting the ERA to the House floor. On August 10, 1970, the ERA went before the House for a full vote, and after an hour's debate, it passed overwhelmingly by a vote of 350–15.[37]

Why did it take an additional eighteen months before the ERA's final passage out of the Senate? Simply put, with chairman of the Judiciary Committee Sam Ervin (D-North Carolina) at the helm, those opposed to the amendment used delaying tactics such as substitute amendments (e.g., resurrecting protective legislation) and unrelated riders (e.g., prayer in the public schools) to forestall a vote. The opponents of the ERA only had to stall the vote until the 91st Congress adjourned in December 1970. In effect, this tactic killed the measure, which meant that the entire process had to begin anew in both chambers of Congress in January 1971.

Once again, ERA supporters in and out of Congress faced the formidable opposition of Celler and Ervin. Once again, feminists launched a lobbying campaign that was both concentrated and wide ranging. On Capitol Hill, a determined and dedicated group of feminists made it their business to speak repeatedly to almost every member of Congress (and the members' congressional staff). They also initiated a nationwide letter campaign designed to overwhelm congressional offices with a floodtide of mail from pro-ERA constituents. One senate office reported receiving over "10,000 letters"; estimates are that the letter-writing campaign "topped out at over 5 million."[38]

In October the amendment reached the floor of the House for a vote, and on October 12, 1971, the ERA sailed through by a wide margin (354–23). In the Senate, Sam Ervin again assumed the role of obstructionist, but eventually he and his substitute amendments ran out of steam. On March 22, 1972, the ERA passed out of the Senate by an 84–8 vote and was sent to the states for ratification. Hawaii proudly became the first state to demonstrate its support for women's equality, and within a matter of months so had eighteen additional states. By the end of the year, twenty-two states had ratified the proposed Twenty-seventh Amendment to the Constitution. Although one of the provisions added to the amendment required its ratification within seven years, feminists were optimistic about the future as 1973 drew to a close. The start of the year had brought a stunning victory for the feminist agenda with the Supreme Court's abortion rights decision in *Roe v. Wade*; and by the year's end with eight more states ratifying the ERA, the total now stood at thirty. With only eight more states to go and five years to the deadline, Alice Paul's fifty-year-old dream of securing "equality of rights under the law" for women no longer seemed a distant vision but a distinct possibility.

## NOTES

1. Betty Friedan, *It Changed My Life: Writings on the Women's Movement* (New York: Random House, 1976), p. 145.

2. For membership information see Susan M. Hartmann, *From Margin to Mainstream: American Women and Politics since 1960* (Philadelphia: Temple University Press, 1989), pp. 69, 101 and Maren Lockwood Carden, *The New Feminist Movement* (New York: Russell Sage Foundation, 1974), pp. 105, 136.

3. Quotes are from Joan Hoff, *Law, Gender, and Injustice: A Legal History of U.S. Women* (New York: New York University Press, 1991), p. 248.

4. Judith Hole and Ellen Levine, *Rebirth of Feminism* (New York: Quadrangle Books, Inc., 1971), pp. 35-37; and Flora Davis, *Moving the Mountain: The Women's Movement in America since 1960* (New York: Simon & Schuster, 1991), pp. 62–64.

5. Barbara Sinclair Deckard, *The Women's Movement: Political, Socioeconomic, and Psychological Issues*, 3rd edition (New York: Harper and Row, Inc., 1983), p. 92.

6. Hole and Levine, *Rebirth of Feminism*, pp. 36–37, 106.

7. Statistics on child care are from Susan M. Hartmann, *The Home Front and Beyond: American Women in the 1940s* (Boston: Twayne Publishers, 1982), pp. 58–59, 84–85.

8. Steven D. McLaughlin et al., *The Changing Lives of American Women* (Chapel Hill: University of North Carolina Press, 1988), p. 115.

9. See Hole and Levine, *Rebirth of Feminism*, pp. 308–9 for statistics on the growth of feminist child-care centers.

10. Davis, *Moving the Mountain*, p. 282.

11. Each source consulted provided a different date for the founding of the National Women's Health Network: 1975 according to Davis, *Moving the Mountain*, p. 228; 1976 according to Winifred D. Wandersee, *On the Move: American Women in the 1970s* (Boston: Twayne Publishers, 1988), p. 86; and 1979 according to Deckard, *The Women's Movement*, p. 430. See Davis, *Moving the Mountain*, pp. 245–47 for health care among women of color.

12. Leslie J. Reagan, *When Abortion Was a Crime: Women, Medicine, and Law in the United States, 1867–1973* (Berkeley: University of California Press, 1997), pp. 187–88.

13. Ibid., p. 221.

14. Ibid., pp. 209–14.

15. Ibid., p. 244.

16. Hoff, *Law, Gender, and Injustice*, p. 301.

17. Carole J. Sheffield, "Sexual Terrorism," in Jo Freeman, ed., *Women, A Feminist Perspective,* 3rd edition (Palo Alto: Mayfield Publishing Company, 1984), p. 16.

18. Susan Griffin, "Rape: The All-American Crime," *Ramparts* 10 (September 1971), pp. 26, 33.

19. bell hooks, *Ain't I a Woman: Black Women and Feminism* (Boston: South End Press, 1981), pp. 51–56, 59 and Paula Giddings, *When and Where I Enter: The Impact of Black Women on Race and Sex in America* (New York: William Morrow and Company, 1984), p. 310.

20. Noreen Connell and Cassandra Wilson, *eds., Rape: The First Sourcebook for Women* (New York: New American Library, 1974), pp. 126–28; and Deckard, *The Women's Movement,* p. 433.

21. Ibid., p. 437.

22. Hartmann, *From Margin to Mainstream*, pp. 121–23 and Davis, *Moving the Mountain,* pp. 310–17.

23. Kathleen J. Tierney, "The Battered Women Movement and the Creation of the Wife Beating Problem," *Social Problems* 29 (February 1982), p. 210.

24. Deckard, *The Women's Movement,* p. 439 and John M. Johnson, "Program Enterprise and Official Cooptation in the Battered Women's Shelter Movement," *American Behavioral Scientist* 24 (1981), pp. 827–42, cited in Tierney, "The Battered Women Movement," p. 212.

25. Ibid., p. 209.

26. Gloria Steinem, "Erotica and Pornography: A Clear and Present Difference," in Laura Lederer, ed., *Take Back the Night: Women on Pornography* (New York: William Morrow and Company, 1980), p. 37.

27. Alice Echols, *Daring to Be Bad: Radical Feminism in America, 1967–1975* (Minneapolis: University of Minnesota Press, 1989), p. 291.

28. Robin Morgan, *Going Too Far: The Personal Chronicle of a Feminist* (New York: Random House, 1977), p. 169. Carole J. Sheffield coined the term "sexual terrorism," which she defined as a "system by which males frighten, and by frightening, control and dominate females." See Sheffield, "Sexual Terrorism," in Freeman, *Women,* pp. 3–20.

29. Irene Diamond, "Pornography and Repression: A Reconsideration of 'Who' and 'What'" in Lederer, *Take Back the Night,* p. 200; Diana E. H. Russell, "Pornography and Violence: What Does the New Research Say?" in Lederer, *Take Back the Night*, pp. 218–38; and Edward Donnerstein, Daniel Linz, and Steven Penrod, *The Question of Pornography: Research Findings and Policy Implications* (New York: The Free Press, 1987), p. 34.

30. Hoff, *Law, Gender, and Injustice,* p. 331.

31. The data on wage differentials comes from the U.S. Census Bureau's reports and are displayed in tables in Deckard, *The Women's Movement,* pp. 118, 134, 136.

32. Davis, *Moving the Mountain,* p. 207; Deckard, *The Women's Movement*, p. 130; and Hole and Levine, *Rebirth of Feminism*, p. 319. According to a 1979 National Research Council survey of men and women who earned doctoral degrees between 1970 and 1974, "men were more than twice as likely as women to have been promoted to full professor [while] more than half the women were still assistant professors or instructors." See Deckard, *The Women's Movement*, p. 130.

33. Wilmington (NC) *Sunday Star-News*, June 22, 1997, Section C, p. 1.

34. Hole and Levine, *Rebirth of Feminism*, pp. 414–27.

35. *Newsweek*, December 10, 1973; Wandersee, *On the Move*, pp. 119–26; Hole and Levine, *Rebirth of Feminism*, 324–25; and Deckard, *The Women's Movement*, pp. 351–52.

36. A. P. Parelius, "Change and Stability in College Women's Orientations Towards Education, Family, and Work," *Social Problems* 22 (1975), pp. 420–32 and M. C. Regan and M. E. Roland, "University Students: A Change in Expectations and Aspirations over the Decade," *Sociology of Education* 55 (1982), pp. 228–33. Both studies are cited in McLaughlin, *The Changing Lives of American Women*, pp. 170–79.

37. Hole and Levine, *Rebirth of Feminism*, pp. 55–56; Hartmann, *From Margin to Mainstream,* p. 105; and Davis, *Moving the Mountain*, pp. 124–27.

38. Davis, *Moving the Mountain*, p. 134.

**WOMEN'S STRIKE**
*AUGUST 26*

FREE Abortion on Demand
EQUAL Opportunities in Jobs & Education
FREE 24-hour Childcare Centers

MARCH: 5:30
59 st & 5th ave

RALLY: 7:30
bryant park

sponsored by the august 26 women's strike committee · 229 lexington · 685-7089

Poster announcing the first Women's Strike for Equality Day Rally in New York City, August 26, 1970.
Library of Congress

A women's liberation march, Washington, D.C., 1970. Library of Congress

Dr. Bernice Sandler, Women's Equity Action League, testifying in the Old Senate Caucus Room on women's second-class status in higher education, 1970. Library of Congress

Gloria Steinem and other members of the board of directors hold a press conference in Washington, D.C., 1972, to announce the formation of the Women's Action Alliance. Library of Congress

Shirley Chisholm thanking her delegates on the last night of the 1972 Democratic National Convention. Library of Congress

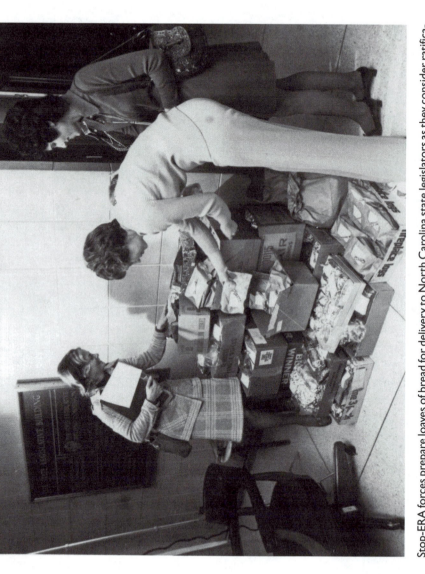

Stop-ERA forces prepare loaves of bread for delivery to North Carolina state legislators as they consider ratification in March 1975. Used by permission of Raleigh, North Carolina, *News and Observer*

Seattle Radical Women host a women's liberation conference at the University of Washington, 1976. Library of Congress

Phyllis Schlafly (center) leads an anti-ERA demonstration in front of the White House to protest First Lady Rosalynn Carter's support for the amendment, 1977. Library of Congress

Pro-ERA parade in Washington, D.C., 1977. Library of Congress

Bella Abzug marches in support for the ERA at a Women's Equality Day demonstration, 1977. Library of Congress

A White House briefing with Esther Peterson on the occasion of her appointment by President Jimmy Carter to the position of Special Assistant to the President for Consumer Affairs, 1977. Library of Congress

A pro-ERA rally in Raleigh, North Carolina, 1982. Used by permission of Raleigh, North Carolina, *News and Observer*.

# 5

## Backlash, The Political Right's War against Equal Rights and Reproductive Freedom, 1972–1992

In August 1967 when Phyllis Schlafly mailed approximately 3,000 copies of the inaugural issue of *The Phyllis Schlafly Report* to like-minded conservative Republican women activists, it is safe to assume that few feminists took any notice of the new publication. After all, why should they have bothered to pay attention to the actions of a woman little known beyond her immediate political circle? Moreover, Schlafly's motivation in starting up the monthly newsletter had nothing to do with an expressed desire to thwart the recent reemergence of feminism. Instead, having recently suffered through and lost a bruising, bitter fight over the presidency of the National Federation of Republican Women, Schlafly was determined to retain the support of conservative women who had voted for her. Snubbed by the "king and queen makers" who had endorsed the candidacy of Gladys O'Donnell (Schlafly coined these terms to deride the more moderate, "eastern establishment" wing of the Republican party), Schlafly also struck back at party regulars by using her newsletter to expand her political base both within and beyond the Republican party.

In an ironic twist of historical fate, the battle for leadership within the Republican women's organization in 1967 eventually claimed an unintended victim: feminism. In the wake of their slim victory over Phyllis Schlafly (the vote was 1,910 for O'Donnell and 1,494 for Schlafly), establishment women within the National Federation of Republican Women moved to undercut Schlafly's influence during the summer of 1967 by amending the organization's bylaws.[1] In effect, these changes made it almost impossible for any individual to amass a local power base within the women's organization that could be used to challenge the national leadership. Much to the dismay of mainstream Republican women, many of whom supported feminist issues, this calculated move backfired. Instead of isolating Schlafly within the Republican women's organization, this tactic encouraged Schlafly to look beyond the narrow constraints of partisanship. Ultimately, this strategy of coalition building, centered on an emotional appeal to traditional family values and gender roles, proved to be a boon for Schlafly's conservative crusade and a disaster for the feminist cause.

By 1970, about the time Schlafly launched the second of her failed attempts to win a seat in the House of Representatives, she had severed ties with the National Federation of Republican Women, whose membership slowly dwindled under O'Donnell's leadership. Nonetheless, she had not forsaken the importance of cultivating a constituency of women. As *The Phyllis Schlafly Report* steadily increased its readership in the early 1970s, it drew together a seemingly incompatible group of women that crossed party, regional, and religious lines. Many of these women had considered themselves apolitical, but thanks to Phyllis Schlafly's knack for organizing, their latent political power did not remain dormant for long. By the late fall of 1972 when Schlafly's opposition to the centerpiece of liberal feminism—the Equal Rights Amendment (ERA)—had grown sufficiently strong enough for her to found STOP ERA, she would have in place all the essential elements needed to launch a powerful, grass-roots movement: a mass communication network (the newsletter), a devoted core of women followers (ripe for political activism), and a trust fund to handle the flow of monetary contributions.

## HOW COULD IT FAIL? THE BATTLE OVER THE ERA, 1972–1982

In December 1971 a friend of Phyllis Schlafly's had urged her to look into the ERA, which was still pending before Congress. "I'm not interested in ERA. I don't even know which side I'm on," Schlafly supposedly replied.[2] Still, her friend persisted. Once Schlafly began to investigate the amendment, however, her indecision quickly vanished; and in its place grew a dogged determination to halt ratification. In keeping with the anti-"big government" philosophy of conservative Republicans, Schlafly's initial objection to the amendment centered on the power it granted to Congress to enforce gender equality. Over time, however, Schlafly developed a much more potent argument that centered on the dangers a "gender-blind" society posed to the sacred institution of the "New (Radical) Right": the American family.

In February 1972, a month before the ERA sailed through Congress, *The Phyllis Schlafly Report* launched a concerted attack on the amendment by devoting an entire issue to "What's Wrong with the ERA?" Schlafly had enough political savvy to recognize that there was little she could do at this late date to prevent the amendment from being voted out of Congress, and she understood that the real war would be waged in successive ratification battles fought in the various state legislatures.

Before Phyllis Schlafly founded STOP ERA, the amendment was strongly supported by a majority of Democrats and Republicans and was on the fast track toward ratification (to become law the amendment needed to be ratified by thirty-eight states and by December 1972 twenty-two states had affirmed their support for the amendment). Though the ratification process slowed somewhat over the next three years—eight "yes" votes in 1973, three in 1974, and one in 1975—feminists remained optimistic about the amendment's eventual passage. After all, a public opinion poll conducted in 1974 had indicated that 74 percent of the Americans queried supported the ERA. By 1975, with only four years to go before the March 22, 1979, deadline and only three more "yes" votes needed for ratification, victory seemed assured.

After 1975, however, the ratification process seemed to stall, and by 1977 it was in a full nosedive. In 1975 sixteen states successfully defeated ratification efforts, and bipartisan support for the amendment had begun to erode. For the first time in over thirty years, Republican women found themselves waging a spirited battle to "retain a pro-ERA plank" in their party's 1976 national platform. Spearheaded by the Republican Women's Task Force, feminists within the party won that fight in 1976, but they lost it in 1980 when the party made a sharp ideological turn to the Right with presidential nominee Ronald Reagan.[3]

Feminists used the 1977 National Women's Conference in Houston, Texas, as a staging ground for what they hoped would be the final push for ratification. Prior to this national gathering, feminists' energies and resources were focused on a myriad of issues, many of which had developed out of localized needs and concerns. At the Houston meeting, equal rights advocates and liberationists put aside their differences in favor of working together to secure ratification of the ERA, only to be frustrated and disappointed when their efforts failed. That same year (1977) only Indiana voted in favor of ratification; nine other states either rejected the amendment outright or succeeded in killing the amendment's chances of coming up for a vote in the legislature by tabling it in committee. Even more worrisome for pro-ERA activists was the success of rescission efforts in several states (Ne-

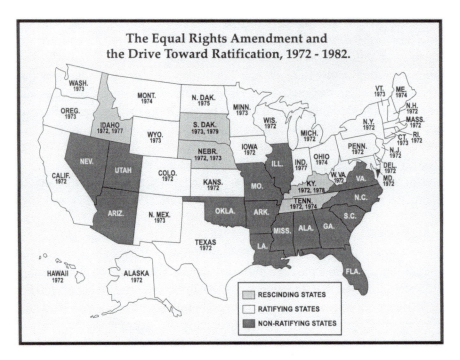

The Equal Rights Amendment and the Drive Toward Ratification, 1972 - 1982.

Source: Data are from Janet K. Boles. *The Politics of the Equal Rights Amendment*, New York: Longman, 1979 and *Facts on File World News Digest*, July 2, 1982.

braska, Tennessee, Idaho, Kentucky, South Dakota) that had previously ratified the amendment.

As it turned out, Indiana (1977) was the last state to vote for ratification. Of course, feminists could not have known this when they pressed for and won from Congress, in the summer of 1978, an unprecedented request for a three-year extension for ratification (the new and final deadline was set for June 30, 1982). By that summer, feminists knew that in order to win over the additional states, they would need foot soldiers and money. The National Organization for Women (NOW) led the way, increasing its membership to well over 200,000 and its annual budget to $8.5 million by 1982, but "the continuing debates over the legality of extension and rescission helped to erode feminists' efforts at consensus-building."[4] These two issues were headed for a showdown in federal court if ratification succeeded; in the end, however, failure to achieve ratification rendered these issues moot.

The final push for ratification came in June 1982 with votes scheduled in three states that had previously rejected or tabled the motion: North Carolina, Illinois, and Florida. The legislators' votes were expected to be close even though public opinion polls suggested that a majority of residents in each state favored the amendment. Pro-ERA sentiments also prevailed nationwide; a Harris Poll conducted in April 1982 "found that support for the ERA was at its highest level since 1976 with 63 percent of Americans in favor of it and 34 percent opposed." Across the country pro- and anti-ERA supporters held their collective breath as the final countdown toward ratification (or its defeat) began. On June 4, North Carolina's Senate tabled the motion; on June 21, Florida's Senate voted against the amendment; and on June 22, the Illinois House turned back equal rights for women.[5] Phyllis Schlafly and her STOP ERA forces had won.

The postmortems began not long after the ERA's defeat, with some of the earliest pronouncements by feminist activists containing heavy doses of self-blame. From Gloria Steinem, the editor-in-chief of *Ms.* magazine, to Eleanor Smeal, then president of NOW, the feminist leadership berated itself for having been too complacent about the prospects for an easy ratification process. Lulled into a false sense of security as the "yes" votes quickly multiplied in 1972, feminists presumably underestimated the strength of the anti-ERA forces and the power of their message. With hindsight, many feminists were convinced not only that the opposition had been better organized at the grass roots, but also that it had quickly gained the upper hand in the publicity wars with clever lobbying tactics. When Schlafly and her army of largely white, middle-class housewives ("middle-aged, well-groomed and frequently dressed in pink for symbolic reasons") visited the offices of state legislators, the women usually came armed with symbolic and tasty reminders of why they opposed the ERA.[6] Homemade loaves of bread with notes attached reading "from the breadmaker to the breadwinner" effectively communicated their position: The ERA's "rigid, unisex, gender-free mandate" would "seriously affect marriage as an economic and social institution by degrading the homemaker role."[7] By the time feminist organizations shifted their national campaigns to state-by-state drives, they discovered a well-entrenched opposition; nothing feminists tried from televised debates to fasting vigils to economic boycotts seemed to resonate with the "white, middle-aged males from business or professional backgrounds" who comprised the majority of legislators in the unratified states.[8]

The accuracy of this early rush to judgment has not stood the test of time and scholarship. If feminists were asleep in 1972, they certainly were wide awake by the spring of 1973. Seven months after Phyllis Schlafly founded STOP ERA, pro-ERA supporters established an ERA Action Committee made up of representatives from a coalition of national women's organizations to coordinate ratification efforts. Feminists were not political neophytes; they knew that ratification would be won or lost at the state level. In 1974 the "National Federation of Business and Professional Women hired a prominent Republican consulting firm" to conduct a detailed survey of the political climate in the seventeen unratified states; soon thereafter all but four of those states had active ratification campaigns. The spirit of bipartisan cooperation was also evident in 1976 with the formation of ERA America jointly headed by Liz Carpenter, a Democrat, and Elly Peterson, a Republican.[9] At the White House, support for the ERA remained strong during the 1970s, regardless of the party in residence, with First Ladies Betty Ford and Rosalynn Carter actively campaigning for the amendment's passage. Ronald Reagan's White House, however, was hostile to the amendment (Nancy Reagan was not a spokesperson for the ERA). Maureen Reagan, the president's daughter from his first marriage, publicly broke with her father over this issue and campaigned actively for its passage.

Why then did the ERA fail? On a very simple level, its failure must be viewed within the context of the amending process that the Founding Fathers "deliberately made difficult," according to historian Mary Frances Berry. While hundreds of amendments have been proposed over the course of this nation's history, only twenty-seven amendments have succeeded to date. The procedure to amend the constitution requires not only a two-thirds majority in the upper and lower chambers of Congress but also a majority vote in at least three-fourths of the states' legislative assemblies. Thus in the case of the ERA, proponents needed to win the support of thirty-eight states; opponents needed only the support of thirteen states to block the amendment. Furthermore, in many of the states that required only a simple majority for a "yes" vote, the strategy to defeat the amendment frequently came down to convincing one state legislator to vote "no." Playing the numbers game is useful, but it has its limitations. While this perspective serves as a reminder that only a plurality of Americans had to find the ERA objectionable, it begs two questions: Who opposed the ERA and why?

To answer these critically linked questions, the narrative returns to an examination of Phyllis Schlafly's message and her constituency. Although organized resistance to the ERA predated Phyllis Schlafly's involvement in the movement, her name has become synonymous with its success. Indeed, long before Schlafly organized STOP ERA in 1972, the John Birch Society (an ultraconservative anticommunist organization founded in the 1950s) had worked against the amendment while it was pending in Congress. The John Birch Society was not alone in these early efforts. Two groups dominated by housewives but supported by their husbands' money sprang into existence in the early 1970s: the California-based Happiness of Womanhood, and the League of Housewives, which claimed a national membership of approximately 10,000 by 1972. Two long-standing, mainstream women's organizations, the Daughters of the American Revolution and the

National Council of Catholic Women also opposed the ERA.[10] None of these groups, however, received the credit that Phyllis Schlafly did for derailing the amendment. Why?

## THE NEW RIGHT VERSUS THE FEMINIST AGENDA

Phyllis Schlafly earned star-billing in the mid-1970s for her political acumen in forging an effective coalition out of the disparate elements of the political Right. Between 1972 and 1975, the years in which Schlafly created STOP ERA and its companion, the Eagle Forum, the political Right stood at a critical juncture in its metamorphosis from the "Old Right" to the "New Right." The Old Right, represented best by the secular-based John Birch Society, had combined the need to defend the United States from communist subversion at home and abroad with the belief that an intrusive "big government" represented a threat to the cornerstones of American democracy: individualism and the free enterprise system (laissez-faire capitalism). In 1964 the Old Right won a victory with the nomination of presidential candidate Barry Goldwater, only to see its candidate defeated in the landslide victory of the Democratic choice, Lyndon Baines Johnson. Many scholars credit Phyllis Schlafly, a longtime supporter of Goldwater, with securing his nomination by promoting the Arizona senator and his ideas in her 1964 self-published handbook for the Right, *A Choice Not an Echo*.

By the early 1970s a different version of the Right was beginning to emerge within American political culture; by the late 1970s, this "New Right" (also referred to as the "Radical Right") was well on its way to taking control of the Republican party. Members of the New Right were convinced that American society was on the verge of losing its public virtue as "secular values" replaced "religious values." The New Right was more interested in halting the acceptence of key social issues—the ERA, abortion, busing, homosexuality, affirmative action—than in promoting the economic and defense issues—welfare, taxes, a balanced budget, anticommunism, a strong national defense system—that had consumed the Old Right.

The New Right also distinguished itself from the Old Right in two ways that proved to be disastrous for feminism. The Old Right "believed that the rational, self-interested individual" stood at the center of American society, whereas the New Right "considered the family to be the sacred unit of society." Along with the New Right's focus on the family came starkly different perceptions about gender relations. Although the Old Right leaned toward the position that the social-cultural roles of men and women were rooted in their distinctive biological makeups, these differences were not equated with concepts of natural superiority/inferiority. For the New Right, however, the differences between men and women were not so much rooted in biology as they were in God's laws. According to this more rigid interpretation of gender, the roles of men (husband, father, breadwinner) and women (wives, mothers, helpmeets) were "divinely ordained and hierarchical with men having natural authority over women." The protection and preservation of these roles were deemed essential to the very survival of the family and society. Any attempt to tinker with this divine order might call forth the biblical consequences of God's wrath. Did the feminist agenda—the ERA, abortion rights, equity in education, child care, domestic violence shelters—fit this bill? Members of the New Right certainly thought so, and beginning with Phyllis Schlafly's anti-ERA campaign, they were determined to save America from the feminists.[11]

By the early 1970s, as Phyllis Schlafly's career as a social activist was taking off, her political philosophy was becoming an amalgam of the ideological tenets of the Old Right and the New Right. Schlafly's old-line, ultraconservative thinking surfaced first in her opposition to the power accorded to the federal government under section two of the ERA (should it pass). At the same time, Schlafly's moral training prepared her to accept the religious fundamentalism of the New Right. Schlafly had grown up in a deeply religious, conservative Catholic household, had received a parochial education (until college), and had married and raised her six children in the church. For Schlafly, the link between the Old Right and the New Right was her deeply held moral obligation to do battle with all the "isms" threatening "the absolute moral authority of God": communism, secular humanism, and feminism. Although Schlafly made these connections explicit in a 1981 introduction to an exposé on secular humanism, she had been acting on these heartfelt beliefs at least since the founding of the Eagle Forum in 1975. Wrote Schlafly:

Just as humanism is based on atheism and the notion that man is at the center of the universe, Feminism puts woman at the center of the universe. They [feminists] chose the word "liberation" because they mean liberation from home, husband, family, and children.[12]

Thus, Phyllis Schlafly and the more than 50,000 women who came to be associated formally with her cause both anticipated and paved the way (in 1979) for Reverend Jerry Falwell's Moral Majority, a Christian Right organization that would lend its considerable financial and voting strength to the war against the ERA and feminism.

Somehow, the ERA, which simply stated that "equality of rights under the law shall not be denied or abridged by the United States or by any State on account of sex," had been reinterpreted by the New Right as a mandate to destroy the American family. Among the things the ERA stood accused of (if it passed) were the following: that married women would lose their "right" to support by their husbands (meaning that the ERA would "require" married women to seek paid employment outside the home); that working parents would "lose" their authority over their children who would be sent to government-sponsored child-care centers; that women would "lose" their automatic "right" to their children in divorce/custody cases; that homosexual relationships would be legalized (through marriage); that women would be required to register for the draft; that the ERA would give women a "constitutional" right to abortion; that rape laws would be invalidated; and that public bathrooms and prisons would become sexually "integrated."[13]

With whom did these messages resonate? The results of numerous polls and surveys conducted by social scientists during and after the ratification process have produced a composite of the men and women opposed to the ERA; not so surprisingly, the social characteristics of this group closely mirrored the demographic makeup of the New Right. In the 1970s, men and women attracted to the anti-ERA/New Right movements tended to come from the middle to upper classes; and more than likely, they were white, married, and middle-aged. Though the vast majority of women were nonworking housewives, those women who did work for wages predominated in the clerical occupations. Meanwhile, their husbands held high-paying, high-status managerial or professional positions. In general, the husbands attained a higher educational level than their wives (the men reported earning more college and advanced degrees, whereas the women indicated that they had attended college). Regular church attendance (especially in a Catholic, Mormon, or fundamentalist Protestant church) reinforced a rigid, moral opposition to the ERA; this religiosity was also strongly associated with conservative political positions on busing, affirmative action, abortion, the civil rights movement, and social welfare.

In the final analysis, the ERA failed largely because of the growing strength of New Right politics in the South and in several central and western states. Had the ERA gotten out of Congress a few years earlier than it did, when it was still "viewed as a narrow, legal issue," it probably would have passed. Once, however, an opposition rooted in a right-wing ideology began to coalesce, the amendment's chances for success became more uncertain. By the late 1970s, the anti-ERA campaign was linked to a much broader "right-wing backlash against feminism, civil rights, and social welfare legislation." Unifying the Old Right and the New Right were the issues of privatism and localism; the desire to "protect the private sphere of the traditional family, private enterprise, and a desire to protect local governments from federal intervention aimed at improving the positions of blacks and other minorities."[14] Between the mid to late 1970s, these ideological sentiments were finding a home in the Republican party.

## INTO THE BREACH: THE ASSAULT ON REPRODUCTIVE RIGHTS

Any attempt to separate the defeat of the ERA from a more concerted assault on feminism falls short when probing the state of reproductive rights during the presidential administrations of Jimmy Carter, Ronald Reagan, and George Bush (1976–1992). Although *Roe v. Wade*, the 1973 landmark judicial decision on abortion, was not completely overturned during this era of increasing political conservatism, its intent was gutted as the New Right's assault on feminism made its presence felt in American political life. As the Republican party swung further to the right during the 1980s, the impact of this new reactionary political movement was demonstrated not only through the implementation of restrictive legislation but also through the judicial decrees of an increasingly conservative federal bench and Supreme Court.

The ink on the *Roe* decision was barely dry when an organized resistance to a woman's constitutional right to privacy in matters pertaining to reproduction developed. The Catholic church took an early lead in the opposition that surfaced almost overnight. Members of the Catholic hierarchy proposed that legislators and parishioners in good standing with the Church be punished for their "proabortion" stance (suggestions ranged from denying communion to excommunication). In 1975 a plan to found "tightly knit and well-organized antiabortion groups in all congressional districts for the purpose of pressuring members of Congress" received the support of Catholic bishops nationwide.[15] This move was followed a year later by the National Conference of Catholic Bishops' support for a political campaign aimed at securing a constitutional amendment banning abortion.

Antiabortion politics encouraged the formation of an unusual political alliance as numerous fundamental Christian sects, the Mormon church, and the Orthodox branch of American Judaism joined the Catholic church's backlash against *Roe*. For some members of this diverse religious coalition, the underlying objection to the Supreme Court's decision was a belief that life begins at conception; thus abortion at any stage of pregnancy was tantamount to murder. For others *Roe* came to symbolize female sexual promiscuity, an attack on male sexual privilege (the double standard), and a selfish act of individualism run amuck and inspired, of course, by the feminist movement.

According to this latter interpretation, only the fear of an unwanted pregnancy had prevented women from engaging in premarital sex; thus, access to legal, safe, and inexpensive abortion services allowed women to be as sexually "free" and active as men and suffer no consequences from their "promiscuity." Fanning the flames of this concern over female sexual "immorality" was the fact that unmarried white teenagers comprised the majority of women seeking abortion services in the years following legalization.[16] A woman's sexual freedom also was linked to feminist demands for independence from men and the institutions of marriage and the family. Abortion foes believed that when a woman opted for an abortion, she was making a "selfish" choice that put her individual needs—schooling, work, the desire to remain single, or limit her family size if married—above those of society, which were defined solely in terms of accepting the primacy of marriage and motherhood. These fears found embodiment in the Family Protection Act of 1981, a legislative program initially designed by the New Right to strengthen the "besieged" American family by promoting "public policies favoring marriage, childbirth, heterosexuality, and the role of the husband as household head."[17]

Before the close of 1973, antiabortion activists founded the National Right to Life Committee; within a few years, local chapters proliferated across the nation. New words and new images emerged in the American political lexicon as "pro-life" and "pro-choice" advocates sought to influence the outcome of political campaigns with emotional appeals, campaign contributions, and the promise of votes delivered. Pro-life forces (also dubbed "anti-choice" activists by feminists) quickly gained the upper hand in this contest by relying on pseudoscientific revisionism.

Despite the fact that "between 92 to 96 percent of the 1.5 million abortions per year occurred within the first trimester and over half within the first eight weeks of the pregnancy," the term embryo (the period from conception to eight weeks) completely disappeared from the literature published by the right-to-life movement and the image of a fetus (from eight weeks to birth) was recast into that of an "unborn child."[18] According to the "scientific" information produced by this movement, at eleven weeks of fetal development this unborn child (often referred to as a "baby") had the ability to "breathe, swallow, digest, urinate, sleep, dream, taste, feel pain, react to light and noise, and learn things."[19] On placards waved at rallies and in pamphlets circulated to voters and legislators, pictures of perfectly formed babies were contrasted with gruesome, bloody images of dismembered limbs, torsos, and heads of aborted fetuses.

In 1985, pseudoscientific support for the right-to-life movement received a political boost with the White House screening of *The Silent*

*Scream*, a controversial documentary produced by Dr. Bernard Nathanson, a gynecologist and former abortion provider. With the help of ultrasound imaging, the film followed the real abortion of a twelve-week fetus. As the viewer watched the fetus "jerking and kicking as its body is sucked from its mother," the voice of Dr. Nathanson narrated: "We see the silent scream of a child threatened imminently with extinction. It is moving away in a pathetic attempt to escape the inexorable instruments which the abortionist is using." Medical experts condemned the film as a "cheap shot—an emotional, unscientific piece of propaganda" (a fetus's central nervous system is not sufficiently developed at twelve weeks to feel and respond to pain). President Reagan, whose habit it was to address the right-to-life demonstrations held each year in Washington, D.C., on the anniversary of the *Roe* decision, responded to the film's message by "encouraging the distribution of hundreds of copies of the film to every senator, representative, and Supreme Court justice."[20]

With few exceptions, pro-choice advocates avoided the use of such grisly sensationalism; when they did, the purpose was to remind viewers of the needless and often life-threatening medical complications women suffered at the hands of "back-street" abortionists (in the immediate pre-*Roe* era, approximately 350,000 women were admitted to hospitals for treatment of complications resulting from illegal abortions). Instead, they attempted to combat the false "reality" of the pro-life position with medical and sociological information about abortion, with appeals to a woman's constitutional guarantee of privacy, and with a nod to feminist principles emphasizing a woman's "right" to control her body. In a chilling replay of the rhetorical contest that had characterized the debates between pro- and anti-ERA activists, however, the strategies of pro-choice advocates were no match for those of the pro-life forces.

By the early 1980s, abortion had become the "wedge" issue in American politics as Congress, the president, and the courts weighed in on the side of the right-to-life movement. Although the antiabortion initiative began with right-wing members of Congress, it was President Reagan's decision to make this stance the litmus test for appointing judges to the federal courts and to the Supreme Court that gave the edge to the right-to-life movement. In this, the president had the support of his political party; since 1980 (the same year the party turned its back on the ERA) the Republican platform supported a constitutional amendment to overturn the *Roe* decision.

The first successful legislative attempt to undermine *Roe* occurred in 1976 with the passage of the Hyde Amendment. Named for Henry Hyde (R-Illinois), this amendment was actually a rider attached to an appropriations bill for the Departments of Labor and Health, Education, and Welfare.

Federal dollars for abortions for poor women had increased rapidly after the *Roe* decision; the intent of this rider was to prohibit the use of Medicaid funds for abortion services unless the mother's life was threatened or the pregnancy resulted from rape or incest. Requests to terminate a pregnancy under these circumstances (rape or incest) would be granted only if the woman reported the sexual assault to federal authorities within sixty days of the incident.

Lawsuits filed on behalf of poor women led to a temporary stay, but only until November 8, 1976, when the Supreme Court refused to uphold the injunction against the Hyde amendment (*Califano v. McRae*). In a 1980 decision, the Supreme Court went one step further in limiting the ability of poor women to secure abortions. While *Harris v. McRae* upheld a woman's constitutional right to an abortion, the Court rejected the idea that the government (under the Medicaid system) should pay for this right. Taken together, these early legislative and judicial decisions made it possible for states to deny poor women public funds for abortions; and by 1987, thirty-eight states had such provisions on the books. Thus had reproductive rights been pushed backward to the pre-*Roe* era when abortion was largely the privilege of middle- and upper-class women.

Women, single or married (but not teenagers), who could afford to pay for an abortion saw their constitutional right to privacy whittled away more slowly. Although many states passed restrictive legislation in the late 1970s and early 1980s, these laws, which focused on a husband's consent, a woman's informed consent, and a mandatory twenty-four-hour waiting period, were overturned in early Supreme Court decisions. In *Planned Parenthood of Central Missouri v. Danforth* (1976), the Supreme Court overturned a law requiring a husband's consent before a woman could have a first-trimester abortion. In a 1983 decision, *City of Akron v. Akron Center for Reproductive Health,* the justices voided a 1978 law requiring both a twenty-four-hour waiting period after a woman had signed an "informed consent" form and hospitalization for all second-trimester abortion procedures (which doubled the costs of the medical procedure).

Following the *Akron* decision, radicals within the right-to-life movement unleashed a terrorist campaign targeting members of the medical community who provided abortion services. In the year following the *Akron* decision, two dozen reproductive clinics reported attacks (arson and bombings), and close to a score of clinic directors were threatened with violence. Though these early assaults did not result in the loss of life, within a decade "pro-life" violence had escalated to murder. A Florida abortion doctor, Dr. David Gunn, was gunned down in 1993; Gunn's replacement, Dr. John Britton, and his volunteer escort, James Barrett, were murdered in 1994; in that same year, a December rampage on two Massachusetts abortion clinics resulted in the deaths of staff members Shannon Lowney and Lee Ann Nichols and the wounding of five others. Testimony presented at all three trials linked the perpetrators to the "hard-core" faction of the pro-life movement.

Two organizations in particular contributed to the heightened tensions over the abortion issue: Terry Randall's Operation Rescue and Joe Scheidler's Pro-Life Action League. Taking a page from the handbook of the political Left, these militant organizations engaged in acts of civil disobedience, forming picket lines and human gauntlets in front of abortion clinics. The purpose was intimidation; demonstrators hoped to frighten patients away from besieged clinics and to harass the medical staff into closing down the clinics. Overzealous members of these and other right-to-life organizations, however, took their campaigns into neighborhoods and to schools; picketing the homes and driveways of "abortion doctors" and leafleting the schools of doctors' children with pamphlets that labeled their parents "murderers." Pro-choice advocates responded by filing lawsuits charging these pro-life organizations with mounting a conspiracy to close down abortion clinics. Guided by the Racketeer Influenced and Corrupt Organizations Act, many judges rendered rulings favorable to the pro-choice side. Although the imposition of stiff fines led Operation Rescue to cease its operations by the early 1990s, the organization's demise did not halt antiabortion protests. Instead, new and more dangerous groups, like the American Coalition of Life Activities and Pro-Life Virginia, sprang into existence and the violence—sniper attacks, bombings, arson, and murder—escalated.

Antiabortion protests also had an adverse effect on women's health-care services. Even though abortion remained legal in this country, "by 1987, 85 percent of the nation's counties had no abortion services" with the rural areas, where these services ceased to exist altogether, the hardest hit. [21] Beyond the immediate loss in the number of doctors willing to put themselves and their families at risk by continuing to provide legal abortions, another chilling effect of the antiabortion crusade has been that only a few medical schools continue to teach interns and residents how to perform abortions. By 1992, "only 12 percent of the programs for residents in obstetrics and gynecology taught first trimester abortions."[22]

Beginning in the mid-1980s, an increasingly politically conservative Supreme Court signaled its willingness to limit *Roe* by reexamining restrictive state laws previously struck down for constituting an "undue burden" for women. In a 1986 case, *Thornburgh v. the American College of Obstetricians and Gynecologists* (named for Reagan's Attorney General, Richard

Thornburgh), the justices turned back a harshly worded Pennsylvania law requiring doctors to provide specific information to women about fetal development, medical risks of an abortion, and alternatives to abortion. A victory for the pro-choice side? Yes, but in a sharply divided 5–4 opinion, several justices indicated their willingness to consider cases that would open the door for a reexamination of *Roe*.

That same year, the justices heard oral arguments in an Illinois case (*Hartigan v. Zbaraz*) pertaining to parental notification for minors, but no decision was reached and the case was held over until the 1988 term. By then, almost two dozen states had passed statutes similar to the one favored by Illinois. Ultimately, the Court decided not to rehear oral arguments in the *Hartigan* case; instead, three abortion cases dealing with variations on parental notification were scheduled for the 1989–1990 Court session. Although the justices finally handed down decisions supporting parental consent in two of the three cases, these rulings seemed almost anticlimactic to the struggle to preserve *Roe*.[23] That battle appeared lost in July 1989 when the Supreme Court rendered its controversial decision in a case it had accepted at the beginning of the year at the urging of the Bush administration.

When the Supreme Court handed down a 5-4 decision in the Missouri case, *Webster v. Reproductive Health Services*, on July 3, 1989, it not only shredded the *Roe* decision but also provided an open invitation for states to draft laws designed to overturn *Roe*. The 1986 Missouri law, which opened with a preamble declaring that human life begins at conception, had been written by William Webster, the state's attorney general, for the express purpose of gutting *Roe*. Key provisions of the state law upheld by the justices in the *Webster* decision included a ban on all abortions performed by public employees in public facilities with or without the use of public funds (private clinics and hospitals receiving public money were included in this ban, too). Abortion counseling in public facilities (or such services provided by public funds) was also prohibited. Under this sweeping ban, legal abortions, which almost ceased to exist in Missouri, were permissible only if the mother's life was threatened. *Webster* also called into question *Roe*'s trimester framework by requiring doctors to order fetal viability testing at twenty weeks (less than 1 percent of abortions nationwide occurred after twenty weeks, and according to neonatal experts at the time, fetal viability became a significant medical factor only after twenty-four weeks). Still, under the *Webster* decision, a woman seeking a second-trimester abortion (at which time the state's only obligation was to protect the mother's life) was required to submit to a needless, expensive medical procedure.

*Webster* opened the door for states to draft even more restrictive abortion laws. Within a year of the decision, dozens of states had done so. In 1990, for example, the Idaho legislature approved an abortion bill designed specifically to meet the objections of the one justice considered by many Court watchers to be the swing vote on abortion cases. " 'What we're after is Sandra Day O'Connor,' said Brian Johnston, Western regional director of the National Right to Life Committee. 'We know Justice O'Connor wants to overturn *Roe v. Wade*. We just want to give her something she's comfortable with.' "[24] With few exceptions—rape, incest, severe fetal deformity, the physical health of the mother—the Idaho abortion statute outlawed abortion. Members of the medical community who violated the law faced up to $10,000 in civil fines and put themselves at risk for civil lawsuits instituted by the father. Women seeking abortions were not penalized, unless they attempted a self-induced abortion. Under this circumstance, the fine was $10,000. The governor of Idaho vetoed the bill eight days after it cleared the state legislature.

In Pennsylvania, pro-choice advocates were not so fortunate; four months after *Webster*, a restrictive abortion measure won approval from the state legislature and the governor. The Abortion Control Act of 1989 mandated a woman's informed consent (based on a graphic description of fetal development), a twenty-four-hour waiting period, a written statement indicating that a married woman had informed her husband of her decision, and parental notification for a minor. The law also required doctors performing late-term abortions (after six months) to select a procedure that would best ensure the survivial of the fetus. In January 1990, pro-choice activists won a temporary injunction against portions of the statute from a federal court judge; once the appeals process began, the stage was set for yet another momentous Supreme Court decision.

The Supreme Court's 1992 decision in *Planned Parenthood Association of Southeastern Pennsylvania v. Casey* took both pro-choice and pro-life supporters by surprise. By a vote of 5–4, the justices upheld the core of the *Roe* decision; namely, a woman's right to an abortion up until the point of fetal viability and beyond that point if her physical and/or mental health was threatened if the pregnancy continued. On this point, feminists applauded. At the same time, however, the majority tossed out the trimester framework that had guided previous Court decisions regarding a state's ability to regulate abortion. On this point, which turned on what constituted an "unfair burden" to women seeking an abortion, the pro-life forces took heart. While the *Casey* decision struck down the Pennsylvania provision requiring a husband's consent (the issue in the 1976 *Danforth* case), it upheld the twenty-four-hour waiting period and an informed consent lecture that required physicians to describe fetal development and counsel women about the alternatives to abortion (striking down the undue burden arguments advanced in the 1983 *Akron* case and in the 1986 *Thornburgh* decision). Other provisions of the Pennsylvania law similar to those upheld in the *Webster* decision (such as the ban on abortions in public facilities) were left intact.

The partial victory for both sides in the *Casey* decision reflected an emerging "middle ground" on the Supreme Court and in American culture. After over two decades of feminist-inspired debates and negotiations over the meaning of personal liberty and the constitutional right to privacy in such matters as sexuality, marriage, and family life, a new but still fragile consensus was in the making. According to a 1993 Gallop Poll, a significant majority of Americans (83 percent) supported the legalization of abortion, but only a fraction of Americans (13 percent) disapproved of abortion no matter the circumstance. At the same time, only a minority (32 percent) favored legalization "under any circumstances." Instead, a slim majority of Americans (51 percent) believed that abortion should be legal, but only under certain circumstances (in cases of rape, incest, or severe fetal deformity, and to save the life of the mother).[25]

On the Supreme Court, this new centrist position (which found expression in the *Casey* decision) was the result of shifting ideological alliances among the justices as the Court's most liberal members—William Brennan and Thurgood Marshall—retired and were replaced, respectively, by the more temperate David Souter (in 1990) and the more conservative Clarence Thomas (in 1991). In the *Casey* decision, the swing votes belonged to justices O'Connor, Souter, and Anthony Kennedy.

Since *Casey*, the Supreme Court's composition has been altered again with the retirements of Byron R. White and Harry A. Blackmun and their replacement with two justices—Ruth Bader Ginsburg (1993) and Stephen G. Breyer (1994)—both nominated by the country's first avowedly pro-choice president, Bill Clinton (elected in 1992). Since *Casey*, the Court has hinted at its reticence to reexamine *Roe* by denying full review to "cases dealing directly with abortion rights, while granting "full review to disputes involving protests outside abortion clinics." An example of the Court's new silence on *Roe* came shortly after its 1997–1998 session opened. On October 20, 1997, in a "rare near-unanimous vote" (with Antonin Scalia the lone dissenter), the justices decided not to hear an appeal of a "Louisiana parental-consent law found by lower courts" to have placed an undue burden on the abortion rights of minors.[26] How long this newfound consensus will continue to preserve the heart of the *Roe* decision is, of course, a matter of conjecture.

What is not a matter of speculation is the success of the antiabortion movement since the mid-1980s and the increase in antiabortion violence

by extremists within the pro-life movement. The addition of five conservative justices during the Reagan and Bush administrations led directly to the
narrowing of the *Roe* decision. This reality raises the question of whose reproductive freedom was put at risk by these Supreme Court decisions.
Twenty-four-hour delays, the denial of public funding, new regulations on
abortion counseling, restrictions on facilities where abortions can be performed, and the implementation of parental consent decrees (that have
ranged from mild to rigid) have adversely affected poor women and teenagers. This is a troubling reality for feminists who struggled to advance and
protect the reproductive rights of all women regardless of their race, ethnicity, class, age, or marital status. And finally, although abortion remains a legal, medical procedure, the lives of those who provide, support, and seek
this service have been placed in extreme jeopardy. Since the late 1970s,
"there have been seven murders, at least 16 attempted murders, more than
200 bombings and arsons, 750 death threats and bomb threats, and hundreds of acts of vandalism, intimidation, stalking, and burglary of abortion
providers across the country (Dr. Barnett A. Slepian's murder in Buffalo,
New York, on October 23, 1998, is the most recent example of antiabortion
violence)."[27] If this undeclared war against abortion continues unchecked,
much more will be at stake in this country than reproductive freedom.

## NOTES

1. Carol Felsenthal, *The Sweetheart of the Silent Majority: The Biography of
Phyllis Schlafly* (Garden City, NY: Doubleday and Company, Inc., 1981), p. 193.

2. Ibid., p. 240.

3. Susan M. Hartmann, *From Margin to Mainstream: American Women and
Politics since 1960* (Philadelphia: Temple University Press, 1989), pp. 83–84.

4. The statistics on the National Organization for Women (NOW) are from
Janet K. Boles, "The Equal Rights Amendment as a Non-Zero-Sum Game," in
Joan Hoff-Wilson, ed., *Rights of Passage: The Past and Future of the ERA*
(Bloomington: Indiana University Press, 1986), p. 59. The quote is from Mary
Frances Berry, *Why ERA Failed: Politics, Women's Rights, and the Amending
Process of the Constitution* (Bloomington: Indiana University Press, 1986), p. 70

5. Berry, *Why ERA Failed*, pp. 80–81; Boles, "Equal Rights Movement," in
Hoff-Wilson, ed., *Rights of Passage*, p. 57; and Mark Daniels, Robert Darcy, and
Joseph Westphal, "The ERA Won—At Least in the Opinion Polls," *Political Sci-
ence* 15 (1982), pp. 578–84.

6. David W. Brady and Kent L. Tedin, "Ladies in Pink: Religion and Political Ideology in the Anti-ERA Movement," *Social Science Quarterly* 56 (1976),
pp. 568–70.

7. Quotes are from Felsenthal, *Sweetheart of the Silent Majority,* p. 260 and Phyllis Schlafly, *The Power of the Positive Woman* (New Rochelle, NY: Arlington House Publishers, 1977), pp. 85, 133.

8. Val Burris, "Who Opposed the ERA? An Analysis of the Social Bases of Antifeminism," *Social Science Quarterly* 64 (1983), p. 315.

9. Berry, *Why ERA Failed,* pp. 66–67.

10. Hartmann, *From Margin to Mainstream,* p. 135.

11. The quotes are from Rebecca E. Klatch, *Women of the New Right* (Philadelphia: Temple University Press, 1987), pp. 4–5, 9.

12. Ibid., p. 130.

13. Schlafly, *The Power of the Positive Woman,* pp. 68–138.

14. Burris, "Who Opposed the ERA?," p. 316.

15. Barbara Sinclair Deckard, *The Women's Movement: Political, Socioeconomic, and Psychological Issues,* 3rd edition (New York: Harper and Row Publishers, 1983), p. 425.

16. Between 1975 and 1984, 65 percent of all women seeking abortions were between the ages of fifteen and twenty-four, and 75 percent of them were unmarried. According to numerous studies, white teenagers and older, poor, and minority women were the primary recipients of legalized abortion services. See Rosalind Pollack Petchesky, *Abortion and Woman's Choice: The State, Sexuality, and Reproductive Freedom* (Boston: Northeastern University Press, 1984), pp. 142–44.

17. Ibid., p. 264 for the quote and pp. 264–67 for an analysis of the bill's provisions.

18. Ibid., p. 347.

19. From a pamphlet distributed by "The Precious Feet People," P.O. Box 730, Taylor, Arizona, produced by Hayes Publishing Company of Cincinnati, Ohio, 1981 (in possession of author).

20. "The Silent Scream: Seeking an Audience," *Newsweek* (February 25, 1985), p. 37.

21. Susan Faludi, *Backlash: The Undeclared War against American Women* (New York: Doubleday and Company, 1991), p. 415; see Leslie J. Reagan, *When Abortion Was a Crime: Women, Medicine, and Law in the United States, 1867–1973* (Berkeley: University of California Press, 1997), p. 252 for information on the absence of abortion services in rural America.

22. Reagan, *When Abortion Was a Crime,* p. 292.

23. In *Ohio v. Akron Center for Reproductive Health,* a 6–3 majority upheld a law requiring the signature of one parent before a minor could obtain an abortion. In *Hodgson v. Minnesota,* a 5–4 majority prevailed in preserving a statute mandating both parents' signatures even when the parents were divorced and only one parent was the legal guardian. *Ragsdale v. Turnock* was dropped. See Joan Hoff, *Law, Gender, and Injustice: A Legal History of U.S. Women* (New York: New York University Press, 1991), pp. 314, 474 (note 92).

24. The *Wilmington* (North Carolina) *Morning Star*, Thursday, March 22, 1990.

25. George Gallop Jr., *The Gallop Poll, Public Opinion 1993* (Wilmington, DE: Scholarly Resources, 1994), pp. 73–74, 145–47, cited in Reagan, *When Abortion Was a Crime*, p. 341, note 28.

26. *Wilmington* (North Carolina) *Morning Star*, Tuesday, October 21, 1997.

27. Frederick Clarkson, "Some Anti-Abortion Zealots Want a Country Governed by Preachers," *Wilmington* (North Carolina) *Sunday Star News*, November 22, 1998.

# 6

## Epilogue: Entering the Twenty-First Century

The September/October 1997 silver anniversary issue of *Ms.* opened with a self-congratulatory, optimistic message to its readers from "the present caretaker of this institution," editor Marcia Ann Gillespie.

And "they" said it wouldn't last. They being all the media soothsayers and social commentators who, when *Ms.* debuted 25 years ago, were as quick to dismiss the viability of this magazine as they were the movement that spawned it. They said we'd run out of things to write about and the movement would run out of steam. Well, here we are 25 years later still going strong and gearing up for a new century.[1]

As Marcia Gillespie's introductory remarks suggest, second-wave feminism has exhibited a remarkable staying power in American society. While its critics note that countless women's groups have come and gone over the last thirty years—primarily those from the more radical women's liberation branch of the movement—and that several objectives previously achieved under the feminist banner have suffered setbacks, feminism does not appear to be in danger of becoming passé as the twenty-first century dawns. Even as old battles are being refought—affirmative action and reproductive rights—new issues and concerns—like the gender gap in employer-provided pensions—are beginning to emerge as the movement's early participants age. Finally, as the current leadership seeks to attract new and younger followers from "Generation X" (the birth cohort between 1964 and 1982), one would expect that their needs and concerns will add a different dimension to feminism. What form(s) the women's movement will take as the next millennium begins is a topic that historians who are not in the business of "reading the future" usually defer to those who are. Still, it is possible to assess the state of feminism as the twentieth century draws to a close and to offer a few thoughts as to its future direction.

## A STATUS REPORT

Though it is impossible to determine the number of feminist organizations that have come and gone over the past thirty years, dozens have withstood the test of time. The most recent edition of the *Encyclopedia of Associations* lists ninety-three women's organizations under the topic of "feminism," with many more women's advocacy groups, like Women Against Pornography, included in this resource under different headings.[2] From the San Francisco-based Radical Women founded in 1967, to the Mexican-American Women's National Association, a national latina organization founded in 1974, to the National Hook-Up of Black Women founded in 1975, and the Coalition for Women in International Development founded in 1976, these thriving organizations continue to promote issues of concern to women from affirmative action to economic development to welfare.

Some of these organizations, like the National Organization for Women (NOW), which celebrated its thirtieth anniversary in 1996, have become venerable institutions. Representative of the equal rights branch of feminism, NOW continues as the largest and most well-established second-wave feminist organization. Although other equal rights groups like Federally Employed Women, 9 to 5 (The National Association of Working Women), and the National Women's Political Caucus continue to make their presence felt, in the minds of most Americans NOW remains the most potent symbol of late twentieth-century feminism.

From its founding in 1966 with twenty-eight charter members and a shoestring, start-up budget of $140, NOW's membership has grown to approximately 250,000 in 1997, with the organization's annual operating budget topping out at over 10 million in recent years. Like *Ms.* magazine, NOW has changed considerably since its early "salad days" although the organization has remained true to its founding principles. Over the past dozen years, NOW has worked diligently toward a more inclusive agenda that recognizes and supports diversity; at the same time, NOW has continued its leadership role in the struggle for reproductive freedom, equity for women in education and the workplace, and inclusion in the political process at all levels of government.

Far fewer of the women's liberation groups survived much past the late 1970s; included among the more well-known liberation groups that dissolved are New York Radical Feminists (1972), Bread and Roses (1973), Cell 16 (1973), and Chicago Women's Liberation Union (1977). Redstockings also disbanded in 1970 only to be reconstituted five years later "in a desperate attempt to reassert radical feminist politics."[3] Even in smaller cities outside the eastern corridor, groups such as Dayton (Ohio) Women's Liberation and Dayton Women Working were gone by 1980; that Radical Women, with its avowedly "socialist-feminist political orientation" continues to thrive with nine chapters in the San Francisco Bay area is, indeed, a rarity in the 1990s.[4]

Clinging to their grass-roots origins, few if any of these women's liberation groups were interested in adopting the more structured (some would say hierarchical) organizational style perfected by equal rights feminists. Internal strife also brought down many of these groups that seemed incapable of weathering either the "gay-straight split" that developed by the early 1970s, or the conflicts that resulted from race and class differences. Still others fell victim to the backlash against feminism that dominated much of the political climate of the 1980s. While not discounting these influences, historian Alice Echols has pinpointed another causal factor in the decline of radical feminism, especially after 1975: the rise of "cultural feminism."

Cultural feminists claimed the existence of an "essential" female culture that was fundamentally different from and at odds with male culture. According to many radical feminists, as cultural feminism became "the dominant tendency within the women's liberation movement," it "threatened to transform feminism from a political movement to a lifestyle movement."[5] The rise of cultural feminism also disturbed many equal rights feminists who objected to any definition of feminism that promoted the concept of "innate differences" between women and men. As many an equal rights feminist understood and feared, a previous generation of social feminists had embraced this view of womanhood and had used it to justify the passage of protective labor legislation that equal rights feminists had fought long and hard to overturn.

The vast majority of women's liberation groups burned brightly for only a few years, but some like the Boston Women's Health Book Collective and Women Against Pornography continued strong in the 1990s. Although these groups never achieved the national stature accorded to NOW, they are recognized as popular authorities on issues pertaining to women's health care and the relationship between pornography and violence against women. The disappearance of the countless women's liberation groups that once existed in communities across the country has not brought an end to many of the causes they once espoused. Their legacy of liberation continues to thrive today in the thousands of rape crisis centers, domestic violence shelters, and other social service organizations that not only cater to women and children in need but also aid them in their search for empowerment.

As this study has sought to demonstrate, second-wave feminism has made an indelible imprint on American culture and society from the language we speak to the laws that govern our society. Indeed, the women's liberation movement has had such a transformative effect on American society that it has been held responsible for societal changes both real and imagined that have occurred over the past thirty years. As noted in the previous chapter, feminism has been blamed for the disappearance of the "traditional American family" (male breadwinner, female homemaker, and dependent children) and the prevalence of divorce. Today when "married couples with children make up just one-fourth of all households," and even fewer American families (19 percent) fit the traditional profile just described, it is folly to deny that the structure of the family has remained unchanged, but those who would point the causal finger at feminism may be confusing a myth with reality.[6]

This specific myth paints a picture of an emancipated woman in hot pursuit of a well-paying, high-powered career that requires her to relegate her family responsibilities to the proverbial "back burner." Central to the creation of this myth is the "fact" that women's labor force participation has increased dramatically since the advent of second-wave feminism, from 41 percent of women sixteen years of age and older in 1972 to 56 percent in 1996. The myth, however, fails to note that this trend has a history reaching back to at least the World War II era, and that this phenomenon may have more to do with the twists and turns of the national (and international) economy than with the rise of feminism. For more than fifty years, American women, especially those married and with children, have marched into the labor force in response to increased demands for their work in times of war and the desire to achieve and maintain middle-class status, which has become increasingly dependent on a second income. The mythic notion attached to this change in the pattern of women's work equated women's increased labor participation with economic gain that (supposedly) enabled women to assert their independence from the traditional family structure.

In truth, women's increased participation in paid work has brought neither economic nor familial independence. The vast majority of women (like men) work not because they want to but because they have to in order to make ends meet. As for the civil rights legislation (Title VII and Title IX) that purportedly ended gender discrimination in the workplace and in higher education, opportunities for women have widened, but gender differences also remain. Scholars attempting to explain why this "gender gap" has closed more quickly in some occupations than in others point to several influential factors: changes in educational attainment among women; the extent to which employment opportunities within specific fields have either expanded or contracted; the complex relationship between gender roles, family responsibilities, and job choices; and, in some instances, the persistence of discrimination.[7]

Occupational advances have occurred for women entering such select fields as higher education, law, medicine, accountancy, and personnel management. According to the most recent (1990) decennial census, women account for 24 percent of lawyers and judges nationwide, compared to 5 percent in 1970; they make up almost 21 percent of physicians, compared to 9 percent in 1970; almost 53 percent of accountants and auditors, compared to 25 percent in 1970; and 40 percent of college and university professors (this category includes faculty from two-year institutions) compared to 28 percent in 1970. Two professional fields have proven more difficult to crack—engineering (9 percent in 1990 compared to 1 percent in 1970) and architecture (15 percent in 1990 compared to 4 percent in 1970). As for women executives, they have discovered that it remains difficult to pass through the doors of America's boardrooms. As late as 1995, over 96 percent of the top corporate executives in the United States were white men. The "glass ceiling" is not glass after all; it consists of a very dense layer of white men. [8]

What has remained unchanged about the American workplace across the twentieth century is that a majority of men and women continue to work in "sex-segregated" occupational categories. In one state, North Carolina, which is not too far off the national mark, three-quarters of the state's labor force still work in jobs that are either 95 percent male or 95 percent female. Nationwide, women still tend to cluster in the lower-paying white/"pink"-collar jobs such as teaching, librarianship, nursing, social work, clerical work, and banking (as tellers not loan officers). Women are dramatically underrepresented in technology and blue-collar jobs and overrepresented in the manufacturing, retail, and service industries (food workers, support personnel, domestics). Even in the area of sales where women comprise almost one out of every two employees, stark differences exist. For example, women "make up 83 percent of apparel sales personnel, but only 31 percent of persons selling securities and financial services."[9]

What accounts for the persistence of occupational segregation? In part this pattern persists because of the lingering effects of prior discrimination and because of structural barriers to advancement that feed off of long-standing cultural assumptions about women's "distinctive nature." An International Gallop Poll conducted in 1996 provides cross-cultural support for this latter supposition. The poll-takers discovered that no matter the culture, women and men perceive females to be emotional, talkative, and affectionate and males to be courageous, aggressive, and ambitious. While the survey documented the existence of a strongly held international consensus that having more women in politics would lead to better government, polltakers also discovered that this positive view of women's leadership abilities vanished when respondents were queried about women in positions of authority in the workplace. Indeed, there was no country in which a majority of the respondents said that they would pick a woman over a man for a boss if they were taking a new job and had a choice. The irony is lost on no one. Even as the popular press and academic journals publish stories proclaiming that women bring a different, more inclusive, more egalitarian and less hierarchical leadership style to management and problem solving, a disturbing cross-cultural image lingers of "difficult" women bosses.[10]

Structural barriers continue to influence women's decisions regarding occupational choices. These obstacles reflect the reality that working women (full- or part-time) continue to bear the primary responsibility for household and child-rearing responsibilities. In one recent study of American family life, the researchers estimated that working wives spend between fifteen and twenty hours a week more than their husbands on housework and child-care responsibilities, "even though men cook and shop more than they did a decade ago."[11] In addition, women's unpaid contributions to the American economy stand at 66 percent compared to 34 percent for men. Many women still tend to select jobs that are more accommodating to their familial responsibilities, even if those jobs are lower in status and pay.

Even after thirty years of feminist demands for equality in the workplace, the reality is that the more a field is dominated by women, the lower the pay scale, whereas the opposite continues to hold true in fields dominated by men. Though it is true that the wage gap separating the earnings of women and men has narrowed from 58 cents for every dollar that men earned in 1963 to 75 cents for every dollar that men earn in 1998, at this rate of progress it will take until at least the second decade of the twenty-first century before wage parity is achieved. According to a 1996 report by the National Committee on Pay Equity, the average working woman earns $420,000 less over a lifetime of earnings than the average working man.[12]

This wage gap holds for women and men working in the same occupation and having the same skill level and/or educational achievement. For example, among sales, retail, and personal service workers, women earn 66 cents for every dollar that men earn; female financial managers earn 67 cents for every male dollar; female lawyers earn 74 cents for every male dollar; female full professors earn 88 cents for every male dollar; female waiters earn 79 cents for every male dollar; and female secretaries and stenographers earn 96 cents for every male dollar, the smallest wage difference. This narrow difference probably reflects the fact that secretarial work remains the most female-dominated job category (at 98 percent) and ranks among the lowest paying of the white/pink-collar occupations; but even in this instance, men still earn a few more pennies per dollar than women. Finally, no matter their race or ethnic identity, males on average earn more money than their female counterparts. White men set the rate at one dollar, with white women earning 80 cents; black men earn 73 cents for every dollar that white men earn, with black women earning 63 cents; and Hispanic men earn 63 cents for every dollar that white men earn, with Hispanic women earning 56 cents.[13]

## THE FUTURE OF FEMINISM

The political, legal, material, and cultural conditions that provided the impetus for the first and second waves of feminism have not been vanquished, completely. As American women continue to stream into the labor force (and estimates are that by the early years of the twenty-first century, women and people of color will dominate the labor force), older labor policies based on the outmoded concept of a family maintained by the male breadwinner and full-time female homemaker will have to yield further.

The Family and Medical Leave Act passed in 1993 represented a tentative step toward a reorientation of workplace values and labor management policies. Yet, far too few working adults covered under the act can afford to take full advantage of the up-to-twelve weeks of unpaid leave in order to care for new babies or sick family members. The next step, some feminists argue, would be to expand workers' coverage by mandating paid leave and by removing exemptions to the act. The current act, for example, limits compliance to businesses with more than fifty employees; however, many women work for companies with far fewer employees.[14]

Other issues of concern to many working women include a national system of health care insurance, equalizing pension coverage, flexible work schedules, a more assertive corporate culture that actively discourages sexual harassment, counseling and training programs that move women into technical and nontraditional jobs, public education reforms that enlarge the range of vocational choices available to women, legislative efforts that focus on comparable worth (because occupational segregation has not disappeared completely), and child care (a feminist objective never fully achieved).

Child care remains a critical issue for working families. Working parents are very concerned about the quality of the care their children receive, especially in institutional settings. They do not want to warehouse their children in large, impersonal facilities where staff turnover is high because the primarily female caregivers are underpaid and overworked (according to a 1998 report, child-care providers earn approximately $13,000 annually and experience a 30 percent turnover in their jobs because of low pay). In addition to the need for quality child care, which necessitates a low staff-child ratio and flexible operating hours to accommodate night-shift workers such as nurses, working families need affordable child care. In North Carolina, which has a female working population approaching 60 percent, child care is the fourth largest family expenditure.

According to many women's studies scholars and feminist writers and activists, the next feminist wave in the United States will have a much stronger international emphasis. It is true that geographic barriers, competing political systems, and cultural differences separate and divide women. Yet, universal obstacles to improving women's status worldwide—poverty, domestic and sexual violence, inadequate health care, unequal access to educational institutions, the perpetuation of cultural values that devalue women and encourage their underutilization in government and the economy—hold the potential for uniting disparate groups of women under the banner of global feminism. At the same time, knotty problems in the United States pertaining to the intertwining of race, class, ethnicity, and gender concerns may further comparisons between the conditions of American women and women in countries around the world. And, as more and more American women take up the cause of "ecofeminism" (the relationship between humans and their environment has grown to include a gendered perspective), they too will embrace the ecologists' motto, "Think globally, act locally." The feminist agenda is not finished, yet.

## NOTES

1. Marcia Ann Gillespie, "We've Only Just Begun," *Ms.* 8 (September/October 1997), p. 1. *Ms.* encountered some bumpy times in the late 1980s and was reissued in 1990 as an ad-free bimonthly with a much more expensive subscription ($45 per year for six issues).

2. *Encyclopedia of Associations*, 32nd edition (Detroit: Gale Research Company, 1996), pp. 1693–1703.

3. Alice Echols, *Daring to Be Bad: Radical Feminism in America, 1967–1975* (Minneapolis: University of Minnesota Press, 1989), p. 260 for the quote and pp. 387–89.

4. Judith Sealander and Dorothy Smith, "The Rise and Fall of Feminist Organizations in the 1970s: Dayton as a Case Study," *Feminist Studies* 12 (Summer 1986), p. 335; and the *Encyclopedia of Associations*, p. 1700.

5. Echols, *Daring to Be Bad,* pp. 240–43, 283.

6. The statistics come from a variety of sources: *Ms*. 8 (September/October 1997), p. 22; a Census Bureau report, "Fertility of American Women: June 1995," excerpted in the *Wilmington* (North Carolina) *Morning Star*, November 26, 1997; a report on the results of a 1996 International Gallop Poll excerpted in Ibid., March 27, 1997; and a report from the Census Bureau released in November 1996, excerpts of which appeared in Ibid., November 27, 1996.

7. Barbara H. Wootton, "Gender Differences in Occupational Employment," *Monthly Labor Review* (April 1997), pp. 15–24.

8. *Ms*. 8 (September/October 1997), pp. 22–24.

9. Wootton, "Gender Differences," pp. 15–16, 19–22 (the quote is found on p. 16).

10. International Gallop Poll Results, *Wilmington* (North Carolina) *Morning Star,* March 27, 1996.

11. See excerpts from John Robinson and Geoffrey Godbey, *Time for Life* (University Park, PA: Pennsylvania State University Press, 1997), cited in *Newsweek* (May 12, 1997), p. 68.

12 "Your Work," *Ms*. 6 (March/April 1986), pp. 36–39 and "Clinton asks $14 Million to Close Gender Pay Gap," *Sunday Star News* (Wilmington, North Carolina), January 31, 1999.

13. "Your Work," *Ms*. 6 (March/April 1996), pp. 36–39. In part, this wage gap reflects differences (within these large occupational categories) in wage and salary scales and practices. In the area of sales, for example, men tend to gravitate toward commission-paying jobs (securities and financial services and large-ticket items, like automobiles), whereas women tend to concentrate in the wage-based, small retail and apparel businesses. In the area of higher education, women professors tend to concentrate in the lower-paying humanities disciplines (English, foreign languages), whereas men tend to dominate in the higher-paying sciences (physics) and professional schools (business and engineering).

14. *Summary of the Family and Medical Leave Act of 1993* (Department of Labor, Employment Standards Administration, 1995 update).

# Biographies: The Women Who Shaped the Women's Liberation Movement

## Bella S. Abzug (1920–1998)

In January 1971 when Representative Bella Abzug took her seat in the 92nd Congress, she was already a public figure, easily identified by her trademark wide-brimmed hat and brassy voice, and her radical feminist politics. Even after hats and radicalism were no longer considered stylish, "Battling Bella" (as she was called by supporters and detractors alike) unabashedly continued to embrace both fashions. In 1961 she had helped found and then became a lobbyist for Women's Strike for Peace. Active in the National Organization for Women (NOW) since the late 1960s, she and fellow NOW members Shirley Chisholm, Betty Friedan, and Gloria Steinem were instrumental in founding the National Women's Political Caucus in July 1971. During her three terms in the House of Representatives (1970–1976), Abzug was an outspoken opponent of the Vietnam War and a central figure in furthering the feminist movement's legislative agenda. After leaving public office, Abzug continued crusading for women's civil, political, and economic rights at home and abroad. In 1979 she became president of the Women's Foreign Policy Council (headquartered in New York) and attended several international women's conferences. In her later years she became interested in the relationship between environmentalism and feminism (ecofeminism) and founded the Women's Environmental and Development Organization, an international advocacy group based in New York. Despite the poor health that marked the last few years of her life, Bella Abzug remained a vital presence in this organization until her death in March 1998.

Bella Abzug was born July 24, 1920, in the Bronx (New York) to Esther (Tanklefsky) and Emanuel Savitsky, both of whom were Russian Jewish immigrants. Her father was, in her words, a "humanist" butcher who managed the "Let Live Meat Market." When he died during the Great Depression, her mother supported the family (Bella and her older sister Helene) by working as a department store clerk. Abzug grew up in a religious household and remained an observant Jew, although she was critical of women's second-class treatment by the Orthodox and Conservative branches of Judaism. She was also a member of two Jewish benevolent organizations—B'nai B'rith and Hadassah—and a strong supporter of Israel. Thus, during her first political race she became incensed when her opponent (who was also Jewish) questioned her loyalty to Israel.

From the time she was young, Abzug had set her sights on the law as a profession. She completed her undergraduate work at Hunter College of New York in 1942 and earned her law degree from Columbia University in 1947. She had entered law school in 1942 but took a temporary wartime leave to work in the shipbuilding industry. In June 1944 she married Maurice M. Abzug, a stockbroker and novelist. Marriage did little to halt her ambitions or her success; when Abzug returned to law school, she did well enough to become editor of the *Columbia Law Review*. Admitted to the New York State Bar in 1947, Abzug accepted a position with a firm that specialized in labor law. Motherhood soon followed with Eve Gail, born in 1949, and Isobel Jo (Liz), born in 1952. The Abzugs' marriage was a long and happy one; when Maurice died in 1986, Bella's loss was inconsolable.

Abzug's legal career in the early 1950s bore the mark of a political radical. She represented labor unions, defended individuals targeted by anti-communist politicians like Senator Joseph McCarthy, and did pro bono work for civil rights and civil liberties groups. Her most "famous" case involved Willie McGee, a black man from Mississippi convicted and sentenced to death by an all white jury for raping a white woman. Although Abzug won a stay of execution twice from the Supreme Court, McGee was eventually put to death.

By the early 1960s, Abzug was also becoming, in her words, a "peacenik." The resumption of nuclear testing had hit a nerve among thousands of women across the United States. With experts issuing warnings about the dangers of radioactive fallout (especially to young children), a women's peace movement seemed to mushroom almost overnight in the nation's major urban centers. Abzug was a founding member of the Women's Strike for Peace (with a membership of approximately 50,000) and served as the group's legislative director until she went to Congress in 1971.

After 1965, Abzug's peace efforts focused on U.S. intervention in Vietnam. She helped organize the anti-[President] Johnson movement in late 1967 and was a strong supporter of Eugene McCarthy's bid for the 1968 Democratic presidential nomination. She also plunged into local politics in 1969, campaigning for John Lindsay, the Republican reform candidate for mayor of New York City. In 1970 she decided to run for Congress and won handily with 55 precent of the vote.

Abzug quickly made her presence known to her congressional colleagues, the majority of whom were white, middle-aged men. When Abzug took the oath of office in 1971, she joined Shirley Chisholm and ten other women in the House and one in the Senate. Abzug angered her male colleagues by publicly challenging the seniority system that controlled congressional committee assignments. She requested, but was refused, a seat on the powerful Armed Services Committee; instead, she was appointed to Government Operations and Public Works (there is little doubt that Abzug's fuss over committee assignments contributed to Patricia Schroeder's appointment, two years later, to the Armed Services Committee). Abzug's first action on the floor of Congress was equally controversial: she introduced a resolution calling for an immediate withdrawal of all American armed forces stationed in Vietnam. A few months later, she sponsored an amendment calling for the abolition of the Selective Service System (the draft).

Abzug's feminism was as uncompromising as her antiwar position, and during her tenure in Congress she worked diligently to advance the feminist agenda. In particular, Abzug testified on behalf of the Equal Rights Amendment (ERA), cosponsored (with Shirley Chisholm) child-care legislation, fought to expand prohibitions on sex discrimination in employment in federally funded programs, sought authorization for abortion and sterilization services at military facilities, extended privacy rights to include marital status (public records no longer referred to men as "Mr." and women as "Miss" or "Mrs."), and integrated the congressional swimming pool (mornings were reserved for women). In 1973 Abzug won a symbolic victory for women's rights by obtaining congressional and presidential support for honoring August 26th (the anniversary of the suffrage amendment) as Women's Equality Day. Two years later symbol became substance when Abzug introduced legislation (which Congress approved) requesting $5 million dollars to help underwrite the National Women's Conference scheduled to take place in Houston, Texas, in November 1977. In an ironic twist of fate, Abzug would go on to chair the Houston Conference after losing a closely contested primary race in 1976 for the Senate seat held by fellow Democrat Daniel Patrick Moynihan.

Feminists applauded when the White House returned to Democratic control with the election of Jimmy Carter in November 1976, in part because Carter had promised to increase the number of women appointed to high-level executive and judicial positions. Acting on his promise, Carter created a forty-member National Advisory Committee on Women and asked Bella Abzug to serve as its cochair; Carmen Votaw, head of the National Conference of Puerto Rican Women, served with Abzug. Soon, however, many feminist leaders, including Abzug, became disenchanted with Carter because of his lukewarm support for abortion rights and the ERA. Under fire from the political Right and plagued by a lagging economy, Carter decided to trim the budget for domestic programs by $15 million while increasing the defense budget. Abzug objected; and acting in her capacity as cochair of the women's advisory committee, she prepared a report and a press release criticizing the president. After a rancorous meeting between Carter and Abzug, he announced her removal from the committee. In the feminist uproar that followed Abzug's dismissal, Votaw and twenty-six members resigned from the committee; the gulf between Carter and the feminist community had widened.

Out of a job (so to speak), Bella Abzug began a grass-roots lobbying group, Women U.S.A., in 1979 and returned to private practice the following year. In 1972 she published the journal she had kept of her first year in Congress, *Bella: Ms. Abzug Goes to Washington* and in 1984 (with Mim Kelber) she published *Gender Gap: Bella Abzug's Guide to Political Power for American Women.* In 1986, and again in 1992, Abzug tried to regain a seat in Congress but failed; undaunted, she continued her advocacy work on behalf of women and the environment. Bella Abzug died March 31, 1998, at Columbia-Presbyterian Medical Center.

### Rita Mae Brown (1944– )

Essayist, poet, and novelist Rita Mae Brown left an indelible mark on feminism by exposing the fault lines of homophobia and class privilege that ran through the women's liberation movement. An early member of the National Organization for Women (NOW), Brown tendered her resignation in January 1970 in response to her removal the previous month from the editorship of the New York chapter's newsletter. Brown's openness about her lesbian identity and her linkage of lesbians' rights to the larger struggle for women's rights worried NOW's top leaders. According to Brown's memoir, *Rita Will: Memoir of a Literary Rabble-Rouser* (1997), they (especially Betty Friedan) moved to silence her, but not for long. Friedan had "won the battle but she had lost the war," Brown remembered. Over the next few years, Brown and a small group of like-minded women increased the pressure on straight feminists to confront their collusion with the American penchant for "lesbian baiting." What Brown and the others wanted was an acknowledgment that lesbianism was a feminist issue, and eventually they succeeded. At the 1971 annual NOW conference, the governing board recognized the futility of ignoring the "lavender menace" by passing a resolution "acknowledging the oppression of lesbians as a legitimate concern of feminism." Two years later, NOW formally established a Task Force on Sexuality and Lesbianism. Rita Mae Brown had indeed "won the war."

Rita Mae Brown was born November 28, 1944, in Hanover, Pennsylvania, not far from the Mason-Dixon line, to an unmarried teenager. According to oft-repeated family lore, the baby was placed in an orphanage in Pittsburgh only to be rescued and adopted by Ralph and Julia Ellen Brown, a cousin of the biological mother. Ralph Brown was a butcher by trade who struggled to keep the family afloat. When Rita Mae Brown was eleven, the family moved to Fort Lauderdale, Florida, but the family's finances never improved. When Ralph Brown died in 1961, Rita Mae estimated that the family's annual income had hovered around $2,000 annually. Brown grew up in a struggling, working-class family, whereas many of her high school and college peers came from much more affluent homes. This contrast between the "haves" and "have-nots" became a major influence in Brown's later life, shaping her feminist politics and her early writings. The other significant influences were her sexuality and her identity as a southerner.

In 1962 Brown entered the University of Florida as a scholarship student, but left two years later when university officials threatened to revoke her scholarship "if she didn't straighten up and fly right." Brown's transgressions were her growing interest in the civil rights movement that was beginning to emerge on her college campus and her sexuality. Her sexual experimentation had begun in high school but had not advanced much beyond a few kisses and love letters. In college, Brown tried to remain circumspect about her lesbianism (she even had a boyfriend), but rumors about her homosexuality eventually came to the attention of the administration. Following a confrontation with a university official, Brown was ordered to undergo psychiatric therapy and she was ostracized by the university community. According to her memoir, she left the university in an effort to safeguard her academic record just in case she applied for scholarship money "somewhere else." After a stint at a junior college in Florida (she earned an A.A. degree), Brown moved to New York and secured a scholarship to New York University where she completed the requirements for an undergraduate degree in English in 1968. In 1976 she earned a Ph.D. from the Institute for Policy Studies in Washington, D.C.

With few exceptions, Brown found a more welcoming climate for her lesbian and feminist activities in New York. During her senior year at New York University she embarked on a joint venture with like-minded Columbia University students and founded one of the first gay and lesbian student organizations, the Student Homophile League (1967). After graduation she joined New York NOW, the organization's largest and most radical chapter, and assumed the task of newsletter editor. Unfortunately for Brown, NOW's "radicalism" did not preclude intolerance. Maneuvered out of power after coming out as a lesbian, Brown quit NOW. A brief association with straight radical feminists did not prove fruitful either, and so in the early months of 1970 she became a founding member of Radicalesbians. Brown played a key role in formulating the collective's widely circulated position paper on the relationship between lesbianism and feminism, "The Woman-Identified Woman," and she was a leading participant in the group's 1970 "lavender menace" demonstration at the Second Congress to Unite Women.

In 1971 Brown moved to Washington, D.C., where she was instrumental in forming the lesbian-feminist collective, the Furies. Life inside the Furies collective, however, was far from peaceful. Conflicts over personalities, political styles, and class differences abounded, and Brown was the lightning rod. The collective's decision to purge Brown in March 1972 did little to halt its disintegration, and it soon folded.

The publication of Brown's semiautobiographical novel *Rubyfruit Jungle* (1973) introduced the nation to the author and to her outrageously funny and irreverent lesbian heroine, Molly Bolt. When Brown first shopped the novel around, no mainstream press was willing to take a chance on it. Instead, it was published by Daughters Publishing Company, a small "women's only" press. To everyone's surprise, *Rubyfruit* became an instant success with over 70,000 copies sold. Eventually, Bantam Press negotiated for the copyright to *Rubyfruit*; its edition appeared in 1977. Since then, over 500,000 copies have been printed.

Brown's most overtly lesbian-feminist material appeared early in her literary career (prior to 1978). These include *The Hand That Cradles the Rock* (1971), a volume of poetry, and *A Plain Brown Rapper* (1976), a collection of essays on the women's liberation movement written between 1969 and 1975. With few exceptions, Brown's works since 1978 have used historical themes and settings and have emphasized family and community issues within a regional (southern) culture. Beginning in 1990, Brown tried her hand at writing mysteries (with some help from her cat, Sneaky-Pie Brown, who served as coauthor).

Rita Mae Brown's shift over the intervening decades from activist-writer to full-time novelist has not come at the cost of her social conscience. AIDS research, the arts, and animals have all benefited from her generosity and her success.

## Shirley Chisholm (1924– )

In 1968 Shirley Chisholm, a member of the National Organization for Women (NOW), made history by becoming the first black woman elected to the U.S. House of Representatives (joining Chisholm in the House were 417 white men, 9 white women, and 8 black men). Four years later, Chisholm (a founding member of the National Women's Political Caucus) made history again when she decided to seek the Democratic party's nomination for the presidency. To be black and female was a political anomaly in the late 1960s and early 1970s, but which "handicap"—race or sex—was the bigger stumbling block to political success? Much to Shirley Chisholm's surprise, "being female put many more obstacles in [her] path than being black." Her political battles, she noted in *Unbought and Unbossed* (1970), were "long, hard, and continual" with her strongest opposition coming from "less competent males, both black and white." "Sexism," she observed, "has no color line." Although Chisholm was a staunch feminist, she was fiercely independent and never hesitated to challenge the feminist establishment if she thought the needs of poor women were being neglected. Throughout her more than twenty years of government service, Shirley Chisholm refused to be typecast as either a "black politician" or a "feminist politician." Instead, she saw herself as a "voice for all out-groups" and an advocate for a government responsive to the "human needs of every citizen."

Shirley Chisholm was born Anita St. Hill (when she took the name Shirley is not known) on November 30, 1924, in Brooklyn, New York, to Ruby (Seale), a seamstress, and Charles St. Hill, an unskilled factory worker. When she was three, she and her younger sisters were sent to live with her maternal grandmother on a farm in Barbados. Her struggling parents hoped to reclaim their children as soon as they had acquired a comfortable nest egg. Although the St. Hills' dream of economic security did not come to pass, Shirley and her sisters returned to Brooklyn in 1934.

Chisholm was a strong student. When she graduated from Girl's High School in 1939, she received several scholarship offers, including ones from Vassar and Oberlin. Family finances, however, dictated that she attend college closer to home. She enrolled at tuition-free Brooklyn College and lived at home. She majored in sociology and minored in Spanish; soon after graduating *cum laude* in 1946, she was hired as a teacher's aide at Mt. Calvary Child Care Center and stayed until 1953. These seven years were fruitful ones for Chisholm. She was promoted to a teacher's position; she married Conrad Chisholm, a private investigator, in 1947 (the childless couple divorced in 1977; that same year she married Arthur Hardwick, a businessman); she earned a master's degree in early childhood education from Columbia University in 1952, and she joined a political club.

In 1964, when Shirley Chisholm decided to run for a seat in the New York State Assembly, she was regarded as a hard-working but highly independent member of her local Democratic club. In addition, her expertise in early childhood education had caught the attention of New York City officials; that reputation had earned her a position, since 1959, as an education consultant for the day care division of the New York City Bureau of Child Welfare. Chisholm was not the first black woman to run for the Brooklyn assembly seat (Maude Richardson had broken that barrier two decades earlier); nonetheless, her candidacy was greeted with hostility. Men and women, white and black, questioned Chisholm's loyalty to her husband; some went so far as to tell her that politics was a man's job. Chisholm persisted and won. In Albany, Chisholm was something of a political maverick, always putting her constituents' needs above the demands of the party's leadership (a practice that would carry over when Chisholm served in Congress). Chisholm's independence did not render her ineffective as a legislator; during her four years in the state assembly, she sponsored bills that created educational opportunities for disadvantaged students, extended unemployment insurance to domestic and service workers, and outlawed discriminatory employment practices directed at pregnant schoolteachers.

When Shirley Chisholm decided to make a historic run for Congress in 1968, her candidacy was greeted, once again, with dismay by black male politicians within her district. Publicly they voiced concern about Chisholm's "independence" from the local Democratic leadership, but privately they objected to her because she was an uppity woman. Chisholm won the primary only to discover that her Republican opponent James Farmer (the former director of the civil rights organization Congress of Racial Equality) planned to make a campaign issue of her gender. His strategy backfired; and Chisholm, who had cleverly responded by organizing the women of her district, beat Farmer by a margin of 2.5 to 1.

Four years later when Chisholm entered the race for the Democratic party's presidential nomination, she faced an even more uphill battle. First, the Democratic front-runners had more money and larger, professionally trained campaign staffs than did Chisholm. Second, Chisholm's race and gender made her candidacy "suspect" in the eyes of the press, the political elite, and among many voters; few people were willing to see her as a "serious" candidate (a point she laments in her account of the 1972 campaign,

*The Good Fight*). Third, Chisholm's candidacy created a political dilemma for two groups, feminists and the civil rights establishment, predisposed to support her. Should they support her because of her strong congressional record on women's rights and civil rights, or should they use their political clout to extract promises of support for their issues from someone (like George McGovern) who stood a better chance of capturing the Democratic party's nomination? In the end, although NOW unofficially endorsed Chisholm's candidacy (an official endorsement would endanger the organization's tax-exempt status), many leading white feminists, like Gloria Steinem and Bella Abzug, tried to "butter both sides of their bread" by supporting Chisholm and McGovern (black and brown feminists rejected this expedient strategy and remained committed Chisholm supporters).

During the years Shirley Chisholm spent in Congress she worked to mold an effective feminist coalition. In 1968 she was one of only eleven women elected to Congress (ten in the House and one in the Senate). By 1981 this number had increased to eighteen, and the year she left office (1983) twenty-one women were prepared to take oaths of office. Chisholm's presence also helped smooth the way for additional black female lawmakers like Barbara Jordan and Yvonne Braithwaite Burke.

When Shirley Chisholm entered Congress, her ambitious list of feminist goals included expanding job training programs, providing adequate public housing, equalizing educational opportunities, getting federal support for day care, and gaining enforcement and expansion of antidiscrimination laws. An early supporter of the Equal Rights Amendment, Chisholm testified on its behalf, and she continued her advocacy of poor women's rights (one of her greatest legislative achievements came in 1974 when Congress overrode a presidential veto and expanded coverage of minimum-wage guarantees to domestic workers). When this outspoken champion for the rights of women and minorities left Congress in 1983, she returned to her first love, teaching.

## Mary Daly (1928– )

Between 1968 and 1973, feminist theologian Mary Daly's intellectual and spiritual journey followed a path taken by many women caught up in second-wave feminism. Initially a reformist, Daly, like her peers in the National Organization for Women (NOW), believed that it was possible to eradicate sexism from society's most basic institutions. Over time, however, Daly became convinced that gender oppression was so deeply embedded in these institutions that reform was not possible. As long as women remained within the traditional boundaries of "patriarchal space, time and consciousness," their quest for spirituality would be stymied. According to Daly, if women wished to experience the "unfolding of God" they would have to "come together as women [and form] a spiritual community unrecognized by institutional religion." In essence, Daly was proposing not only a separate worship space for women, but a new, female-centered theology.

Mary Daly was born on October 16, 1928, in Schenectady, New York, to Anna Catherine (Morse) and Frank X. Daly. Raised in a Catholic household, she was educated at Catholic institutions. Daly received an undergraduate degree from the College of St. Rose in 1950, a master's degree in 1952 from the Catholic University of America, a Ph.D. from St. Mary's College, Notre Dame, in 1954, and a doctorate of theology (1963) and a second Ph.D. (1965) from the University of Fribourg in Switzerland.

Daly's progress up the professorial career ladder followed the typical academic pattern until the spring of 1969. She supported herself as a visiting lecturer in English at St. Mary's College until she completed her Ph.D. at the same institution (1952–1954); then she accepted a position at Cardinal Cushing College in Brookline, Massachusetts, where she taught philosophy and theology from 1954 to 1959. In 1959 she moved to Switzerland, teaching theology and philosophy at the University of Fribourg while she completed two more advanced degrees. In 1966 Daly's first and only conventional book, *Natural Knowledge of God in the Philosophy of Jacques Maritain* was published, and she returned to the United States, settling in at Boston College (a Jesuit institution) as an assistant professor of theology. The publication of her second book, *The Church and the Second Sex* (1968), almost derailed her career at Boston College.

By the late 1960s, no institution in American society remained safe from feminists' demands for inclusion and equity with men; not government, industry, the professions, schools and colleges, the media, the judiciary, labor unions, political parties, or the churches. Mary Daly was hardly the first feminist to criticize the Christian church for its antifeminism. Indeed, almost three-quarters of a century ago, women's rights activist Elizabeth Cady Stanton had created a stir among the more conservative leaders of the suffrage movement by publishing her feminist critique of organized religion, the *Woman's Bible*.

Daly was not necessarily inspired by the distant feminist past when she questioned women's second-class status within the Catholic church. The church itself had opened this particular door from 1962 to 1965 with the Second Vatican Council's reexamination of almost every tenet of church doctrine. Indeed, Daly was especially encouraged by Pope John XXIII's *Pacem in Terris,* which recognized "the equality of women and the fact of their oppression." In 1967 NOW created the Ecumenical Task Force on

Women and Religion headed by Dr. Elizabeth Farians, a Catholic theologian like Mary Daly. Thus, by the late 1960s, religious reformers from within and beyond the church were calling for a more active role for nuns, an end to the use of sexist liturgical language, and the participation of girls and women in rituals and practices heretofore denied to them (within a few years, reformers would add one more demand to their list: ordination of women).

Given the direction Mary Daly's subsequent works would take, *The Church and the Second Sex* was quite mild in its criticism of the church and clearly within the reform tradition. Indeed, by 1975, when the book was reissued with the author's new introduction, Daly had repudiated her "reformist views" in favor of a "postchristian radical feminist" perspective that put her beyond the purview of Christianity. Apparently, however, her second book was still daring enough to shake the college's administrative hierarchy; in the spring of 1969, Boston College moved to dismiss Daly. The campus erupted in protest for almost three months: while witches tossed spells, "1,500 students marched on the college president's house, and over 2,500 students and faculty signed a petition" calling for Daly's rehiring. The administration capitulated, and Mary Daly was awarded tenure and promotion to associate professor status.

Between 1969 and 1973, the years in which radical feminism flourished, theologian Mary Daly rejected church reform in favor of a theological revolution. Her own spiritual and intellectual quest had led her to question the very foundation of the Judeo-Christian tradition: Is God male? Was woman's subordination to man ordained by God? Daly's answer to each was a resounding No! In *Beyond God the Father: Toward a Philosophy of Women's Liberation* (1973), Daly challenged almost every patriarchal precept upon which Western civilization was founded. In her next book, *Gyn/Ecology: The Metaethics of Radical Feminism* (1978), patriarchy and its flip side, misogyny, were placed within a worldwide context: all religions are patriarchal, all religions objectify (and therefore oppress) women. In Daly's alternative religion, women's search for spirituality took them on a journey of discovery through a world that existed beyond the boundaries of patriarchy. This journey was more fully explored in Daly's 1984 "sisterwork," *Pure Lust: Elemental Feminist Philosophy* and on a more personal note in her autobiography, *Outercourse: The Be-Dazzling Voyage: Containing Recollections from My Logbook of a Radical Feminist Philosopher* (1992).

In moving toward a theological perspective she described as "postchristian radical feminism," Daly found the sexism inherent in (all) languages to be a stumbling block to her explanation of female spirituality. Her solution was the creation of an alternative feminist vocabulary that reclaimed and reinterpreted pejorative words (crones, hags, and harpies became powerful and positive symbols), modified the spelling of familiar words (dis-ease, dis-passion, e-motion, cat/egory, man-ipulated), and created new words (cronehood, phallogrammar, gynocide). To aid readers eager to unlock the secrets of her prose, Daly and co-collaborator Jane Caputi produced their version of a feminist dictionary in 1987: *Websters' First New Intergalactic Wickedary of the English Language.*

Mary Daly's work has been both praised and scorned for its shocking and brilliant deconstruction of Western culture. Many feminists consider her radicalism visionary; others have accused Daly of falling into cultural feminism "with its insistence upon women's sameness to each other and their fundamental difference from men." Still, despite these criticisms, Mary Daly's reputation as one of the most daring and unconventional feminist thinkers of the late twentieth century endures, and her works (especially *Beyond God the Father* and *Gyn/Ecology*) have become required reading in philosophy, theology, and women's studies courses.

### Betty Friedan (1921– )

Betty Friedan is best known as the author *of The Feminine Mystique* (1963), considered in popular lore to be the spark that ignited second-wave feminism, and for her role in founding the National Organization for Women (NOW) in 1966, the first national civil rights organization for women. Friedan served as NOW's first president, a post she held until 1970. Under her leadership, NOW formulated its controversial 1968 Bill of Rights for Women. Despite strong opposition from both radical and conservative members, Friedan argued forcefully for the inclusion of the two most radical feminist issues of the day: passage of the Equal Rights Amendment (ERA) and repeal of all laws limiting a woman's access to contraception and abortion. On the occasion of her farewell address in 1970, the outgoing president challenged NOW members to organize a twenty-four-hour national strike in order to galvanize support for the feminist agenda. On August 26, 1970 (the date marked the fiftieth anniversary of the Nineteenth Amendment granting women the right to vote), "Women's Strike for Equality Day" rallies took place in over ninety cities. In New York City, the site of the largest march (crowd estimates ranged between 35,000 and 50,000), Betty Friedan led the way.

Betty Friedan was born Bettye Naomi Goldstein on February 4, 1921, in Peoria, Illinois, to Miriam (Horowitz) and Harry Goldstein, a jeweler. The oldest of three children, she was raised in a middle-class Jewish household. A talent for writing, an affinity for journalism, and a social conscience appeared early in Betty Friedan's life. She entered Smith College in 1938, and just before her senior year began, she became editor-in-chief of the student newspaper. Under her tutelage, the paper's editorials reflected a populist, left-of-center ideology. In 1942 Friedan graduated from Smith *summa cum laude* and entered a graduate program in psychology at the University of California at Berkeley only to depart a year later. From then until the early 1950s, Friedan honed her journalistic style, her radical political sensibilities, and her emerging feminism by working for the Federated Press, a leftist news service, by writing for the *UE News,* the most radical union paper of the era, and by free-lancing.

She also fell in love with Carl Friedan, a World War II veteran, working as a summer theater producer. They married in June 1947, and between 1948 and 1956 the Friedan family expanded to include three children. Precarious family finances led Carl to abandon the theater for the more lucrative field of public relations work; like many a baby-boom couple, the Friedans eventually joined the middle-class exodus from the city to the suburbs by the time the last child was born. Several sources hint that from the beginning, the Friedans' marriage was marked by periodic strife, and in May 1969 the couple quietly divorced.

Following her departure from NOW's presidency, Friedan used her organizational skills to further feminism's political objectives. In July 1971 Friedan joined Bella Abzug, Shirley Chisholm, and Gloria Steinem in guiding the formation of the National Women's Political Caucus. Conceived as a diverse and bipartisan effort, the four spokeswomen made sure that a cross section of women's organizations was present at the founding and that these different groups would have a voice on the governing board. Although the National Women's Political Caucus was dedicated to identifying and supporting women candidates for national, state, and local offices, the organization was also interested in promoting "women's issues" and willingly endorsed male candidates if they ran on a feminist platform.

By the mid-1970s, Betty Friedan found herself at odds with the direction feminism was taking, and her relationship with some of the movement's most prominent leaders, most notably Gloria Steinem and Bella Abzug, was becoming strained. Friedan's leave-taking from NOW had occurred just as lesbianism was surfacing as a potent feminist issue. Lesbianism was a "lavender herring," Friedan had supposedly remarked; she believed that it was not only a divisive issue but also a diversionary one. Friedan also worried that radical feminism's emphasis on "sexual politics" was both antimale and antifamily. Friedan's ideas were quickly labeled "reactionary" by radical feminists. Following the 1977 Houston Conference, where Friedan believed that she had been maneuvered out of power by her critics, she took a hiatus from organized feminism.

A year before the Houston Conference, Friedan's official memoir of the women's movement, *It Changed My Life,* had appeared in print. In the aftermath of the power play at Houston, Friedan increasingly turned her efforts to college lecture tours, writing, and promoting her vision of feminism. In 1981 this vision appeared in the form of a new direction for feminism. In *The Second Stage,* Friedan criticized the women's movement for replacing the "feminine mystique" with an equally crippling "feminist mystique." This mystique not only encouraged the "polarization of men and women" but also created rifts between women. An increasingly narrow vision of feminism pitted work against family; and in doing so, Friedan argued, many women felt forced to deny the fulfillment they received from home and family life. Calling for an end to this feminist trap as well as the equally devastating myth of the "supermom" who could "do it all," Friedan insisted that it was time for feminists to come to terms with family life and end the battles for power between men and women. The second stage, she wrote "may not be a women's movement. Men may be at the cutting edge of the second stage." Published at the moment when the backlash against feminism was shifting into high gear (the ERA would be defeated within a year, and serious legal challenges to *Roe v. Wade* were underway), many feminists expressed anger and betrayal with *The Second Stage.*

Betty Friedan has remained committed to a feminist vision for America even as she has continued to rework its meaning. In *The Fountain of Age* (1993) she tackled the issue of ageism, and in 1997 she returned to a familiar theme, but with a twist, in *Beyond Gender: The New Politics of Work and Family.* An enigmatic figure in the feminist world, Friedan has been labeled, paradoxically, a radical by the political Right and a reactionary by the feminist Left. Undaunted by her critics, Friedan has continued to demonstrate her commitment to a life well-lived in the service of others.

### Ruth Bader Ginsburg (1933– )

Frequently described as the "legal architect of the modern women's movement," Ruth Bader Ginsburg's feminist credentials date back to the late 1960s when the New Jersey chapter of the American Civil Liberties Union sought her assistance in litigating sex discrimination cases. Ginsburg's success with these local cases earned her the attention of the organization's national director, and in 1971 he handed Ginsburg her first case, and subsequent victory, before the Supreme Court. In *Reed v. Reed,* the justices struck down an Idaho law that automatically privileged men over women in the selection of an executor of an estate. The law's unstated premise assumed that because of their sex, men were simply more competent than women. Rejection of this arbitrary assumption was historic, marking the first time that the Supreme Court invalidated a state law because of its inherent sex bias. The following year, the American Civil Liberties Union established its Women's Rights Project and hired Ginsburg for the directorship. She held that post until 1980 when President Jimmy Carter appointed her to the United States Court of Appeals for the District of Columbia. In her thirteen years on the bench, Ginsburg wrote hundreds of decisions and earned a reputation for being a moderate-to-liberal jurist. In June 1993 President Bill Clinton nominated Ruth Bader Ginsburg to replace retiring associate Supreme Court Justice Byron R. White. On August 10, 1993, Ginsburg became the second woman to sit on the Supreme Court (the distinction of being first belongs to Sandra Day O'Connor, a 1981 Ronald Reagan appointee).

Ruth Bader Ginsburg was born on March 15, 1933, in Brooklyn, New York, to Celia (Amster) and Nathan Bader, and grew up in a Jewish household only recently removed from the immigrant experience. An excellent student, she won a scholarship to Cornell University in 1950 and graduated with high honors four years later. In 1954 she married Martin D. Ginsburg, and the couple moved to Cambridge, Massachusetts, in anticipation of Martin Ginsburg's entrance to Harvard Law School. His schooling was interrupted by a stint in the military, which he served in Oklahoma where the couple's first child, a daughter, was born (a son was born in 1965). When the Ginsburgs returned to Cambridge in 1956, Martin resumed his studies and Ruth began law school. Despite the pressure of being "only one of nine women in a class of five hundred," Ruth Ginsburg excelled and became editor of the *Harvard Law Review.* When Martin graduated in 1958 and took a position with a New York firm, Ruth decided to complete her studies at Columbia University Law School. Once again she made law review, and in 1959, she graduated at the top of her class.

Her accomplishments in school accounted for very little in the profession. Ginsburg made the painful discovery that few judges were willing to hire female clerks and few law firms were willing to extend job offers to female law school graduates. Eventually Ginsburg secured a clerkship with federal district court judge Edmund L. Palmieri. After working with him for two years, she returned to Columbia University Law School and served a two-year stint as a researcher and project administrator. Ruth Bader Ginsburg's pioneering efforts continued in 1963 when she accepted a faculty position at Rutgers University Law School at a time when women comprised approximately 1 percent of law professors in the nation. Nine years later

Ginsburg was still a rarity in the legal and academic professions when she returned to her law school alma mater as its first tenured female professor. As late as 1980, the year Ginsburg left Columbia Law School for her appointment to the bench, women accounted for only 5 percent of the law school faculty nationwide.

Ginsburg wore many professional hats during the 1970s: law professor, director of the Women's Rights Project, general counsel to the American Civil Liberties Union, and board member of the National Organization for Women's Legal Defense and Education Fund. Building on her initial success in the *Reed* case, Ginsburg made five more appearances before the Supreme Court between 1973 and 1976, and lost only once. The issue before the Court in this case concerned a Florida property law that excluded widowers from special benefits granted to widows; Ginsburg, who believed that the legal system must turn a blind eye toward gender differences, represented the widower.

Her most famous case was *Frontiero v. Richardson* (1973). In this 8–1 decision, the justices invalidated a military policy that routinely denied spouses of servicewomen the same dependents' benefits automatically granted to spouses of servicemen. Here the inherent sex bias turned on the assumption that a serviceman's wife was legally "dependent" on her husband; therefore she was automatically entitled to dependents' benefits. The husband of a servicewoman, however, was legally independent of his wife, and therefore not entitled to dependents' benefits. Ginsburg had argued that "sex, like race, was a suspect basis for classification"; thus any law based on sex was subject to "strict scrutiny" under the Fourteenth Amendment's "equal protection clause." Though four of the eight concurring justices found this aspect of Ginsburg's argument compelling, the other four opted for a less demanding scrutiny (the state had to prove a compelling interest in maintaining sex discrimination). In the absence of a majority decision, the latter view prevailed. In an ironic twist of fate for feminism, one justice who favored "making sex a suspect classification" did not take this position in the *Frontiero* decision. Instead, he preferred to see this issue settled in the near future by a constitutional amendment (in 1973, ratification of the Equal Rights Amendment appeared inevitable).

Throughout her career as a lawyer, professor, judge, and Supreme Court justice, Ruth Bader Ginsburg has been guided by a philosophy grounded in the doctrine of equal rights. Her judicial voice has been moderate and restrained, but her message is clear: the law cannot build in privilege for any one group over another.

## Kate Millett (1934– )

In 1970 Kate Millett gained instant fame as a feminist literary sensation with the publication of *Sexual Politics,* a witty, scholarly feminist critique of the misogynous works of such prominent literary figures as Henry Miller, D. H. Lawrence, and Norman Mailer. The book was an overnight commercial and critical success. Thrust into the limelight by the press (she was dubbed the "high priestess" of the women's movement), Millett found herself in an uneasy relationship with many feminists. While the media was intent on creating a "spokeswoman" for feminism, radicals within the movement resented "celebrities" who were presumed to represent feminists everywhere. Caught in the political crossfire between radical feminists and the mainstream press, Millett became a target of both. For Millett, the feminist truism, "the personal is political" soon became all too real.

Katherine (Kate) Murray Millett was born in St. Paul, Minnesota, on September 14, 1934, to Helen (Feely) and James Albert Millett, an engineer. When Kate, the middle of three daughters, was fourteen, her father abandoned the family. Her college-educated mother had a difficult time finding a position that paid enough to support the family comfortably, and Kate helped out by working after-school jobs.

Millett graduated from the University of Minnesota in 1956 with a Phi Beta Kappa key. The sponsorship of a wealthy aunt (who became the subject of Millett's 1995 book *A.D.*), made graduate study in England possible; in 1958, she completed a master's degree (with high honors) in English literature at St. Hilda's College, Oxford University. Back in the United States, she briefly taught college in North Carolina before moving to New York City where (from 1959 to 1961) she concentrated on learning how to paint and sculpt. She also spent two years in Tokyo, Japan, working on her sculpting and paying her bills by teaching English at Waseda University. Her first show was held at the Minami Gallery in 1963, the same year she returned home to the United States.

By 1964 Millett was teaching at Barnard College in New York City and had joined the civil rights movement as a member of the Congress of Racial Equality. A year later she married the Japanese sculptor Fumio Yoshimura, an act that halted efforts to deport Yoshimura whom she had met while living in Japan (the couple divorced in 1985). The mid- to late 1960s were frenetic and heady times for Millett. She had begun attracting the attention of the local art world, the outcome of which was a second exhibit at the Judson Gallery in Greenwich Village in 1967, and she discovered feminism. By 1967 she had joined the National Organization for Women's New York chapter and New York Radical Women, the city's first radical women's liberation group. At the same time, she was working on her dissertation (*Sex-*

*ual Politics*) at Columbia University, organizing a women's liberation group on the campus, and putting the final touches on "Sexual Politics: A Manifesto for Revolution" (1968), one of the most widely read early position papers on the relationship between feminism and sexual freedom.

For many radical feminists, a key component of the women's movement was the permission it granted women to escape from the "repression of enforced heterosexuality." Sexual "self-expression," which many in the movement interpreted as lesbianism, was a "hot potato" during the early years of the movement. Kate Millett's part in this confrontation had its roots in a lesbian relationship that began when she was preparing for graduate study in England. There was also her statement in the "Sexual Politics" manifesto about feminism ending "enforced heterosexuality." Then in May 1970, following the Radicalesbians' spoof of the "lavender menace" at the Congress to Unite Women conference, Kate Millett was one of several women willing to talk about her sexual identity.

In May, Millett's sexual preference was hardly a big deal; after all, she was still an obscure figure within the movement. By November, however, she was earning star-billing with *Sexual Politics* and had become fair game. At a public meeting on sexuality held at Columbia University, a radical lesbian feminist directly confronted Millett, asking that she embrace her lesbianism; a *Time* magazine reporter covering the event noted Millett's response. A month later, Millett's sexual preference would not only find its way into the magazine's story, "Women's Lib: A Second Look" (December 14, 1970), but it also would be used in an attempt to discredit feminism. Three days after the magazine hit the newsstands several leading feminists called a press conference to demonstrate their support for Millett and to salvage feminism from the press's attacks.

Millett, who had left Barnard College prior to completing her Ph.D., soon found temporary employment at Bryn Mawr College. Teaching, however, was always secondary to her need to create, and by the early 1970s Millett was focused on her writing. Following her 1971 documentary on prostitution, *Three Lives,* Millett produced a written companion piece, *Prostitution Papers* (1973). Then came two of her four autobiographical works that focused explicitly on her lesbianism: *Flying* (1974) and *Sita* (1977). *The Basement: Meditations on Human Sacrifice,* a gripping tale about the real-life torture and murder of a teenage girl, appeared in 1980. Next came *Going to Iran* (1981); based on her two-week sojourn in Iran in 1979 (shortly after Islamic fundamentalists took control of the country), the book was both a travelogue and feminist political commentary. Millett's third autobiographical piece, *The Loony-Bin Trip* (1990), was a marked departure from her two previous personal narratives. This book revealed Millett's decades' long struggle with mental illness (she suffered from bipolar disorder and had made several suicide attempts both before and after being medicated and institutionalized). *The Politics of Cruelty: An Essay on the Literature of Political Imprisonment* came out in 1994. The fourth installment of her life, *A. D.* came in 1995.

Kate Millett's contribution to second-wave feminism differed significantly from many of her peers. Whereas most leaders are remembered for their organizational skills, their political acumen, or even their popular writings, Millett is best remembered for her intellectual insights. When *Sexual Politics* burst onto the literary scene in 1970, feminist literary criticism did not really exist. Millett and others (like feminist theologian Mary Daly) were scholarly pioneers mapping what would soon become the fertile intellectual terrain of feminist theory; for many, the personal and professional costs of producing such path-breaking works were too high. Certainly, Millett was unprepared for and uncomfortable with the glare of publicity (she referred to it as the "pain of public scrutiny"); whether this was a contributing factor in her battle with mental illness is a matter of conjecture. Seeking an alternative to medication, Millett created a refuge for herself on a working Christmas tree farm located in upstate New York; since the late 1980s, the farm has also served as a summer sanctuary for women artists.

## Robin Morgan (1941– )

Robin Evonne Morgan jokingly rejected the phrase, "Le Mouvement, c'est moi" in her introduction to *Going Too Far: The Personal Chronicle of a Feminist* (1977). She should not have been so modest, however, for her metamorphosis from New Left militant to radical feminist mirrored the conversion experience of thousands of young, educated, white middle-class women during the tumultuous 1960s. Morgan emerged as one of the most influential voices and powerful personalities in the radical wing of the women's liberation movement.

Robin Morgan was born January 29, 1941, in Lake Worth, Florida, to Faith Berkeley Morgan and grew up in Mt. Vernon, New York. Morgan's parents divorced before she was born, and for the first twelve years of her life she was raised by her mother and her maternal aunt. Published sources about Morgan barely mention her father; in a rare and fleeting reference to him, Morgan noted that they did not meet until she was eighteen and then only "infrequently and disappointingly." A similar silence cloaks any detailed references to Morgan's childhood, her religious training, or her education. Her memoir merely notes that she was a child-actress from ages two to sixteen (she was the youngest child, Dagmar, on the TV show *I*

*Remember Mama*), that she grew up in an "apostate Jewish household," and that at some point in her spiritual journey she became a "wiccean atheist" (Wicca is the pre-christian folk religion also known as witchcraft). She attended Columbia University from 1956 to 1959, but, according to the available records, she never earned a degree. She met her future husband, the twenty-seven-year-old writer Kenneth Pitchford, when she was seventeen and married him when she was twenty-one. Robin Morgan and Kenneth Pitchford had one child born in 1969, a son they named Blake (the "genderless" name was a deliberate choice according to Morgan). They divorced in 1990.

By the mid-1960s, Robin Morgan was a free-lance editor and professional writer whose works were finding a home in the numerous journals published by the political Left during the 1960s; from 1969 to 1973 she served as a consulting editor for Grove Press. In addition to writing for leftist periodicals, Morgan also participated in demonstrations sponsored by the civil rights, student, and peace movements. Although a founding member of New York Radical Women in 1967, Morgan remained a committed leftist; thus, she strongly believed that women's liberation was only an "arm" of the Left's much larger "revolutionary movement." This political perspective dominated Morgan's thinking even as she helped organize the first major demonstration of the women's liberation movement, the September 1968 Miss America Beauty Pageant protest.

In the aftermath of the Miss America protest, New York Radical Women attracted so much interest that it grew too large to accommodate all interested parties; spin-off groups began to form. Some women joined the Redstockings, a radical feminist group that emphasized consciousness-raising more than protests. Women who were still tied to the ideology of the "male-dominated Left" founded the more political, action-oriented Women's International Terrorist Conspiracy from Hell. Still a leftist more than a feminist, Morgan was a member of this latter group, and played a key role in organizing its "zap action" hexing of Wall Street on Halloween in 1968 and its February 1969 Bridal Fair protest at Madison Square Garden.

The year 1970 marked a turning point in Morgan's odyssey toward radical feminism with several factors influencing her rejection of the "male-dominated" Left. Among these were the take-over of the *Rat* by women staff members fed up with the sexism of leftist men (Morgan's contribution to the women's inaugural issue was the soon-to-be classic essay "Goodbye to All That"), the publication of Shulamith Firestone's *The Dialectic of Sex: The Case for Feminist Revolution,* Morgan's efforts to bring out her own feminist anthology, *Sisterhood Is Powerful*, and the recent birth of her son (motherhood was a "transformative and radicalizing" experience for Morgan personally and politically). Following the publication of *Sisterhood,* Morgan was in high demand as a speaker on college campuses across North America; according to Morgan, by 1971 she had become a "feminist outside agitator."

Although Morgan distanced herself from the Left by the early 1970s, she continued to define herself as a political radical. This perspective shaped her early view of the National Organization for Women, which she described as "bourgeois and reformist," and the causes its members championed. In these early years, Morgan was especially dismissive of the Equal Rights Amendment, but by the late 1970s, after the radical edge of the women's movement faded, her respect for liberal feminism increased.

The emergence of the gay-straight split within the women's movement created a different dilemma for Morgan. Her identity as a radical made her support for the lesbian presence within the movement a given, but she worried that the increasing emphasis on lesbian-separatism would drive straight women out of the movement. At one point, Morgan declared herself a lesbian, but since she lived with her young son and her husband (he was gay), many lesbians considered her assertion political posturing. As tensions over sexual politics heightened, Morgan increasingly found herself playing the role of movement peacemaker, emphasizing women's commonalities and downplaying their sexual differences.

The 1980s brought new challenges and opportunities for Robin Morgan. At the national level, she focused on women's health issues and the problems stemming from sexual violence. Her board memberships included the Feminist Women's Health Network, the National Battered Women's Refuge Network, the National Network of Rape Crisis Centers, and Women Against Pornography, which she cofounded. Her feminist vision also expanded globally during this decade. In 1984 she cofounded the Sisterhood Is Global Institute, and by the late 1980s she was serving as a special consultant on global feminism to the United Nations.

In addition to her activism, Robin Morgan has produced an extensive body of works on modern feminism. Morgan has written several volumes of poetry—*Monster* (1972), *Lady of the Beasts* (1976), *Death Benefits* (1981), *Depth Perception* (1982), and *Upstairs in the Garden* (1990). As a companion piece to her 1970 *Sisterhood* anthology, she edited *Sisterhood Is Global: The International Women's Movement Anthology* (1984) and wrote *The Demon Lover: On the Sexuality of Terrorism* (1989). A novel for adults, *Dry Your Smile,* appeared in 1987, and a children's story, *The Mer-Child: A Legend for Children and Other Adults* came out in 1991. She also played a pivotal part in shaping *Ms.* magazine as a contributing editor in the late

1970s, as editor-in-chief between 1989 and 1993, and as an international contributing editor since 1993.

## Pauli Murray (1910–1985)

This granddaughter of a slave was a pioneering civil rights and feminist lawyer-activist, a member of the President's Commission on the Status of Women, and a founding member of the National Organization for Women (NOW). She was also a scholar, author, and (in 1977) the first black woman to be ordained as an Episcopalian priest. Denied admission to two prestigious universities, the first time because of her race and the second time because of her gender, Pauli Murray developed an early understanding that racism and sexism were but opposite sides of the same coin. For Pauli Murray, social justice could never be achieved by sacrificing the rights of one group over that of another; thus she devoted her life to the struggle for human rights.

Pauli Murray was born November 20, 1910, in Baltimore, Maryland, to Agnes (Fitzgerald), a nurse, and William Murray, a teacher and principal in Baltimore's segregated school system. The Murrays' eleven-year marriage was rocky, and on more than one occasion, the couple separated. During such periods, brought on by her father's physical and mental deterioration, Pauli was sent to the North Carolina home of her maternal grandparents, the Fitzgeralds, and her beloved Aunt Pauline and Aunt Sallie (both of whom were unmarried school teachers). When Pauli's mother died when she was three, she returned to Durham, North Carolina, to live with her aging grandparents and was legally adopted by Aunt Pauline (Murray's tribute to her family's history was published in 1956 as *Proud Shoes: The Story of an American Family*).

Pauli Murray graduated from her segregated North Carolina high school in 1926 determined to attend an integrated northern college, and she set her sights on Columbia University. When she arrived in New York, Murray discovered that Columbia did not accept women (of any color) and that her inferior southern education was a barrier to her acceptance at Barnard College (Columbia's sister institution) or Hunter College, a prestigious public women's college. Undaunted, Pauli Murray arranged to live with a distant cousin and enrolled for a second senior year at Richmond Hill High School. In 1928 Pauli Murray entered Hunter College, one of only two black women in the freshman class. A year later the Great Depression began, and by 1930 a penniless Pauli Murray had to drop out of school for a year. It was during this period that Murray met, married, and separated from an equally poor, struggling student known only as Billy (the marriage was later annulled). Murray returned to school in 1931 and graduated in 1933.

For the next few years, Pauli Murray worked an assortment of jobs for the National Urban League and for several New Deal agencies. In 1938 she decided to return to college and applied to law school at the University of North Carolina. Her application was denied because "members of your race are not admitted to the University." In 1941 Murray entered law school at Howard University, the nation's most prestigious black university. There, as the only woman in her class (and one of three in the entire law school), she experienced another form of discrimination: sexism. Women, Murray discovered, were not taken seriously as students, they were the butt of tasteless jokes, and they were excluded from joining the school's legal fraternity. According to Murray's autobiography, *Song in a Weary Throat* (published posthumously in 1987), she had entered Howard with the single-minded purpose of using her law degree to dismantle segregation, but left the university in 1944 a committed feminist determined to bring down "Jim and Jane Crow."

In the years following Murray's graduation from Howard, her recognition that "the rights of women and the rights of Negroes are only different phases of the fundamental and indivisible issue of human rights" would grow sharper and become more focused. Personal experience was a great teacher; Harvard, for example, denied her application for graduate study in 1944 not because of her race but because of her gender (undeterred, she applied and was accepted to the University of California at Berkeley, where she earned a master's degree in law in 1945). Prior to and during her years at Howard, Pauli Murray had participated in demonstrations against segregation and had spent time in jail. Though she continued to think of herself as an activist, she became less of a demonstrator (although she participated in the historic 1963 March on Washington) and more of a scholar, a writer of prose and poetry, and an organizer (her collection of poetry appeared in 1970 under the title *Dark Testament and Other Poems*).

In 1962 an old friend who worked for the Women's Bureau (a division of the Department of Labor) invited Pauli Murray to serve on the President's Commission on the Status of Women. Murray, who had been working on a doctoral degree in law at Yale University (awarded in 1965), was assigned to the Committee on Civil and Political Rights. This invitation put her in touch with some of the most powerful feminists working in the nation's capital: Congresswoman Edith Green (D-Oregon), Marguerite Rawalt, an attorney for the Internal Revenue Service, and Mary O. Eastwood, a lawyer with the Department of Justice. The committee's task was to reconcile the conflicts between pro- and anti-Equal Rights Amendment feminists and to produce written recommendations for improving women's legal and political status. Murray's contribution came in the form of a well-researched memorandum pressing for litigation on behalf of women's civil rights under the Fifth and Fourteenth Amendments (the final report also opened the door to pursuing a constitutional amendment if judicial clarification failed).

With the committee's work complete in the summer of 1963, Murray returned to her dissertation research only to have Eastwood and Rawalt ask her to prepare another memo in the spring of 1964. Led by the powerful Senator Everett M. Dirksen, a handful of Republicans were preparing to amend the proposed 1964 Civil Rights Act by removing the word "sex" from the legislation's Title VII provision. Murray's reasoned, persuasive memo pointed to an historical link between the civil rights struggles by black Americans and women and emphasized that in the absence of either provision (race or sex), black women's civil rights would be at risk. In the hands of the right people, Murray's memo was a powerful weapon; Dirksen backed down, and the sex provision was maintained.

Pauli Murray's reputation as a feminist legal scholar was enhanced by an October 1965 lecture she delivered on Title VII before the National Council of Women of the United States and by her article, "Jane Crow and the Law: Sex Discrimination and Title VII," which appeared two months later in the *George Washington Law Review*. Murray's speech criticized the government for its law enforcement of Title VII's proscription against sex discrimination; she closed by hinting that organized resistance by women might compel the government to uphold its own policy. The next morning when Murray's chance remark about the wisdom of demonstrating made the *New York Times,* it caught the attention of Betty Friedan. A phone call followed, and the seeds of a feminist partnership were planted.

Historical and popular histories of NOW generally credit Betty Friedan as the organization's inspirational founder. Few accounts, however, name the equally important behind-the-scenes actions of the fifteen to twenty women who met in Friedan's hotel room one evening in June 1966 to hatch the idea of founding a "civil rights movement" for women (the occasion was the Third National Conference of State Commissions on the Status of Women). Pauli Murray was one of those women. According to legend, the next day's closing lunch session found the fifteen to twenty feminist conspirators grouped at two tables. As they said their good-byes and ran for cabs to the airport, they paused long enough to scribble their names on napkins and ante up $5.00 as dues for the new feminist organization. Murray was hastily appointed to a committee of six charged with developing a structure for the new organization and drafting its principles.

Pauli Murray's humanitarian vision led to tangles in the late 1960s with Black Power militants (she opposed their divisive rhetoric) and the Episcopalian church in the 1970s (for its sexism). Pauli Murray believed in the powers of acceptance, inclusion, and activism, and she preached this message from pulpits that were both secular and religious. She died of cancer at her Pittsburgh home on July 1, 1985.

## Eleanor Holmes Norton (1937– )

A civil rights and black feminist activist and lawyer, Congresswoman Eleanor Holmes Norton has represented the city of her birth, Washington, D.C., since her election in 1990. Born on June 13, 1937, this proud Washingtonian was educated in the district's (then) segregated public schools. Nurtured and encouraged by her family and teachers, Norton learned early on that "empowerment comes from within [the family and the community]." Married to Edward Norton, a lawyer, the couple have two children, Katherine Felicia and John Holmes.

Norton's interest in the civil rights movement dates back to her undergraduate days at Antioch College in Ohio where she served as president of the local chapter of the National Association for the Advancement of Colored People. After earning her bachelor's degree in 1960, Norton simultaneously began a graduate program in American Studies and entered law school at Yale University. There she met civil rights and feminist lawyer Pauli Murray who was working on her doctoral degree in law. As Norton's and Murray's friendship deepened, the latter's experiences as a civil rights demonstrator inspired and informed Norton's life and work.

At Yale, Norton joined the more radical civil rights organization, the Student Nonviolent Coordinating Committee; and during a summer reprieve from the pressures of law school, she went south to participate in the Student Nonviolent Coordinating Committee's Mississippi voter registration drive. There she met Fannie Lou Hamer, the heart and soul of the Mississippi Freedom Democratic Party, who inspired an entire generation of young black activists. Norton and Marian Wright Edelman (who would go on to lead the Children's Defense Fund) helped write the Mississippi Freedom Democratic Party's legal challenge to unseat the state's all-white, male delegation to the 1964 Democratic National Convention. That the party failed to achieve its goal only hardened Norton's resolve to seek black inclusion in American politics.

Following the awarding of her advanced degrees in 1963 (the M.A.) and 1964 (law), Norton was admitted to the New York State Bar. She clerked for Federal District Court Judge A. Leon Higginbotham for a year before going to work for the American Civil Liberties Union. In the wake of a controversial case in 1968 involving Alabama governor and third-party presidential candidate George Wallace (well-known for his support for segregation), Norton was elevated to the position of assistant legal director of the New York City chapter (Norton defended the governor's constitutional right to hold a political rally in the city). Norton remained with the American Civil Liberties Union until the election of the city's reform-minded mayor John Lindsay in 1970. He asked her to chair New York City's Commission on Human Rights, which she did until 1977; a year after Lindsay took office, Norton joined his staff.

Dating Norton's feminist awakening is more difficult than identifying her conversion to the civil rights cause. One source traces Norton's feminist activities back to the mid-1960s when she served as a legal advisor to the Student Nonviolent Coordinating Committee's Black Women's Liberation Committee; the same source also links Norton to the American Civil Liberties Union's Women's Rights Project. Although there is no evidence indicating that Norton joined either the liberal women's rights or the radical women's liberation wings of the feminist movement, she did contribute an article, "For Sadie and Maude" to Robin Morgan's feminist classic, *Sisterhood Is Powerful: An Anthology of Writings from the Women's Liberation Movement* (1970).

Try as they might, both wings of the feminist movement (dominated by white, middle-class women) remained susceptible to charges by black women that ranged from indifference to racism. Although the National Organization for Women managed to attract a few "famous" black women—Pauli Murray, Shirley Chisholm, Fannie Lou Hamer—many more black feminists embraced the goals of the women's movement but kept their distance. At the same time, black feminists recognized that the male-dominated black liberation movement was not free of sexism. By the early 1970s, recognition of the "simultaneity of [race and sex] oppression" led many black feminists to found independent black feminist organizations. One of the first such groups was the National Black Feminist Organization, which began in May 1973; founding member Eleanor Holmes Norton has been credited with writing the group's statement of purpose (see the May 1974 issue of *Ms.*). By 1974, the National Black Feminist Organization (headquartered in New York City) had approximately ten chapters nationwide, claimed 2,100 members (one source puts the membership figure closer to 400), and had established task forces on the media, drug addiction, prisons, lesbianism, and sexual violence.

During this period of feminist activity, Norton's excellent work on the New York City Commission on Human Rights caught the attention of

Jimmy Carter; early in his presidency, he appointed Norton to chair the Equal Employment Opportunity Commission (EEOC), the first woman to do so. When Norton took over the almost moribund agency, there existed a backlog of over "130,000 affirmative action and discrimination cases." With Norton at the helm, the agency's productivity rate rose by 65 percent in four years and she made enforcement of the Equal Pay Act and the Age Discrimination Act her top priorities. During the 1980s, when Republicans controlled the White House, Norton taught law at Georgetown University (she became a tenured professor). Eventually, Norton's concern for the steady erosion of the EEOC under Presidents Reagan and Bush led to her decision to stand for Congress in 1990.

The four-term congresswoman from the District of Columbia holds a unique position in the House of Representatives. As the capital city's delegate, Norton has limited voting privileges (she votes in committee but does not have the right to vote on the floor of Congress). Despite this limitation, Norton has earned a reputation as an able legislator; only a handful of her peers have introduced more bills than she, and her success rate for enacting legislation puts her within the top third of House members. An ardent, unabashed defender of affirmative action, she has strong words for those who attempt to discredit affirmative action as a "quota system." She has been successful in increasing funding for the agency she once headed (the EEOC), and although she did not achieve victory in her fight for statehood for the District of Columbia, she made her point about the district's right to equal representation. An important voice in the Democratic party, Norton served as vice chair of the platform committee for the 1992 Democratic National Convention, is a member of the Executive Committee of the Democratic Study Group (the policy-making body of House Democrats), and is active in several congressional caucuses, including the Women's Caucus (which she has cochaired), the Black Caucus, and the Progressive Caucus.

### Esther Peterson (1906–1997)

A pioneering consumer advocate, labor activist, feminist, and advisor to three Democratic presidents (John Kennedy, Lyndon Johnson, and Jimmy Carter), Esther Peterson was born in Provo, Utah, in 1906 to Annie and Lars Eggertsen, Mormon immigrants from Denmark. Her father was the superintendent of the local school system, and her mother supplemented the family's income by boarding students from Brigham Young University in the family home.

Following in the footsteps of her siblings, Esther Peterson attended Brigham Young University where she prepared for a career in teaching.

Graduating with honors in 1927, Peterson taught physical education and dance at the Branch Agricultural College in Cedar City, Utah, for the next three years. Wanting something more for herself, however, Peterson left Utah in 1930 for graduate school at Columbia University Teachers College.

When Esther Peterson arrived in New York City, she considered herself a "strict conservative Mormon Republican [who was] very anti-union" (see her 1995 autobiography, *Restless: Memoirs of Labor and Consumer Activist Esther Peterson*). Her radical transformation into a labor activist began soon thereafter when she met Oliver Arthur Peterson, the man she married in 1932. Peterson's political perspective was decidedly radical, and he introduced Esther to a world she had been sheltered from by her parents, her community, and her faith.

Soon after their marriage (which lasted until Oliver's death from cancer in 1979), the couple moved to Boston where Oliver attended Harvard and Esther taught physical education at an exclusive preparatory school for girls. She also taught an evening course on "current events" to working girls at the local Young Women's Christian Association. As it turned out, her students gave Peterson a lesson she would never forget.

One evening in the fall of 1932, half of Esther Peterson's class failed to show; the reason for their absence was a strike. When the owner of the sweatshop refused to bargain with the underpaid workers, Esther Peterson found herself walking the picket line and calling in reinforcements from the Young Women's Christian Association and the Women's Trade Union League. Within a matter of weeks, the women workers had formed a local chapter of the International Ladies Garment Workers Union and had negotiated a successful end to the strike, and Esther Peterson had become a convert to trade unionism.

Peterson's discovery of trade unionism's potential for empowering women nurtured her growing feminism and encouraged her entrance into the related field of consumer activism (as the primary consumers for their households, women were encouraged to use their purchasing power to demand healthier and safer products for their families and to improve the conditions under which workers labored). Even as her interest in consumerism grew, Peterson remained committed to workers' education. This interest led to her six-year association with Bryn Mawr College's Summer School for Women Workers, an experimental educational program sponsored by the elite women's college from 1921 until 1935. There, her association with some of the country's brightest and most progressive professors led directly to her becoming a union organizer for the American Federation of Teachers and the Amalgamated Clothing Workers in the late 1930s. Although a fervent unionist, Peterson was not a wide-eyed innocent. She tangled with male labor leaders who paid female organizers less than male organizers, and she noted with dismay the relationship between organized labor and organized crime.

During the period in which she worked for Amalgamated, the Petersons started a family. After two miscarriages, their daughter Karen was born in 1938 and three sons—Eric, Iver, and Lars—soon followed. In 1944 when Oliver's career took the family to Washington, D.C., Esther switched from organizing to lobbying. Working the halls of Congress for the next four years, Peterson's top priorities were raising the minimum wage and extending coverage of the Fair Labor Standards Act to agricultural and service workers. In 1948 when Oliver began working for the State Department, Esther resigned from Amalgamated. For the next nine years (1948 to 1957) she played the traditional role of a diplomat's wife. Still, Peterson managed to give this staid position a unique twist. While the family was stationed in Brussels, she worked with other foreign service wives to establish the International School for Working Women based on the Bryn Mawr program.

The Petersons' return to the United States in 1957 marked another turning point in Esther's personal and professional life. In 1958, she bumped into John F. Kennedy, an old acquaintance on the Hill. The Massachusetts senator was considering a run for the 1960 presidential nomination, and he asked Peterson to join his campaign. When he won, Peterson was rewarded with a post in the Kennedy administration. Asked what she would like to do, she replied "[head] the Women's Bureau."

Created in 1920, the Women's Bureau was housed under the Department of Labor and was the domain of social feminists. Intent on protecting and expanding the interests of working women, social feminists, with whom the pro-labor Peterson clearly identified, remained united in their opposition to political feminists' proposal for an Equal Rights Amendment (ERA). Although Peterson clearly understood that "laws to protect women could also be laws that kept women subordinate to men," she preferred to err on the side of maintaining protective labor legislation. According to Peterson, too many pro-ERA feminists "wanted a symbolic emancipation from male expectations of womanhood, but did nothing to support bread-and-butter issues [like minimum wage]."

Credit for President Kennedy's Commission on the Status of Women belongs to Esther Peterson. Peterson, whose motto was "specific bills for specific ills" saw the commission as the ideal vehicle for documenting women's second-class status and then making policy recommendations to correct specific inequities (thus avoiding the need for a blanket ERA). That President Kennedy signed the Equal Pay Act in June 1963 (four months before the commission's final report) was proof enough for Peterson that her strategy was sound.

At the time of President Kennedy's death, Esther Peterson was also serving as an assistant Secretary of Labor (which made her the highest ranking woman in the Kennedy administration). Concerned about the high rate of occupational injuries, Peterson laid the groundwork for the bill that would eventually create the Occupational Safety and Health Administration. Peterson also encouraged Kennedy's growing interest in the consumer movement, and she had high hopes that he would follow through with his pledge to create a consumer advisory council. When the president's death cut short this plan, his successor, Lyndon Johnson, appointed Peterson the first Special Assistant to the President for Consumer Affairs.

Peterson's tenure as special assistant lasted until her resignation in January 1965, when she returned to her former position in the Department of Labor. For a year she had collected information about price-gouging, truth in lending in the credit industry, deceptive advertising and packaging practices. Peterson expected strong opposition from the advertising, manufacturing, and credit industries but was unprepared for the lack of support inside the White House (one of President Johnson's top advisors had been an advertising executive). When the stress proved too much, she quit. In 1971 the president of Giant Foods hired Esther Peterson as vice president for consumer affairs, and over the next six years she revolutionized grocery shopping. In 1977 President Jimmy Carter asked Esther Peterson to return to government service, continuing her fight for consumers' rights from the Office of Consumer Affairs. In January 1981 the outgoing president paid tribute to Esther Peterson by awarding her the Presidential Medal of Freedom. Thanks to her vision and her determination, an ordinary shopper "can tell a product by its label." Unit pricing, product dating, ingredient labeling, nutritional guidelines, environmentally friendly products, energy-efficiency labels on products, and permanent care labels on clothing—all are on the list of Peterson's accomplishments.

During the 1980s, Esther Peterson expanded her consumers' crusade onto the global stage. She represented the International Organization of Consumer Unions before the United Nations. She also devised a set of standards for developing countries interested in creating consumer protection programs similar to those in the United States (the United Nations Guidelines for Consumer Protection were adopted in 1985), and she put the finishing touches on the United Nations Code of Conduct on Transnational Corporations (pressure from the Reagan White House killed this measure). In 1988, Peterson became the consumer advisor for the National Association of Professional Insurance Agents, and following the 1992 election of

President Bill Clinton, she joined the U.S. delegation to the UN. Esther Peterson's remarkable career in public service ended with her death in Washington, D.C., on December 20, 1997.


## Phyllis Schlafly (1924– )

Mention the name Phyllis Schlafly and feminists shudder. Schlafly, a self-styled homemaker (and lawyer) acquired a national following in the 1970s and 1980s because of her achievements as a conservative, political activist. Schlafly was the creative force behind the founding of *The Phyllis Schlafly Report,* a monthly newsletter begun in 1967; STOP ERA, a national single-issue organization that operated between 1972 and 1982; and the Eagle Forum, organized in 1975 as an "alternative to women's lib." Although Phyllis Schlafly's career as a political operative predated the rise of the women's liberation movement, her fame increased in direct proportion to the growing popularity of the antifeminist backlash (she made *Good Housekeeping*'s list of the "ten most admired women of the world" from 1977 to 1990). Indeed, many political analysts both within and outside of the feminist movement credit Schlafly for the defeat of the Equal Rights Amendment (ERA: 1972–1982).

Phyllis Schlafly was born Phyllis MacAlpin Stewart on August 15, 1924, in St. Louis, Missouri, to Odille (Dodge) and John Bruce Stewart, a salesman. Her family was middle-class, Republican, and devoutly Catholic, and Schlafly's early education reflected her family's faith. Her high school years and her first year of college were spent at Sacred Heart institutions; after a year at Maryville College, she transferred to Washington University where she majored in political science and graduated with honors in 1944. She received a graduate fellowship to Radcliffe College and earned a master's degree in political science in 1945. Thirty years later, she returned to school to earn a law degree from her undergraduate alma mater in 1978.

Her first professional job was with the American Research Association (now the American Research Institute), a privately supported conservative think tank located in the nation's capital. She worked there a year before returning home to St. Louis in 1946. She quickly landed a position as campaign manager for Claude Bakewell, a staunchly conservative, anticommunist Republican lawyer, who was preparing a run for the congressional seat held by the popular Democratic incumbent, John Sullivan. When Bakewell won and left for Washington, D.C., Schlafly remained behind in St. Louis and found employment as a librarian/speech writer/newsletter editor for two local banks. In 1949 she met and married Fred Schlafly, a lawyer fifteen years her senior with impeccable Catholic and conservative

Republican credentials. After the wedding, Phyllis Schlafly retired from the work force to become a full-time wife and mother (the couple would have six children between 1950 and 1964); or so she thought.

The lure of politics proved too much for Phyllis Schlafly. When her husband turned down an opportunity to run for Congress in 1952, she jumped at the chance. She won the primary but lost the general election. Despite this defeat, Schlafly was hooked on politics; and though she never won public office (a second congressional bid failed in 1970), Schlafly found another outlet for making her mark on public policy.

She joined the National Federation of Republican Women and served as president of the Illinois chapter from 1960 to 1964. Next she succeeded to the national office of first vice president, a position she held from 1964 to 1967. She set out to win the presidency but lost the election to Gladys O'Donnell in 1967. The campaign between the two women had been bitter. O'Donnell, a moderate Republican (who would join a bipartisan effort in 1970 to secure Congress's support for the ERA), had the support of party leaders; Schlafly did not. In part, the Republican leadership's antipathy toward Schlafly stemmed from the part she played in the party's debacle at the polls in the 1964 presidential race between President Lyndon Johnson and Senator Barry Goldwater (R-Arizona). Schlafly admired the conservative senator's politics and had written a book, *A Choice Not an Echo* (1964), promoting his candidacy. Although moderate Republicans trashed the book, its popularity (3 million copies sold) is credited with securing Goldwater's nomination. Embarrassed by Johnson's landslide victory over Goldwater, the Republican party spent the next several years distancing itself from the Goldwater contingency. Schlafly labeled this strategy a "purge" and was convinced that O'Donnell's victory had been engineered by establishment Republicans.

Schlafly's response to Goldwater's loss in 1964 and her defeat in 1967 was to come out fighting. More books touting the conservative position (and critical of the party's establishment wing) appeared between 1964 and 1967: *The Gravediggers* (1964), *Strike from Space* (1965), and *Safe Not Sorry* (1967). Schlafly also struck back at the party's elite by starting a monthly newsletter, The *Phyllis Schlafly Report,* that not only kept her in touch with the conservative women who had supported her candidacy but also allowed her to expand her political base beyond the narrow constraints of partisanship.

Initially, *The Phyllis Schlafly Report* was devoted to traditional conservative issues—anticommunism, opposition to the welfare state and to busing, low taxes, support for law-and-order campaigns on college campuses and in urban ghettos, a strong national defense. By 1970, however, Schlafly had begun worrying about a new threat to American society—feminism. Her growing concern for the ill effects a gender-blind society would have on the American family found a welcome reception from her growing list of newsletter subscribers (estimated at 35,000 by the early 1970s). By 1972 Schlafly was prepared to battle feminism's most potent symbol of gender equality, the ERA; all she had to do was organize her troops and publicize her message (in her 1977 book, *The Power of the Positive Woman*, the "positive woman" battles the "femlib fanatics").

Feminists may have achieved some of their biggest victories in the 1970s, but they soon suffered their greatest defeat. When Schlafly and her anti-ERA forces prevailed in 1982, their triumph marked a critical turning point for second-wave feminism. STOP ERA disbanded, but Schlafly's Eagle Forum did not. Having succeeded in derailing the ERA, Schlafly and her Eagles were ready to tackle other items on the feminist agenda (reproductive freedom, federally funded child care), and in Ronald Reagan's White House (1980–1988), both the antifeminist message and its messengers received a warm welcome.

## Gloria Steinem (1934– )

Gloria Steinem's name is synonymous with *Ms.*, the feminist magazine she founded in 1972 and guided as its editor-in-chief until 1987. Soon after the magazine was up and running, Steinem helped establish the *Ms.* Foundation for Women (a nonprofit agency that funds programs in areas such as employment, reproductive freedom, and domestic violence prevention). In 1979 Steinem responded to the escalating political attacks on abortion rights by cofounding Voters for Choice. A charismatic speaker, Steinem was in high demand at rallies, fund-raisers, and public hearings during the 1970s and 1980s; consequently, she became something of a media darling. Steinem paid dearly within feminist circles for her celebrity status; revered by many within the movement for her ability to popularize feminism, she also was castigated as a "media creation" by some of the movement's more radical members.

Gloria Steinem was born March 25, 1934, in Toledo, Ohio, to Leo and Ruth (Nuneviller) Steinem. Her parents' marriage was strained by poor finances and her mother's constant battle with depression. In 1944, Leo and Ruth separated; their divorce came a year later. Steinem seldom saw or communicated with her father, and with her mother's hold on reality tenuous at best, Steinem grew up quickly.

Gloria Steinem followed in her older sister's footsteps by also attending Smith College (on scholarship) and graduated magna cum laude in 1956.

She became engaged during her senior year but backed out of the pending marriage soon after graduation. While Steinem was reconsidering her decision to marry, she applied for and won a postgraduate fellowship to India offered by Smith for the 1957–1958 year.

After Steinem's return to the United States, she spent a brief interlude (1959–1962) working for the government in the newly founded Independent Research Service, an agency ostensibly created to open up communications between communist and noncommunist delegates who were attending a series of international youth festivals. That Steinem knew of the Central Intelligence Agency's (CIA) involvement with this agency is clear (she admitted as much in interviews with the *New York Times* and the *Washington Post* in 1967); that she was naive about the CIA's motives for establishing links between youths from communist and noncommunist countries is open to interpretation.

By the early 1960s, Steinem was beginning to make a living as a freelance writer in New York, with her work appearing in such publications as *Esquire, Show, Glamour, Ladies' Home Journal,* and the *New York Times Magazine.* Her most famous piece from these early years was the 1963 exposé, "I Was a Playboy Bunny," published in *Show* (Steinem had spent two weeks "working undercover" at the New York club). Her first sustained political writing occurred during the period (1964–1965) she spent working for NBC's television show, *That Was the Week That Was.*

The year 1969 was transformative for Steinem. In her new role as a writer for *New York,* a magazine she had recently cofounded with a friend, Steinem found a vehicle for her politics. Although she had begun following the women's liberation movement for the magazine, she did not consider herself a feminist—yet. Then, during the winter of 1969, Steinem covered a demonstration sponsored by the National Organization for Women (NOW) to integrate the dining room of a prominent New York hotel (the hotel had a "men's only" policy at lunchtime and seated women for dinner only if they were in the company of men) and a "speakout on abortion" rally organized by the radical feminist group the Redstockings. These two events helped crystallize Steinem's thoughts on feminism, and the result was "After Black Power, Women's Liberation," which appeared in the April 7, 1969, issue of *New York.* Soon after the women's liberation story ran, Steinem was asked to elaborate on her views about feminism before an audience of college students at New York University; her dynamic lecture style earned her high marks, and she was asked to join a college speakers' bureau, which she did. Her career as a public speaker had begun.

By the late 1960s, the feminist movement existed as an umbrella under which groups with widely divergent political perspectives operated. From the beginning of her association with feminism, Steinem had worked more closely with the liberal wing of the movement than with the radical wing. She marched with Betty Friedan and Bella Abzug at the "Women Strike for Equality Day" rally on August 26, 1970; the following year she joined Friedan, Abzug, and Shirley Chisholm in founding the National Women's Political Caucus. Nevertheless, Steinem's relationship with this group was not free of conflict. Friedan, in particular, may have viewed Steinem as too radical, and too flamboyant for the liberal wing of the movement; by the mid-1970s they were rivals (Friedan would later blame Steinem and Abzug for easing her out of power at the 1977 Houston Conference).

At the same time that Friedan was typecasting Steinem as too radical, radical feminists were condemning Steinem for selling out to the establishment. The surrender of the radical political fugitive Jane Alpert to federal authorities in November 1974 had driven a bitter wedge between feminists. While in hiding, Alpert had condemned the Left's sexism and had converted to feminism. When accusations flew that Alpert was cooperating with federal authorities, radical feminists labeled Alpert a collaborationist and called on the feminist community to condemn her. Instead, many leading feminists such as Robin Morgan and Gloria Steinem defended Alpert. Steinem was especially vulnerable on the issue of collaboration, for it was common knowledge that she had worked (indirectly) for the CIA during her years at the Independent Research Service. In May 1975 the Redstockings publicly accused Steinem of selling out the feminist movement to the government by reviving the story of Steinem's long-ago connection with the CIA and by hinting that the agency might be funneling funds to *Ms.* magazine.

Although it seems ludicrous that a handful of radical feminists would consider *Ms.* a front for the CIA, their attack on the magazine is understandable. Radical feminists had been suspicious of the political orientation of *Ms.*'s editorial board from its inception, criticizing the magazine for its stereotypical advertising and dismissing many of the articles as fluff pieces. Indeed, some radical feminists believed that *Ms.* had become a forum for a conservative, bourgeois feminism. That their dislike of *Ms.*'s politics took the form of a personal attack on Steinem strongly suggests that by the mid-1970s Steinem had become one of the most recognizable symbols of liberal feminism. The Redstockings' attempt to trash Steinem and *Ms.* also hints at the radical feminists' recognition of their growing isolation within the larger feminist movement. According to feminist scholars, radical feminism was fast being eclipsed by both liberal and cultural feminism by mid-decade; thus in many respects, the attack on Steinem may have symbolized the last gasps of radicalism within second-wave feminism.

Gloria Steinem emerged from this internal conflict with her leadership within the women's movement unrivaled. For the next several years, Steinem seemed to be everywhere at once: fund-raising, lobbying, and protesting. All eyes were focused on the prize as feminists of all persuasions (gay, straight, radical, liberal) united at the 1977 Houston Conference to secure passage of the Equal Rights Amendment. Its defeat in 1982 was a stunning blow to feminists.

Although Steinem did not put organizing and speaking aside, she spent the better part of the 1980s and early 1990s editing her early works and writing. *Outrageous Acts and Everyday Rebellions*, a collection of two decade's worth of essays appeared in 1983; in 1986 Steinem's feminist revision of the life of Marilyn Monroe, *Marilyn: Norma Jean* appeared. Relinquishing the editorship of *Ms.* after its sale in 1987, Steinem's focus shifted to the "inner self." Her next two books, *Bedside Book of Self-Esteem* (1989) and *Revolution from Within: A Book of Self-Esteem* (1992), were Steinem's contribution to the popular genre of self-help books (several feminist critics viewed these books as a retreat from feminism). In 1993 Steinem returned to form with *Moving beyond Words*.

An enigmatic figure, Gloria Steinem's feminism defies easy classification. Castigated, sometimes simultaneously, for being too liberal and too conservative, Steinem's politics aptly reflects the movement she helped guide.

# Primary Documents of the Women's Liberation Movement

## Document 1

### FROM *AMERICAN WOMEN: REPORT OF THE PRESIDENT'S COMMISSION ON THE STATUS OF WOMEN, WASHINGTON, D.C., OCTOBER 11, 1963*

On December 14, 1961, President John F. Kennedy issued Executive Order 10980 establishing the President's Commission on the Status of Women. The idea for an executive commission to study the status of women was hardly new with requests from women's organizations dating back to the immediate post–World War II era. For President Kennedy there was much political capital to be gained and little political risk taken by creating an executive commission to study the progress of women.

Eleanor Roosevelt, a former First Lady and the first U.S. Ambassador to the United Nations, accepted the figurehead position of commission chair. Kennedy's decision in this matter actually reflected the political savvy of two members of his administration: Esther Peterson, Assistant Secretary of Labor and the Director of the Women's Bureau, and her boss, Arthur Goldberg, Secretary of Labor. Peterson stepped into the powerful, behind-the-scenes working position of executive vice chair, and Richard A. Lester, an economics professor, was asked to serve as the second vice chair. In addition, the President's Commission on the Status of Women included "twenty members with a competency in the area of public affairs and women's activities," five cabinet members (from the departments of Labor; Justice; Health, Education, and Welfare; Commerce; and Agriculture), and the head of the Civil Service Commission.

The initial life of the President's Commission on the Status of Women was brief; the final report was due on the president's desk by October 1, 1963. The committee was charged with making "recommendations for constructive action in [federal and state] employment policies and practices, insurance and tax laws, labor laws, legal differences [between men and women] in political, civil, and property rights, and new and expanded services in education, counseling, training, home services, and child care" for women juggling the multiple responsibilities of wife, mother, and worker.

The President's Commission on the Status of Women's creation would result in unintended, positive consequences for second-wave feminism. Many of the women instrumental in securing the addition of Title VII (on sex discrimination) to the 1964 Civil Rights Act and in founding the National Organization for Women (NOW) in 1966 had cut their political teeth and honed their feminist ideals by participating in either the federal commission or in one of the state commissions that sprang into existence after 1963 (by 1964 there were thirty-two state commissions and by 1967 there were fifty).

Dear Mr. President:

In presenting the report of your Commission on the Status of Women, we are mindful that we transmit it bereft of our Chairman. Today is Eleanor Roosevelt's birthday. In handing you the work started with her participation, we wish to pay tribute to a great woman.

On behalf of the Commission, we submit to you this unanimous report. In inviting action on its recommendations, we count on a varied initiative, private and public, in all parts of the country [the letter is signed by Ester Peterson and Richard A. Lester. Recommendations follow].

EDUCATION AND COUNSELING

Good basic instruction must be within reach of all children from the time they start school.

- Means of acquiring or continuing education must be available to every adult at whatever point he or she broke off traditional formal schooling. The structure of adult education must be revised [to] provide practicable and accessible opportunities, developed with regard for the needs of women, to complete elementary and secondary school and to continue education beyond high school. Vocational training [for a] skilled and highly educated manpower, should be included at all educational levels. Financial support should be provided by local, State, and Federal governments and by private groups and foundations.

- The education of girls and women for their responsibilities in home and community should be thoroughly reexamined with a view to discovering more effective approaches with experimentation in content and timing.

## HOME AND COMMUNITY

The Commission recognizes the fundamental responsibility of mothers and homemakers and society's stake in strong family life. Demands upon women in the economic world, the community, and the home mean that women carry on different kinds of activity. Women can do a more effective job as mothers and homemakers when communities provide appropriate resources.

- For the benefit of children, mother, and society, child care services should be available at all economic levels. Cost should be met by fees scaled to parents' ability to pay, contributions from voluntary agencies and public appropriations

- Tax deductions for child care expenses of working mothers should be commensurate with the median income of couples when husband and wife are employ[ed].

## WOMEN IN EMPLOYMENT

American women work in their homes, unpaid, and outside their homes, on a wage or salary basis. Among the majority of women the motive for paid employment is to earn money.

- Equal opportunity for women in hiring, training, and promotion should be the governing principle in private employment. An Executive Order should state this principle and advance its application to work under Federal contracts.

## LABOR STANDARDS

Many of the lowest paid jobs in industry and service occupations have been filled by women, driven by economic necessity. They have labored and been exploited as textile and needle trade workers, as laundresses and waitresses, as doers of industrial homework. Trade unions raise wages and improve working conditions [but] even now only a little over 3.5 million out of 24 million women [workers] are union members.

- The Fair Labor Standards Act, including premium pay for overtime, should be extended to employment subject to Federal jurisdiction now uncovered, such as work in hotels, motels, restaurants, and laundries, in retail, in agriculture, and in nonprofit organizations.

- State legislation, applicable to men and women, should be enacted, strengthened, and extended to provide minimum wage levels approximating Federal law.

- State laws should establish the principle of equal pay for comparable work.

## SECURITY OF BASIC INCOME

The Social Security Act (1935) instituted the Federal system of old-age, survivors, and disability insurance and the program for unemployment compensation. These programs have widened their coverage, but some important gaps remain.

- A widow's benefit should be equal to the amount her husband would have received at the same age had he lived.

- The coverage of unemployment insurance should be extended to small establishments and nonprofit organizations. Practicable means of covering household workers and agricultural workers should be explored.

- Paid maternity leave or comparable insurance benefits should be provided for women workers.

## WOMEN UNDER THE LAW

Equality of rights under the law for all persons, male or female, is basic to democracy and its commitment must be reflected in the fundamental law of the land. The Commission believes that this principle is embodied in the 5th and 14th amendments to the Constitution. In the face of these amendments, however, there remain distinctions based on sex which discriminate against women. The Commission considered methods of achieving greater recognition of the rights of women: test litigation seeking redress under constitutional safeguards, amendment to the Constitution—the proposed equal rights amendment, legislative action to eliminate discriminatory State laws.

- Early and definitive court pronouncement, by the U.S. Supreme Court, is urgently needed under the 5th and 14th amendments to the end that the principle of equality become firmly established in constitutional doctrine.

- Interested groups should give high priority to bringing under court review cases involving laws and practices which discriminate against women.

- Appropriate action, including enactment of legislation, should be taken to achieve equal jury service in the States.

- State legislatures concerned with improvement of statutes affecting family law, personal and property rights of married women should move to eliminate laws which impose legal disabilities on women.

## WOMEN AS CITIZENS

Since the 19th amendment to the Constitution, political participation by women has grown, but full participation is not yet a fact.

- Women should be encouraged to seek elective and appointive posts at local, State, and National levels and in all three branches of government.
- Public office should be held according to ability, experience, and effort, without preferences or discriminations based on sex. Consideration should be given to the appointment of women of demonstrated ability to policy-making positions.

## CONTINUING LEADERSHIP

Federal Action taken as a result of the Commission's proposals [should] become operative through regular and existing Federal Government structure.

- Designate a Cabinet officer responsible for carrying out the Commission's recommendations.
- Designate heads of agencies involved in those activities to serve as an interdepartmental committee.
- Establish a citizens committee to evaluate progress made, provide counsel, and serve as a means for suggesting action. This is our call to move ahead.

*Source*: *American Women: Report of the President's Commission on the Status of Women* (Washington, D.C.: Government Printing Office, 1963), pp. i, v, 9, 13, 15, 17, 19, 20–23, 27, 30, 35–37, 40, 42–47, 49, 52–53, 54.

## Document 2

## FROM *THE FEMININE MYSTIQUE*, 1963

The genesis for The *Feminine Mystique* was an "intimate open-ended" questionnaire Betty Friedan sent to 200 Smith College classmates on the eve of their fifteenth year reunion in 1957. The results from the 189 responses were startling, or perhaps not. First and foremost, these college graduates considered themselves primarily wives and mothers (approximately only 15 percent reported full-time employment). Almost the entire class had married (183), only four had divorced, and motherhood was almost a universal condition (family size averaged three children). Yet, these women were hardly "happy housewives." Instead, they suffered from a "nameless, aching dissatisfaction" and sought relief from their doctors who reported, bewilderingly, the rise of a new disease, "housewife's fatigue."

Published in February 1963, The Feminine Mystique was a best-seller by the time the President's Commission on the Status of Women released its report eight months later. A series of television talk-show interviews and other public appearances soon made Betty Friedan's name a household word. After 1963, her participation as a delegate to the annual meetings of the State Commissions on the Status of Women and her research for a book on "sex discrimination in employment" put Friedan at the center of a small feminist nucleus taking shape in the nation's capital. When this group's frustration with the federal government's foot-dragging on sex discrimination reached a boiling point in 1966, Betty Friedan seemed a likely figure to channel this discontent into a national "civil rights organization for women." Tapped to serve as the first president of the National Organization for Women (NOW), Friedan held this position until 1970. Although this activist/writer has several books to her credit, The Feminine Mystique, a harbinger of second-wave feminism, remains her most popular work; as a feminist classic, this text appears frequently on required reading lists for courses in women's studies.

## CHAPTER 1, "THE PROBLEM THAT HAS NO NAME"

Gradually, I came to realize that something is wrong with the way American women are trying to live their lives today. I sensed it first, as a question mark in my own life, as a wife and mother of three small children, half-guiltily and half-heartedly, using my abilities and education that took me away from home. It was this personal question mark that led me in 1957 to my college classmates, fifteen years after our graduation from Smith. The problems and satisfaction of their lives and mine did not fit the image of the modern American woman written about in magazines [and] studied in classrooms and clinics. There was a discrepancy between the reality of our lives and the image to which we were trying to conform, the image I call the feminine mystique. I wondered if other women faced this schizophrenic split. And so I began to hunt down the origins of the feminine mystique, and its effect on women who lived by it, or grew up under it.

The problem lay buried, unspoken, for many years in the minds of American women. It was a sense of dissatisfaction, a yearning. Each suburban housewife struggled with it alone as she made beds, shopped for groceries, matched slipcover material, ate peanut butter sandwiches with her children, chauffeured Cub Scouts and Brownies, lay beside her husband at night—she was afraid to ask the silent question—"Is this all?"

For fifteen years [following World War II] in books and articles by experts, women heard that they could desire no greater destiny than to glory in their own femininity. Experts told them how to catch a man and keep him, how to breastfeed children and handle their toilet training, how to buy a dishwasher, bake bread, cook gourmet snails; how to dress, look, and act more feminine and make marriage more exciting. They were taught to pity the neurotic, unfeminine, unhappy women who wanted to be poets or physicists or presidents. They learned that feminine women did not want careers, higher education, political rights—the independence and opportunities that the old-fashioned feminists fought for.

The suburban housewife—she was the dream of young American women and the envy of women all over the world. She was healthy, beautiful, educated, concerned only about her husband, her children, her home. She had found true feminine fulfillment, free to choose automobiles, clothes, appliances, supermarkets; she had everything that women everywhere dreamed of.

Millions lived the image of the suburban housewife, kissing their husbands goodbye, depositing children at school, smiling as they ran the new waxer over the spotless kitchen floor. They baked bread, sewed their and their children's clothes, kept new washing machines and dryers running all day. They changed the sheets on the bed twice a week, took the rug-hooking class, and pitied their poor frustrated mothers who had dreamed of having a career. Their only dream was to be perfect wives and mothers; their highest ambition to have five children and a beautiful house, their only fight to get and keep their husbands.

If a woman had a problem in the 1950s and 1960s, she knew that something must be wrong with her marriage, or with herself. Other women were satisfied with their lives. What kind of woman was she if she did not feel this mysterious fulfillment waxing the kitchen floor? She was so ashamed to admit her dissatisfaction that she never knew how many other women shared it. Women found it harder to talk about this problem than about sex.

But on an April morning in 1959, I heard a mother of four, having coffee with four other mothers in a suburban development, say in a tone of quiet desperation, "the problem." And the others knew without words that she was not talking about a problem with her husband or her children, or her home. Suddenly they realized that they all shared the same problem, the problem that has no name. They began to talk about it.

Just what was this problem that has no name? Sometimes a woman would say "I feel empty." Or she would say, "I feel as if I don't exist." Sometimes she blotted out the feeling with a tranquilizer. Sometimes she thought the problem was with her husband or her children or that what she needed was to redecorate her house, move to a better neighborhood, have an affair, or another baby.

In 1960, the problem that has no name burst like a boil through the image of the happy housewife from the *New York Times* and *Newsweek* to *Good Housekeeping*. Some said the problem [was] education which naturally made [women] unhappy in their role as housewives. "The road from Freud to Frigidaire, from Sophocles to Spock has turned out to be a bumpy one," reported the *New York Times* (June 28, 1960).

Home economists suggested more realistic preparation for housewives, such as high school workshops on home appliances. College educators suggested more discussion groups on home management and the family to prepare women for the adjustment to domestic life.

A number of educators suggested that women no longer be admitted to colleges and universities [that] the education girls could not use as housewives was needed by boys to do the work of the atomic age.

The problem was dismissed by telling the housewife she doesn't realize how lucky she is—her own boss, no time clock, no junior executive gunning for her job. What if she isn't happy—does she think men are happy? Does she still want to be a man?

The problem was dismissed by shrugging that there are no solutions: this is what being a woman means, and what is wrong with American women that they can't accept their role gracefully?

It is no longer possible to ignore that voice, to dismiss the desperation of so many women. This is not what being a woman means, no matter what the experts say.

It is no longer possible to blame the problem on loss of femininity: to say that education and independence and equality with men have made American women unfeminine.

The problem that has no name is not a matter of loss of femininity, or too much education. It is far more important than anyone recognizes. It may be the key to our future as a nation and a culture. We can no longer ignore that voice within women that says: "I want something more than my husband and my children, and my home."

*Source*: Betty Friedan, *The Feminine Mystique* (New York: W.W. Norton and Company, 1963, renewed 1991), pp. 7, 11, 13–19, 21–22, 27.

## Document 3

## FROM STUDENT NONVIOLENT COORDINATING COMMITTEE *POSITION PAPER*, NOVEMBER 1964 (NAME WITHHELD BY REQUEST)

Following the Student Nonviolent Coordinating Committee's 1964 Mississippi Summer Project, the paid staff planned a retreat at Waveland, Mississippi, to discuss revamping the organization's administrative structure and its goals for the coming year. In preparation for the November meeting, veteran civil rights activist Mary King produced a "working paper" on possible changes with the organization's communications system. After much soul-searching, King also decided to prepare (with input from Casey Hayden) a position paper on the "woman question" to be distributed "informally" at the retreat. That King chose to conceal the document's authorship for fear that raising the issue of sexism within the movement would engender contempt from her male colleagues was but one indication that the Student Nonviolent Coordinating Committee's ideal of a "beloved community" was being shaken to its core.

King's (and Hayden's) fears were soon realized. "Mocked and taunted" by many of their peers (the identity of the author/s was soon discovered), the issue of the unjust, "second-class" treatment of women within the movement was quickly dismissed. Although a few members of the organization's inner circle were privately sympathetic to the points raised in the working paper, they were reluctant to lend public support to discussing the "woman question."

Over the next year, King and Hayden took stock of the relationship between men and women, not only within the Student Nonviolent Coordinating Committee, but also within the larger peace and social justice movements. In November 1965 they collaborated on a manifesto, signed it, and mailed it to forty activists. On receiving the King-Hayden memo, a majority of black women retained a collective silence, but among white women the response was electric. They used it as a reference point for organizing "women's caucuses" at male-dominated conventions.

In April 1966 King's and Hayden's "Memo To A Number Of Other Women in the Peace and Freedom Movements" reached a wider audience when it appeared in the *Liberation*, a publication of the War Resisters League. Though second-wave feminism may have been in its infancy in the spring of 1966 (neither the National Organization for Women nor any of the more radical women's liberation groups existed at the time), a public dialogue on the "woman question" had begun. Change was in the air.

1. Staff was involved in crucial constitutional revisions at the Atlanta staff meeting in October. A large committee was appointed to present revisions to the staff. The committee was all men.

2. Two organizers were working together to form a farmers league. Without asking any questions, the male organizer immediately assigned the clerical work to the female organizer although both had had equal experience in organizing campaigns.

3. Although there are women in the Mississippi project who have been working as long as some of the men, the leadership group in COFO [Council of Federated Organizations] is all men.

4. A woman in a field office wondered why she was held responsible for day-to-day decisions, only to find out later that she had been appointed project director but not told.

5. A fall 1964 personnel and resources report on Mississippi projects lists the number of people in each project. The section on Laurel, however, lists not the number of persons but "three girls."

6. One of SNCC's main administrative officers apologizes for the appointment of a woman as interim project director in a key Mississippi project area.

7. A veteran of two years' work for SNCC in two states spends her day typing and doing clerical work for other people in her project.

8. Any woman in SNCC, no matter what her position or experience, has been asked to take minutes in a meeting when she and other women are outnumbered by men.

9. The names of several new attorneys entering a state project this past summer were posted in a central movement office. The first initial and last name of each lawyer was listed. Next to one name was written: (girl).

10. Capable, responsible, and experienced women who are in leadership positions can expect to have to defer to a man on their project for final decision making.

11. A session at the recent October staff meeting in Atlanta was the first large meeting in the past couple of years where a woman was asked to chair.

Undoubtedly this list will seem strange to some, petty to others, laughable to most. The list could continue as far as there are women in the movement. Except that most women don't talk about these kinds of incidents, because the whole subject is not discussable.

The average white person finds it difficult to understand why the Negro resents being called "boy," or being thought of as "musical" and "athletic," because the average white person doesn't realize that *he assumes he is superior*. And, naturally, he doesn't understand the problem of paternalism. So too the average SNCC worker finds it difficult to discuss the woman problem because of the assumption of male superiority. Assumptions of male superiority are as widespread and deep-rooted and every much as crippling to the woman as the assumptions of white supremacy are to the Negro. Consider why it is in SNCC that women who are competent, qualified, and experienced are automatically assigned to the "female" jobs such as: typing, desk work, telephone work, filing, library work, cooking, and the assistant kind of administrative work but rarely the "executive" kind.

The woman in SNCC is often in the same position as that token Negro hired in a corporation. The management thinks that it has done its bit. Yet, every day the Negro bears an atmosphere, attitudes, and actions which are tinged with condescension and paternalism, the most telling of which are seen when he is not promoted as the equally or less skilled whites are.

This paper is anonymous. Think about the kinds of things the author, if made known, would have to suffer because of raising this kind of discussion. Nothing so final as being fired or outright exclusion, but the kinds of things which are killing to the insides—insinuations, ridicule, overexaggerated compensations.

This paper is presented anyway because it needs to be made known that many women in the movement are not "happy and contented" with their status. It needs to be made known that much talent and experience are being wasted by this movement, when women are not given jobs commensurate with their abilities. It needs to be known that just as Negroes were the crucial factor in the economy of the cotton South, so too in SNCC, women are the crucial factor that keeps the movement running on a day-to-day basis. Yet they are not given equal say-so when it comes to day-to-day decision making.

What can be done? Probably nothing right away. Most men in this movement are probably too threatened by the possibility of serious discussion on this subject. Perhaps this is because they have recently broken away from a matriarchal framework under which they may have grown up. Then, too, many women are as unaware and insensitive to this subject as men, just as there are many Negroes who don't understand they are not free or who want to be part of white America. They don't understand that they have to give up their souls and stay in their place to be accepted. So, too, many women, in order to be accepted by men, on men's terms, give themselves up to that caricature of what a woman is—unthinking, pliable, an ornament to please the man.

Maybe the only thing that can come out of this paper is discussion—amidst the laughter—but still discussion. (Those who laugh the hardest are often those who need the crutch of male supremacy the most.) And maybe some women will begin to recognize day-to-day discrimina-

tions. And maybe sometimes in the future the whole of the women in this
movement will become so alert as to force the rest of the movement to stop
the discrimination and start the slow process of changing values and ideas
so that all of us gradually come to understand that this is no more a man's
world than it is a white world.

In Mary King, *Freedom Song: A Personal Story of the 1960s Civil Rights Movement* (New
    York: William Morrow and Company, 1987), pp. 567–69.

## Document 4

## FROM THE NATIONAL ORGANIZATION FOR WOMEN, STATEMENT OF PURPOSE, 1966

The idea for an action-oriented, national women's organization with a
strong feminist agenda had been brewing for some time; in the summer of 1966, the time seemed ripe. Since 1963 an emerging feminist
network centered in Washington, D.C., had sought to advance many of
the recommendations made by the Presidential Commission on the
Status of Women. Working behind the scenes with some of the long-
standing women's organizations, this network managed a political
coup when Title VII was added to the 1964 Civil Rights Act. An important victory, Title VII gave women both a "legal and psychological
edge" in their fight for equality by fostering the concept of women as a
"class" with the wherewithal for seeking "legal redress" for their
second-class status.

    By 1966, key members of this network were angry with the Equal
Employment Opportunity Commission's (EEOC) foot-dragging on
the numerous sex discrimination cases pending before the agency.
Topping the list of "hot-button" issues was the EEOC's refusal to outlaw sex-segregated job listings in the classified section of newspapers
where high-paying jobs appeared on the "men's pages" and low-paying
jobs on the "women's pages."

    On the eve of the third annual convention of State Commissions on
the Status of Women, Betty Friedan, Catherine East, and Mary Eastwood were among those holding a series of informal talks. When it became clear that none of the existing women's organizations were
willing to advocate openly for women's rights (for fear of being labeled
"too feminist"), this inner circle floated a proposal to create a national
women's rights organization and tapped Friedan to lead such an effort.
Supportive of the concept, Friedan initially sidestepped the issue of her
leadership role. This would change over the course of the two-day
meeting in June when it became clear that the "power" to influence

public policy on women's issues through the state commissions was only advisory.

Commandeering a table at the conference's closing luncheon, Betty Friedan coined the new organization's name on the spot while scribbling potential members' names on a napkin. Before the conference adjourned, the National Organization for Women (NOW) had twenty-eight charter members and a start-up budget of $140. Four months later, NOW presented its statement of purpose and introduced its slate of officers to the press. Elected to the presidency, Betty Friedan served in that capacity until 1970. Still going strong after more than thirty years, NOW's membership hovers around 250,000 with an annual budget of over $10 million.

We, men and women who hereby constitute ourselves the National Organization for Women, believe the time has come for a new movement toward true equality for all women in America, and toward [an] equal partnership of the sexes, as part of the world-wide revolution of human rights now taking place within and beyond our national borders.

The purpose of NOW is to take action to bring women into full participation in the mainstream of American society now, exercising all privileges and responsibilities in equal partnership with men.

We believe the time has come to move beyond the abstract argument, discussion, and symposia over the status and special nature of women which has raged in American in recent years; the time has come to confront, with action, the conditions that prevent women from enjoying equality of opportunity and freedom of choice which is their right as Americans and as human beings.

We organize to initiate or support action, nationally or in any part of this nation, to break through the silken curtain of prejudice and discrimination against women in government, industry, the professions, churches, political parties, the judiciary, labor unions, in education, science, medicine, law, religion and every other field of importance in American society.

Enormous changes taking place in society make it possible to advance the unfinished revolution of women toward equality. With a life span lengthened to nearly seventy-five years, it is no longer necessary for women to devote the greater part of their lives to childrearing, yet childbearing and rearing—which continues to be [an] important part of most women's lives—is still used to justify barring women from equal participation.

Despite all the talk about the status of American women in recent years, the actual position of women has declined. Although 46.4 percent of all women between eighteen and sixty-five work outside the home, the majority—75 percent—are in clerical, sales, or factory jobs, or they are household workers, cleaning women, hospital attendants. About two-thirds of Negro women workers are in the lowest paid service occupations. Full-time women workers today earn 60 percent of what men earn and that gap has been increasing over the past twenty-five years.

In professions considered [important] to society, in the executive ranks of industry and government, women are losing ground. Women comprise less than 1 percent of federal judges; less than 4 percent of lawyers; 7 percent of doctors. Yet women represent 53 percent of the U.S. population. And men are replacing women in top positions in secondary and elementary schools, in social work, in libraries—once thought to be women's fields.

The excellent reports of the President's Commission on the Status of Women and of the state commissions have not been fully implemented. Such commissions have power only to advise. They have no power to enforce their recommendations. The reports of these commissions have, however, created a basis upon which to build.

Discrimination in employment on the basis of sex is now prohibited by federal law, in Title VII of the Civil Rights Act of 1964. Although nearly one-third of the cases brought before the Equal Employment Opportunity Commission during the first year dealt with sex discrimination, the commission has not made clear its intention to enforce the law with the same seriousness on behalf of women as of other victims of discrimination. Until now, too few women's organizations have been willing to speak out [for] fear of being called "feminist."

There is no civil rights movement to speak for women as there has been for Negroes and other victims of discrimination. The National Organization for Women must begin to speak.

WE BELIEVE that the power of American law, and the protection guaranteed by the U.S. Constitution to the civil rights of all individuals, must be applied and enforced to remove patterns of sex discrimination, to ensure equality of opportunity in employment and education, and equality of civil and political rights.

WE DO NOT accept the token appointment of a few women to high-level positions in government and industry as a substitute for a serious effort to recruit and advance women according to their abilities.

WE BELIEVE that this nation has [the] capacity to innovate new social institutions which will enable women to enjoy equality of opportunity in society without conflict with their responsibilities as mothers and homemakers. We do not accept the traditional assumption that a woman has to choose between marriage and motherhood, on the one hand, and participation in industry or the professions on the other. We question the expectation that women will retire from job or profession for ten or fifteen years, to devote full time to raising children, only to reenter the job market at a minor level. True equality of opportunity and freedom of choice for women requires a nationwide network of child-care centers.

WE REJECT current assumptions that a man must carry the burden of supporting himself, his wife, and family and that a woman is entitled to life-long support by a man upon her marriage, or that marriage, home, family are primarily woman's world and responsibility—hers to dominate, his to support. We believe that proper recognition should be given to the economic and social value of homemaking and childcare. To these ends, we will seek a reexamination of laws and mores governing marriage and divorce.

IN THE INTERESTS OF THE HUMAN DIGNITY OF WOMEN, we will protest and endeavor to change false images of women in the mass media, in the texts, ceremonies, laws, and practices of our major social institutions. Such images perpetuate contempt for women by society. We are opposed to all policies and practices which, in the guise of protectiveness, deny opportunities [and] foster self-denigration, dependence, and evasion of responsibility.

WE BELIEVE THAT women will do most to create a new image by *acting* now, and by speaking out in behalf of their equality, freedom, and human dignity—not in pleas for special privilege, nor in enmity toward men, who are also victims of the current half-equality between the sexes—but in active partnership with men. By doing so women will determine the conditions of their life, their choices, their future and their society.

(National Organization for Women, Washington, D.C.)

By the mid-1960s, white women working in various peace and social justice organizations had discovered that even though their male counterparts were more than willing to challenge race and class oppression and American imperialism, they were unable or unwilling to confront their own chauvinism. White women who sought to raise the issue of sexism within New Left organizations were belittled at public forums by New Left men. That these men used degrading sexual words and gestures to dismiss the women's claims of sexism seems ironic. For black women, the issue of sexism within the civil rights/black power movement remained more problematic. Many were hesitant to speak out against sexism for fear of being labeled disloyal to their race; for others, the fight against sexism was far less important to them than the struggle against racism.

For white women, the turning point in the formation of the radical wing of second-wave feminism—women's liberation—came in August 1967. At a national meeting representing more than 200 New Left organizations, the efforts of some fifty women to bring forward their issues were dismissed as unimportant by the men running the convention. The women walked, and a week later the first autonomous women's liberation group was founded.

From its inception, the women's liberation movement was hardly cohesive. Liberationists were united in their determination to eradicate female oppression, but they disagreed over ideology and strategy. "Politico" groups like The Women's International Terrorist Conspiracy from Hell (1968) believed that the root cause of female oppression was capitalism, whereas "feminist" groups like New York Radical Feminists (1969) identified male supremacy as the stumbling block to women's liberation. Politicos tended to favor "zap" actions—protests, pickets, street theater—whereas feminists stressed consciousness-raising.

The heyday of women's liberation was 1969 to 1975; thereafter, the internal differences that had marked radical feminism and the division between liberationists and women's rights activists became less pronounced. In its earliest days, the women's liberation movement had functioned effectively as the "shock troops" for second-wave feminism. With few exceptions, like that of abortion rights, women's liberationists were more inclined to address politically and socially sensitive problems than were women's rights' activists; and though both branches of second-wave feminism exhibited some homophobia, lesbian women's groups were more closely aligned with the liberationists.

By the late 1970s, the shift toward conservatism within American society had produced a political backlash against feminism; within this harsh climate radical feminism seemed to wither away. Some groups disbanded, others merged with local chapters of the more mainstream feminist organization, the National Organization for Women, and surprisingly enough, a handful survived. Still, no matter how temporary its existence, the legacy of the women's liberation movement lives on with the establishment of rape crisis centers, women's health clinics, and domestic violence shelters in communities across the country.

The following document is an example of one of the earliest "politico" groups associated with feminism's radical wing. Note the differences in philosophy, language, and strategies between this women's liberation group, and the "feminist" organization highlighted in Document 6.

## Document 5

## WOMEN'S INTERNATIONAL TERRORIST CONSPIRACY FROM HELL, 1968–1969

WITCH was born on Halloween, 1968, in New York, but within a few weeks Covens had sprung up in such diverse spots as Boston, Chicago, San

Francisco, North Carolina, Portland (Oregon), Austin (Texas), and Tokyo (Japan). They're still spreading. A certain common style—insousciance, theatricality, humor, and activism, unite the Covens—which are otherwise totally autonomous, and unhierarchical to the point of anarchy.

The fluidity and wit of the Witches is evident in the ever-changing acronym: the basic original title was Women's International Terrorist Conspiracy from Hell, but on Mother's Day, one Coven became Women Infuriated at Taking Care of Hoodlums; another group, working at a major Eastern insurance corporation, became Women Indentured to Traveler's Corporate Hell; still another set of infiltrators, working at Bell Telephone manifested themselves disruptively as Women Incensed at Telephone Company Harassment. When hexing inflationary prices at supermarkets, a Midwest Coven appeared as Women's Independent Taxpayers, Consumers, and Homemakers; Women Interested in Toppling Consumption Holidays was another transfigutory appellation—and the latest heard at this writing [this is a reference to Robin Morgan's anthology] is Women Inspired to Commit Her Story.

## FROM THE NEW YORK COVENS

WITCH is an all-woman Everything. It's theater, revolution, magic, terror, joy, garlic flowers, spells. It's an awareness that witches and gypsies were the original guerrillas and resistance fighters against oppression—particularly the oppression of women—down through the ages. Witches have always been women who dared to be: groovy, courageous, aggressive, intelligent, nonconformist, explorative, curious, independent, sexually liberated, revolutionary. They bowed to no man, being the living remnants of the oldest culture of all—one in which men and women were equal sharers in a truly cooperative society, before the death-dealing sexual, economic, and spiritual repression of the Imperialist Phallic Society took over and began to destroy nature and human society.

WITCH lives and laughs in every women [sic]. She is the free part of each of us, beneath the shy smiles, the acquiescence to absurd male domination, the make-up or flesh-suffocating clothes our sick society demands.

Whatever is repressive, solely male-oriented, greedy, puritanical, authoritarian—these are your targets. Your weapons are theater, satire, explosions, magic, herbs, music, costumes, cameras, masks, chants, stickers, stencils and paint, films, tambourines, bricks, brooms, guns, voodoo dolls, cats, candles, bells, chalk, nail clippings, hand grenades, poison rings, fuses, tape recorders, incense—your own boundless beautiful imagination.

Confront the Whoremakers at the Bridal Fair, February 1969.

Marriage is a dehumanizing institution—legal whoredom for women. *Confront* the perpetrators of our exploitation as women. *Confront* the institutions which make us pawns in a male dominated culture. *Confront* the structure which forces men into the dehumanizing roles of our oppressors. *Confront* the Bridal Fair, which encourages vulnerable young women to be dutiful, uncomplaining, self-sacrificing, "loving" commodities on the marriage market, and well-packaged, fully automated, brand-conscious consumers. *Confront* the exhibitors of this commercial extravaganza: "Big Boys" of the world of business and finance who are at the same time enslaving and murdering our sisters and brothers in Asia, Africa, and Latin America.

*Come* witches, gypsies, feminists, students. Come all oppressed women of every age and marital status. Come to New York's first *and* last "Bridle Un-Fair."

*We will create* our own rituals and festivals, perform our own anti-fashion shows, meet each other and the brides-to-be attending the fair in self-defense against the common enemy. *Bridal Fairs must not happen. Here's why:*

1. ALWAYS A BRIDE, NEVER A PERSON. A woman is taught from infancy that her only real goal in life is to fulfill the role of wife and mother of male heirs. An unmarried girl is considered a freak—a lesbian or a castrating career girl.

2. HERE COMES THE BRIBE. The corporations are quick to capitalize on our insecurities. Will I be a good housekeeper and cook? How do I keep my husband from having affairs with other women?

Isolated from her sisters[,] she is alone in her suburb, or apartment, or job as a clerk-typist—dehumanized[,] she is manipulated—by the giant corporations who need consumers on which to unload their over-productivity.

Buy cosmetics and fancy clothes to be beautiful. Buy gourmet foods to win your man's heart. Buy fashionable home furnishings. Buy deodorant to be "dainty" and "safe." With this drivel the corporations transform our self-doubts and emotional needs into commodities and sell them to us at a profit.

3. YOU HAVE A FRIEND AT CHASE MANHATTAN. The corporations exhibiting at this Bridal Fair include Chase Manhattan Bank—major investor in racist South Africa; International Coffee, which condemns its South America workers to poverty and slave labor; J.P. Stevens, a fabric supplier with large government defense contracts (Is J.P. Stevens making military uniforms and soldiers' shrouds at the same time he is filling our hope chests with shoddy linens?). *Imperialism begins at home.*

4. THE RITUAL IS THE REALITY. Our wedding day is the "only" day in our lives. We commence, consummate, consume, and are consumed on

that single day, having spent our childhood playing "house." The wedding ceremony is the symbolic ritual of our legal transference from father's property to husband's property. The name is changed from one man's to another's and our role as chattel in a male's house remains the same. SISTERS! Let us confront the whoremakers at the Bridal Fair but more important, confront and overthrow the institutions of marriage and capitalism which make such bridal fairs possible!

In Robin Morgan, ed., *Sisterhood Is Powerful: An Anthology of Writings from the Women's Liberation Movement* (New York: Random House, 1970), pp. 538–40, 543–46.

## Document 6

## FROM AN INTRODUCTION TO THE NEW YORK RADICAL FEMINISTS, 1970

Dear Sisters,

The following represents the basic philosophy, structures, and techniques of the New York Radical Feminists. We hope this information will help you in understanding the position of radical feminism in the women's liberation movement and will assist you in setting up small groups for the purposes of consciousness-raising.

### THE PHILOSOPHY OF RADICAL FEMINISM

Radical feminism recognizes the oppression of women as a fundamental political oppression wherein women are categorized as an inferior class, based upon their sex. It is the aim of radical feminists to organize politically to destroy this sex class system.

We believe that the purpose of male chauvinism is primarily to obtain psychological ego satisfaction and only secondarily does this manifest itself in economic relationships. We do not believe that capitalism, or any other economic system, is the cause of female oppression, nor do we believe that female oppression will disappear as a result of purely economic revolution. The political oppression of women has its own class dynamic, namely the politics of the ego.

As women we are living in a male power-structure, and our roles become necessarily a function of men. The services we supply are services to the male ego. If we do not choose to perform these ego services, but instead assert ourselves as primary to ourselves, we are denied alternatives wherein we can manifest our self-assertion. Our creative efforts are *a priori* judged not serious because we are females, our day-to-day lives are judged failures because we have not become "real women."

The oppression of women is manifested in particular institutions, such as marriage, motherhood, love, and sexual intercourse, constructed and maintained to keep women in their place. Through those institutions the woman is taught to confuse her biological sexual differences with her total human potential. Biology is destiny, she is told. Because she has childbearing capacity, she is told that motherhood and childbearing are her main *function*, not her *option*, and her function is to marry and have the man economically maintain her and make her decisions. She is told that sexual intercourse too is her function, rather than a voluntary act which she may engage in [as] an expression of her general humanity. In each case *her* sexual difference is rationalized to trap her with it, while male sexual difference is rationalized to imply access to all areas of human activity. Love has been used politically to justify an oppressive relationship between men and women, but there is no genuine love until the need to *control* the growth of another is substituted by the love *for* the growth of another.

We must begin to destroy the notion that we are only servants to the male ego; we must construct alternate selves that are independent and self-assertive. It remains for us as women to develop a new dialectic of sex class—an analysis of the way in which sexual identity and institutions reinforce one another.

## STRUCTURAL APPROACH OF THE NEW YORK RADICAL FEMINISTS

As established by its founding cell, the Stanton-Anthony Brigade, on December 5, 1969, we hereby set up New York Radical Feminists in answer to the largely unmet political and organizational needs as set down below:

We are committed to the building of a mass-based radical feminist movement. To this end we have proposed a structure, consisting of small, closely coordinated groups: nuclear, leaderless, structureless groups of no more than fifteen, where women, over a period of time, develop a personal intimacy, a political awareness, and a positive group experience.

We suggest the following schedule of activity as a period of preparation and development which has proved useful to beginning groups:

1. *Consciousness-raising—For a minimum of three months.*

a. to develop personal sensitivity to the various levels and forms that oppression take in our daily lives;

b. to build group intimacy and thus group unity, the foundations of true internal democracy;

c. to break down in our own heads the barriers between "private" and "public" (the "personal" and the "political"), in itself one of the deepest aspects of our oppression.

2. *Reading and discussion of current literature—For a minimum of six weeks, on the women's movement, both feminist and nonfeminist.*

a. to acquaint each person with the broad spectrum of politics already apparent in the women's liberation movement;

b. to discuss the position of radical feminism within the spectrum.

3. *Intensive reading and discussion of feminist history and theory—For a minimum of six weeks.*

a. to acquaint each member of the group with her own history and to give her a sense of continuity within the feminist tradition;

b. to give the group a good foundation in basic theory on which to build their own analysis;

c. to give the group some basis on which to choose its name. This period of preparation should lead the group to an understanding of the character of action which it will undertake, e.g., research, theory, action, theater, etc.

In Noreen Connell and Cassandra Wilson, eds., *Rape: The First Sourcebook for Women*, by New York Radical Feminists (New York: New American Library, 1974), pp. 253–55.

## Document 7

## FROM "DOUBLE JEOPARDY: TO BE BLACK AND FEMALE," 1970

Women of color, especially black women, have maintained an uneasy alliance with organized feminism in the United States since its inception following the Civil War. During both the first wave of feminism when the suffrage campaign dominated the agenda and the second wave when the feminist platform was more diverse, black women found themselves (sometimes simultaneously) embracing the movement's philosophy while distancing themselves from organizations controlled by white, middle-class women.

The "double jeopardy" of being black and female frequently translated into feelings of divided loyalties and divided duties among black women activists. Their internal debate centered on determining which struggle took precedence—the fight against racism or sexism. Black women wondered if joining the fight for racial uplift would also bring about an end to sex discrimination. Would male race leaders accept black women as their equals or were they (black men) as guilty of sexism as white men? If the latter was true, were black women disloyal to their race if they challenged their men's sexism? Would acknowledging sexism within the movement for social justice undermine or divert attention from the struggle against racism?

Black women also debated whether or not it was truly possible to seek common cause with white women. Was the pull of sisterhood strong enough to overcome race and class tensions? Was the feminist agenda inclusive of race and class concerns or was it shaped primarily by the interests of white middle-class women? These were but some of the questions bedeviling black women as they contemplated where to place their allegiance and how best to use their energies and resources.

Befitting the complexity of resolving race, class, and gender conflicts in the United States, black women sought a variety of solutions to their double jeopardy. Black women joined black men in all the major civil rights organizations with many also participating in the mainstream white women's organizations. At times, however, their unique status led them to recognize the necessity for organizing separately from black men and white women; thus the formation of such organizations as the National Association of Colored Women (1896), the National Council of Negro Women (1935), and the National Black Feminist Organization (1972).

The following document by Frances Beale of the Third World Women's Alliance, a feminist group with strong ties to the Student Nonviolent Coordinating Committee, was written during the period in which the civil rights movement was on the defensive and the women's movement was on the upswing.

In attempting to analyze the situation of the Black woman in America, one crashes into a solid wall of grave misconceptions, outright distortions of fact, and defensive attitudes on the part of many. The system of capitalism (and its afterbirth—racism) under which we all live has attempted to destroy the humanity of all people, and particularly the humanity of Black people.

America has defined the roles to which each individual should subscribe. It has defined "manhood" in terms of its own interests and "femininity" likewise.

The ideal model that is projected for a woman is to be surrounded by hypocritical homage and estranged from all real work, spending idle hours primping and preening, obsessed with conspicuous consumption, and limiting life's functions to simply a sex role. We unqualitatively reject [this model]. A woman who stays at home, caring for children and the house often leads an extremely sterile existence. She must lead her entire life as a satellite to her mate. He goes out into society and brings back a little piece of the world for her. His interests and his understanding of the world become

her own and she cannot develop herself as an individual having been re-
duced to a biological function. This kind of woman leads a parasitic existence that can aptly be described as legalized prostitution.

Furthermore it is idle dreaming to think of Black women simply caring
for their homes and children like the middle-class white model. Most Black
women have to work to help house, feed, and clothe their families. Black
women make up a substantial percentage of the Black working force and
this is true for the poorest Black family as well as the so-called "middle-
class" family.

Black women were never afforded such phony luxuries. Though we have
been browbeaten with this white image, the reality of the degrading and dehumanizing jobs that were relegated to us quickly dissipated this mirage of
womanhood.

There seems to be some confusion in the Movement as to who has been
oppressing whom. Since the advent of Black power, the Black male has ex-
erted a more prominent leadership role in our struggle for justice. He sees
the system for what it is for the most part, but where he rejects its values and
mores on many issues, when it comes to women, he seems to take his guidelines from the pages of *Ladies' Home Journal*. Certain Black men are maintaining that they have been castrated by society and that Black women
somehow escaped this persecution and even contributed to this emascula-
tion.

Black women are not resentful of the rise to power of Black men. We
welcome it. We see in it the eventual liberation of all Black people from this
corrupt system of capitalism. Nevertheless, this does not mean that you
have to negate one for the other. It is fallacious reasoning that in order for the
Black man to be strong, the Black woman has to be weak.

Those who are exerting their "manhood" by telling Black women to step
back into a domestic, submissive role are assuming a counter-revolutionary
position. Black women have been abused by the system and we must begin
talking about the elimination of all kinds of oppression.

Those who project how great and rewarding this role [motherhood] will
be and who feel that the most important thing they can contribute to the
Black nation is children are doing themselves a great injustice. This line of
reasoning negates the contributions that Black women have historically
made to our struggle for liberation.

Much has been written recently about the white women's liberation
movement in the United States, and the question arises whether there are
any parallels between this struggle and the movement on the part of Black
women for total emancipation. While there are certain comparisons that

one can make, simply because we both live under the same exploitative system, there are certain differences, some of which are quite basic.

The white women's movement is far from monolithic. Any group that does not have an anti-imperialist and anti-racist ideology has nothing in common with the Black woman's struggle. Black people are engaged in a life-and-death struggle and the main emphasis of Black women must be to combat the capitalist, racist exploitation of Black people. While it is true that male chauvinism has become institutionalized in American society, one must look for the main enemy—the fundamental cause of the female condition.

Another major differentiation is that the white women's liberation movement is basically middle-class. Very few of these women suffer the extreme economic exploitation that most Black women are subjected to day by day. This is the factor that is most crucial to us. It is not an intellectual persecution alone; it is not an intellectual outburst for us; it is real. We Black women have got to deal with the problems the Black masses deal with, for our problems are one and the same.

If the white groups do not realize that they are in fact fighting capitalism and racism, we do not have common bond. If they do not realize that the reasons for their condition lie in the system and not simply that men get vicarious pleasure out of "consuming their bodies for exploitative reasons" (this reasoning seems to be prevalent in certain white women's groups), then we cannot unite with them around common grievances or discuss these groups in a serious manner because they're irrelevant to the Black struggle.

Frances Beal, "Double Jeopardy: To Be Black and Female," in Toni Cade, ed., *The Black Woman, An Anthology* (New York: New American Library, 1970), pp. 90–94, 98–99.

## Document 8

### THE EQUAL RIGHTS AMENDMENT, 1972–1982

On March 22, 1972, the Equal Rights Amendment (ERA) was sent to the states for ratification. By the end of that year, twenty-two of the thirty-eight states needed for ratification were in the "yes" column, and feminists looked forward to a quick victory. Over the next three years, the ratification process slowed to eight "yes" votes in 1973, three in 1974, and one in 1975; nonetheless, with a 1974 Gallop poll indicating that 74 percent of those queried supported the ERA, feminists remained optimistic about its passage. After 1975, however, only one more state ratified the ERA (Indiana in 1977).

By 1977, feminists had become alarmed. Although they needed to move only three more states into the "yes" column, an increasingly powerful STOP ERA movement had bested pro-ERA forces in several key states. More ominous was the recent decision of three "yes" states to rescind ratification of the amendment (Nebraska, Tennessee, and Idaho). In the summer of 1978, feminist groups marched in the nation's capital and lobbied Congress to extend the 1979 ratification deadline by three years (by 1979 two additional states—Kentucky and South Dakota—had voted to rescind ratification). Feminists won, the new deadline was set for June 30, 1982, but their victory was short-lived. The drive to make the ERA the Twenty-Seventh Amendment to the Constitution ended in June 1982 with defeats in North Carolina, Florida, and Illinois. Throughout the 1980s, feminists made several attempts to restart the ratification process in Congress, but they never succeeded.

It seems paradoxical that throughout most of its almost sixty-year history, the ERA was a contentious factor within American feminism. From the time Alice Paul, president of the National Woman's Party, first proposed the amendment in 1923 until the eve of its success in Congress in 1972, the amendment had been a divisive issue among feminists. Political feminists had been the amendment's strongest supporters, social feminists comprised the opposition. Political and social feminists remained divided over the ERA until the late 1960s when enforcement of Title VII of the 1964 Civil Rights Act struck down protective labor legislation (thereby accomplishing what social feminists had feared the ERA would do). With the disappearance of this bone of contention, the ERA could and did become the symbol and centerpiece of a united feminist front.

It is also ironic that just as the feminist movement was uniting around the ERA, the Radical Right—a conservative political force bent on halting the feminist agenda—was gathering strength. In actuality, the Radical Right's antifeminist stance was part of a broader political opposition to changes that had begun in the 1960s. For those who joined the Radical Right's cause, the ERA, which called for a "gender-blind" society, became one of the more potent symbols of all that was wrong with America. Killing the ERA might just excise the social/moral decay that was eroding "traditional" American values and institutions.

Section 1: Equality of rights under the law shall not be denied or abridged by the United States or by any State on account of sex.

Section 2: The Congress shall have the power to enforce, by appropriate legislation, the provisions of this article.

Section 3: This amendment shall take effect two years after the date of ratification.

## Document 9

## FROM "THE RIGHT TO BE A WOMAN," 1972

In August 1967 long-time conservative Republican activist Phyllis Schlafly founded *The Phyllis Schlafly Report* with the hope that the newsletter would expand her political base within and beyond the Republican party. Far more concerned with traditional conservative Republican values—law and order, anticommunism, a strong defense system, opposition to "big government" and the welfare state—Schlafly paid no attention to the emerging feminist movement. By 1970, however, when Schlafly launched her (unsuccessful) bid for Congress, she had become aware of the growing "dangers" second-wave feminism posed to traditional American values and institutions. Over the next two years, as the federal government's support for the feminist agenda grew, so too did Schlafly's concerns about feminism.

As late as December 1971, Phyllis Schlafly professed little interest or knowledge in the proposed Equal Rights Amendment (ERA) still bottled up in Congress; at the request of a friend, however, Schlafly agreed to study the amendment. Quickly, her indifference and ignorance turned to dismay and then to action. Her newsletter with its growing list of subscribers provided her with a forum for her anti-ERA rhetoric; then in November 1972 Schlafly took the next step in her national campaign to derail ratification. She founded STOP ERA, an organization composed primarily of white, middle-class housewives. Dressed in their trademark pink color and bearing homemade gifts of bread, jam, and apple pie, these women lobbied their representatives to protect the traditional homemaker's role and preserve the American family by voting against ratification.

Women's magazines and talk shows have been filled for months with a strident advocacy of the "rights" of women to be treated on an equal basis with men. But what about the rights of the woman who doesn't want to compete on an equal basis with men? Does she have the right to be treated as a woman—by her family, society, and the law?

The laws of our 50 states guarantee the right to be a woman—protected and provided for in her career as a woman, wife, and mother. The proposed Equal Rights Amendment will wipe out our laws which guarantee this right. ERA will replace these laws with a doctrinaire equality under which women must be treated the same as men. ERA has passed the U.S. Congress and [been] ratified by 21 states. If it is ratified by 38 states, it will become part of the United States Constitution. Is this what American women [and men] want?

The laws of the 50 states require the *husband* to support his wife and children—to provide a home for them to live in, to protect a woman's right to be a full-time wife and mother[;] her right *not* to take a job outside the home, her right to care for her baby in her home while being financially supported by her husband. ERA will remove this sole obligation from the husband, and make the wife equally responsible to provide a home for her family and to provide 50 percent of the financial support of her family.

Some advocates tried to deny that [ERA] will wipe out the husband's present obligation to support his wife and children and to provide them with a home. When the courts adjudicate cases which will arise if [the ERA is] passed, they will refer to law books and to the opinions of eminent constitutional lawyers.

### PROFESSOR PAUL FREUND'S STATEMENT, ERA'S EFFECT ON WIVES

Probably *the* leading expert in the U.S. on the subject of the ERA is Professor Paul A. Freund of Harvard Law School. His study of the ERA covers 25 years and his recent research has convinced him that the case *against* ERA is stronger now than ever before.

As Professor Freund makes clear, if the ERA is passed, *every wife and mother will lose her right to be supported by her husband unless she has pre-school children, and she even loses the right to be supported by her husband while she has preschool children if child care centers are available.*

It is obvious that the ERA would cause massive dislocations in the entire fabric of family relationships, and deprive women of other privileges that they now possess such as the presumption of custody of their children in case of divorce.

### ARE WOMEN DISCRIMINATED AGAINST?

Are women discriminated against in employment? They certainly have been. When I started to work at age 18, I discovered I was doing exactly the same work for $105 per month for which men were paid $125 per month.

The reason the ERA has gotten so far is that Americans believe that it means "equal pay for equal work."

"Equal pay for equal work" is guaranteed by the Civil Rights Act of 1964 which forbids discrimination in every aspect of employment. If any woman is discriminated against she can file a claim with the Equal Employment Opportunity Commission.

There is absolutely nothing the ERA can add in terms of fair employment practices for women.

## ARE WOMEN EXPLOITED BY MEN?

Are women exploited by men? Yes, some women are, and we should wipe out such exploitation.

There is plenty of work for those who want to eliminate the real exploitation of women, but they are 100 percent wrong when they blame husbands and the institution of marriage.

## WHO IS PROMOTING ERA?

There are two types of women lobbying for the ERA. One group is the women's liberationists. Their motive is radical. They hate men, marriage, and children. They are out to destroy morality and the family. They look upon husbands as exploiters, children as an evil to be avoided (by abortion if necessary), and the family as an institution which keeps women in "second-class citizenship" or "slavery."

Anyone who doubts the radical objectives and tactics of the women's liberationists should read their literature, such as the magazine *Ms.*

There is another type of women [*sic*] supporting the ERA from the most sincere motives. It is easy to see why business and professional women support the ERA—many of them have felt the keen edge of discrimination in employment.

To these women, we say:

1) We support your efforts to eliminate all injustices and we believe this can be done through the Civil Rights Act and the Equal Employment Opportunity Act.

2) If the Hayden modification had remained in the ERA we would have supported it [a rider attached and subsequently defeated that attempted to retain some privileges for women].

3) Without the Hayden modification, the ERA won't give you anything—but it will take away fundamental rights and benefits from the rest of women. You have the right to lobby for the extension of *your* rights—but not at the expense of the rights of *other* women.

Urge your State Legislators to vote **NO** on the ERA. It will take away from girls their exemption from the draft and their legal protection against predatory males. It will take away from wives and mothers their right to be provided with a home and financial support from their husbands. It will take away from senior women their extra social security benefits. It will take away a woman's present *freedom of choice* to take a job—*or* to be a full-time wife and mother. In short, it will take away the right to be a woman.

*The Phyllis Schlafly Report* 6 (November 1972).

## Document 10

## FROM *ROE V. WADE*, 1973 (DECISION BY JUSTICE HENRY BLACKMUN)

On January 22, 1973, in *Roe v. Wade*, the Supreme Court handed down a 7–2 decision supporting a woman's right to an abortion based on her constitutional right to privacy (Roe was the pseudonym of Norma McCorvey and Wade was Henry Wade, the Dallas, Texas, district attorney). On that same date, the Court handed down another 7–2 decision in the companion abortion case, *Doe v. Bolton*. (Doe was the pseudonym of Sandra R. Cano and Bolton was Arthur Bolton, the Georgia attorney general). In the more famous *Roe v. Wade* case, the Court struck down a mid-nineteenth-century Texas statute that had made abortion illegal except when the mother's life was threatened. In *Doe v. Bolton,* the Court invalidated a Georgia law that restricted legal abortion to the dictates of a hospital-based therapeutic abortion committee.

Abortion was never completely outlawed in the United States, but for almost a century it had been strictly regulated by the state and medical community. After World War II, liberal members of the medical community had begun to chafe under the states' regulatory powers over physicians' professional decisions regarding therapeutic abortions. By the early 1960s, a movement for abortion reform was gaining ground; by the late 1960s, several states had passed reform statutes (California, Colorado, North Carolina, and Georgia).

Abortion reform was not abortion repeal; thus, it was left to second-wave feminists to take up this challenge. The National Organization for Women (NOW) led the way in 1967 with a position paper calling for the repeal of all existing state criminal abortion laws on the grounds that women have the right to control their reproductive lives; this position was formally adopted in NOW's 1968 Bill of Rights. In 1969, the year in which a Harris Poll found that "almost two-thirds of those surveyed agreed that abortion was a private matter," a new lobbying group, the National Association for the Repeal of Abortion Laws, organized.

Although feminists heralded the Supreme Court's two landmark abortion decisions in 1973, they fell far short of the feminist demand for a woman's sole and absolute right to terminate her pregnancy. Instead, both decisions made abortion a legal and safe medical procedure. Women were accorded some degree of constitutional protection under the right to privacy, but the Court's ruling was tempered by a physician's right to render a medical judgment during the first trimester of pregnancy, and the state's right to regulate and even prohibit abortion during the second and third trimesters (in the inter-

est of maternal health and the potential life of the fetus). Contrary to
popular myth, neither *Roe v. Wade* nor *Doe v. Bolton* guaranteed a
woman unrestricted access to abortion throughout all stages of her
pregnancy.

This Texas federal appeal and its Georgia companion, *Doe v. Bolton,*
present constitutional challenges to state criminal abortion legislation. The
Texas statutes are typical of those in effect in many States for approximately
a century. The Georgia statutes have a modern cast and are a product that reflects the influences of recent attitudinal change, advancing medical knowledge and techniques, and new thinking about an old issue.

We acknowledge our awareness of the sensitive and emotional nature of
the abortion controversy, of the vigorous opposing views, even among physicians, and of the deep and seemingly absolute convictions that the subject
inspires. One's philosophy, one's experiences, one's exposure to the raw
edges of human existence, one's religious training, one's attitude toward
life and family and their values, and the moral standards one establishes and
seeks to observe, are likely to influence and color one's thinking and conclusions about abortion.

Our task is to resolve the issue by constitutional measurement, free of
emotion and predilection. We seek to do this, and because we do, we have
inquired into and in this opinion place some emphasis upon medical and
medical-legal history and what that history reveals about man's attitudes toward abortion procedures over the centuries.

[Jane Roe petitioned] that she was unmarried and pregnant; that she
wished to terminate her pregnancy by an abortion "performed by a licensed physician, under safe, legal conditions"; that she was unable to get
a "legal" abortion in Texas because her life did not appear to be threatened
by the continuation of her pregnancy; and that she could not afford to
travel to another jurisdiction to secure a [safe] legal abortion. She claimed
that Texas statutes were constitutionally vague and that they abridged her
right of personal privacy, protected by the First, Fourth, Ninth, and Fourteenth Amendments.

The principal attack on the Texas statutes is that they improperly invade a
right, said to be possessed by the pregnant woman, to choose to terminate
her pregnancy. Appellant would discover this right in the concept of personal "liberty" embodied in the Fourteenth Amendment's Due Process
Clause or in personal marital, familial, and sexual privacy said to be protected by the Ninth Amendment. Before addressing this claim we feel it de-
sirable to survey the history of abortion, and then examine the state
purposes behind criminal abortion laws.

It is perhaps not appreciated that the restrictive criminal abortion laws in effect in a majority of States today are of relatively recent vintage. Those laws proscribing abortion at any time during pregnancy except when necessary to preserve the pregnant woman's life, are not of ancient or common-law origin. Instead, they derive from statutory changes effected in the latter half of the 19th century.

Three reasons have been advanced to explain historically the enactment of criminal abortion laws in the 19th century and to justify their continued existence.

It has been argued that these laws were the product of a Victorian social concern to discourage illicit sexual conduct. Texas does not advance this justification in the present case, and it appears that no court or commentator has taken the argument seriously. [Roe contends] that this is not a proper state purpose and suggests that if it were the Texas statutes are overbroad in protecting it since the laws failed to distinguish between married and unwed mothers.

A second reason is concerned with abortion as a medical procedure. When most criminal abortion laws were first enacted, the procedure was a hazardous one for the woman. Thus it has been argued that a State's concern in enacting a criminal abortion law was to protect the pregnant woman from submitting to a procedure that placed her life in serious jeopardy.

Modern medical techniques have altered this situation[,] medical data [indicates] that abortion in early pregnancy, prior to the end of the first trimester, is now relatively safe. Mortality rates for women undergoing early abortions, where the procedure is legal, appears to be as low or lower than the rates for normal childbirth.

The third reason is the State's interest in protecting prenatal life. Some of the argument for this justification rests on the theory that a new human life is present from the moment of conception. The State's interest and obligation to protect life then extends to prenatal life.

The Constitution does not explicitly mention any right of privacy [but in] a line of decisions the Court has recognized a right of personal privacy, or guarantee of zones of privacy, does exist under the Constitution.

This right of privacy is broad enough to encompass a woman's decision whether or not to terminate her pregnancy. The detriment that the State would impose upon the pregnant woman is apparent. Specific and direct medical harm may be involved. Maternity may force upon the woman a distressful life and future. Psychological harm may be imminent. Mental and physical health may be taxed by child care. There is also the distress associated with an unwanted child. All these factors the woman and her responsible physician will consider in consultation.

On the basis of elements such as these, appellant argue[ed] that a woman's right is absolute and that she is entitled to terminate her pregnancy [as] she chooses. The Court's decision recognizing a right of privacy acknowledges that some state regulation is protected and appropriate. [A] State may assert important interests in safeguarding health, in maintaining medical standards, and in protecting potential life. The privacy right cannot be said to be absolute.

We conclude that the right of personal privacy includes the abortion decision, but that this right is not unqualified and must be considered against important state interests in regulation.

Measured against these standards, Art. 1196 of the Texas Penal Code sweeps too broadly. The statute makes no distinction between abortions performed early in pregnancy and those performed later, and it limits to a single reason, "saving" the mother's life, the legal justification for the procedure. The statute cannot survive the constitutional attack made upon it.

To summarize and to repeat:

1. A state criminal abortion statute of the current Texas type, that excepts from criminality only a *lifesaving* procedure on behalf of the mother, without regard to pregnancy stage and without recognition of other interests involved, is violative of the Due Process Clause of the Fourteenth Amendment.

(a) For the stage prior to approximately the end of the first trimester, the abortion decision must be left to the medical judgment of the pregnant woman's attending physician.

(b) For the stage subsequent to approximately the end of the first trimester, the State, in promoting its interest in the health of the mother, may, if it chooses, regulate the abortion procedure in ways that are reasonably related to maternal health.

(c) For the stage subsequent to viability, the State in promoting its interest in the potentiality of human life may, if it chooses, regulate, and even proscribe, abortion except where it is necessary, in appropriate medical judgment, for the preservation of the life or health of the mother.

410 U.S. Reports, 113 (1973)

## Document 11

### FROM *THE TOTAL WOMAN,* 1973

Even as the feminist movement was on the upswing in the 1970s, a two-prong backlash was in the making. On the political front, the goals of creating a gender-blind society and empowering women encountered stiff resistance as the Radical Right gradually made its presence felt in American politics. Encouraged by the success of Phyllis Schlafly's STOP ERA campaign and the emergence of a potent right-to-life movement, the Republican party reversed its forty-year support for the Equal Rights Amendment (ERA) in 1980 and endorsed a constitutional amendment banning abortion.

A second front in the war against feminism also opened up in the early 1970s with battle lines drawn over differing interpretations of family life. The feminist critique of the traditional American family focused on the power of the patriarch as derived in law and custom. At its most radical, this perspective called for the abolition of the institution of marriage, not only because it upheld male privilege but also because of its emphasis on the monogamous, heterosexual relationship as the norm. For the vast majority of feminists, however, the problem with marriage and family life lay in the unequal distribution of power and obligations among husbands and wives, fathers and mothers. Their solution called for a realignment of authority and duty within the family such that men and women reached a more equitable and gender-blind balance in decision-making, domesticity, and sexuality.

Though it is easier to understand why some men might oppose the call for an egalitarian family life, it is more difficult to comprehend why so many women were threatened by this concept. In acknowledging that something was amiss within the American family and that many marriages were unhappy (the divorce rate was rising), a few entrepreneurs offered a popular solution that amounted to an implicit assault on the feminist family model. The key to a successful, revitalized marriage and happy family life was to become a better, traditional wife who willingly submitted to her husband.

Among the more successful promoters of this philosophy was Marabel Morgan. In 1973 the "thirty-six year old former beauty queen, wife, and mother" produced a "how-to-save your marriage" guidebook based on the four "A's": accept, admire, adapt to, and appreciate your husband. Billed as an "anti-feminist bible for old-fashioned housewives," *The Total Woman* became a best-seller and served as the basis for a flourishing cottage industry in marrige enrichment classes taught by Morgan and her disciples.

PART TWO, "MAN ALIVE" AND PART THREE, "SEX 201"

Psychiatrists tell us that a man's most basic needs, outside of warm sexual love, are approval and admiration. Women need to be loved; men need to be admired. We women would do well to remember this one important difference between us and the other half.

Try this test for a week. Starting tonight determine that you will admire your husband. By an act of your will, determine to fill up his cup, which may be bone dry. Be positive. Remember that compliments will encourage him to talk.

Admire him as he talks to you. Concentrate on what he's saying. Let him know you care. Put your magazine down and look at him. Even if you don't care who won yesterday's football game, your attention is important to him, and he needs you. Let him know he's your hero.

Tell him you love his body. If you choke on that phrase, practice until it comes out naturally. If you haven't admired him lately, he's probably starving emotionally.

Look for his admirable qualities. Even the ugliest man has certain qualities worth admiring. Pick out his most masculine characteristics and let him know they please you.

In class one day, I gave the assignment for the girls to admire their husband's body that night. One girl went right to work on her homework. That evening while he was reading the paper, she sat down next to him and began stroking his arm. After a bit, she stopped at the bicep and squeezed. He unconsciously flexed his muscle and she said, "Oh, I never knew you were so muscular!"

The next day she told this to her girl friend, who decided to try it herself. Her husband had thin arms, but she admired his muscles anyway. Two nights later she couldn't find him at dinner time. He was out lifting his new set of weights in the garage!

ASSIGNMENT

Man Alive

1. Accept your husband as he is. Write out two lists—one of his faults and one of his virtues. Take a long, hard look at his faults and then throw the list away. Only think about his virtues. Carry that list with you and refer to it when you are mad, sad, or glad.

2. Admire your husband every day. Refer to his virtue list if you need a place to start. Say something nice about his body today.

3. Adapt to his way of life. Accept his friends, food, and life-style as your own. Ask him to write the six most important changes he'd like to see take place at your house. Read the list in private, react in private and then set out to accomplish these changes with a smile.

4. Appreciate all he does for you. Sincerely tell him "Thank you." Give him your undivided attention, and try not to make any telephone calls after he comes home.

One of your husband's most basic needs is for you to be physically attractive to him. Many a husband rushes off to work leaving his wife slumped over a cup of coffee in her grubby undies. His once sexy bride is now wrapped in rollers and smells like bacon and eggs. All day long he's surrounded at the office by dazzling secretaries who emit clouds of perfume.

Remember[,] a man thinks differently than we do. Before a man can care who a woman is, he must first get past that visual barrier. So your appearance at 6:00 p.m. should have top priority. Those first four minutes when he arrives home sets the atmosphere for the entire evening. Greet him at the door with your hair shining, your beautifully made-up face radiant, your outfit sharp and snappy—even though you're not going anywhere.

One morning Charlie [Marabel Morgan's spouse] remarked about the pressures of the day that lay ahead of him. All day I remembered his grim face as he drove away. I wondered how I could revive him when he came home.

For an experiment I put on pink baby-doll pajamas and white boots. When I opened the door to greet Charlie I was unprepared for his reaction. My quiet, reserved, nonexcitable husband took one look, dropped his briefcase and chased me around the dining-room table.

Have you ever met your husband at the front door in some outrageously sexy outfit? Nope, I'm not kidding. You don't think you're the type? I didn't either. But my silly costumes got fabulous results.

[One] graduate appeared in a sheer black lace gown. Her husband was speechless when he opened the front door. She told me after that the evening was not only lots of fun, but he had also suggested a cruise to Nassau the following week.

A woman's most important sex organ is her brain. Super sex is 20 percent education and 80 percent attitude.

Sex is an hour in bed at ten o'clock; super sex is the climax of an atmosphere carefully set all day. Your attitude during your husband's first four waking minutes in the morning sets the tone for his entire day. Give him a kiss first thing tomorrow morning. Rub his back as he's waking up. Whisper in his ear.

Prepare now for making love tonight. This is part of our class assignment. In fact by the second week, the women are to be prepared for sexual intercourse every night for a week.

## ASSIGNMENT

### Sex 201

1. Be an atmosphere adjuster in the morning. Set the tone for love. Be pleasant to look at, be with, and talk to. Walk your husband to the car each morning and wave until he's out of sight.

2. Once this week call him at work an hour before quitting time, to say. "I wanted you to know that I just crave your body!" Then take your bubble bath shortly before he comes home.

3. Thrill him at the front door in your costume. A frilly new nighty and heels will probably do the trick as a starter. Variety is the spice of sex.

4. Be prepared mentally and physically for intercourse every night this week. Be sure your attitude matches your costume. Be the seducer, rather than the seducee.

Marabel Morgan, *The Total Woman* (Old Tappan, N.J.: Fleming H. Revell Company, 1973), pp. 57, 59–63, 87–88, 92–97, 111, 114, 117, 127–28.

## Document 12

## FROM *OUR BODIES, OURSELVES*, 1976

The Boston women's liberation movement was in its infancy when some of its participants organized a conference in the spring of 1969. Among the many sessions women attended was one on "women and their bodies." Talking about their bodies and communicating their frustrations about male doctors who spoke condescendingly to their female patients was a liberating experience for the participants. When the conference ended, some women continued meeting and sharing their experiences; consciousness-raising, they understood, was the first step toward empowerment.

They also decided that they had more to learn about their bodies, and a "summer project was born." Participants researched a topic and summarized the results in a formal paper. Then, in the best tradition of radical feminism, this still unnamed collective of eleven white, middle-class women decided to share their knowledge by offering a free course in the fall of 1969 called "Women and Their Bodies."

They also revised their papers and sought the services of a small, nonprofit press (the New England Free Press) to reproduce an inexpensive edition of *Women and Their Bodies*. In addition to its use as a text for the course, the book was distributed to women's clinics and resource centers around the greater Boston area (in 1969 these clinics and centers were new, community-based institutions staffed and supported by radical feminists). Demand for the book quickly outstripped supply; recognizing that the small press's staff was unable to handle the volume of requests, the collective made two life-altering decisions in 1972. Closing its membership to newcomers, the collective filed formal incorporation papers with the state of Massachusetts, becoming the nonprofit Boston Women's Health Book Collective. Under the auspices of the state, this small band of radical feminists (Norma Swenson, Pam Morgan, Judy Norsigian, Nancy Hawley, Paula Brown Doress, Ruth Bell, Esther Rome, Jane Pincus, Wendy Sanford, Wilma Vilunya Diskin, and Joan Sheingold Ditzion) pledged to work collaboratively "to empower women with knowledge of their bodies, health, & sexuality." They also signed a book deal with Simon & Schuster. In 1973, *Women and Their Bodies* became *Our Bodies, Ourselves*.

An overnight success, *Our Bodies, Ourselves* was instrumental in launching the populist-based women's health movement in the 1970s, but it has not grown stale with the passage of time. New perspectives and information have found their way into subsequent editions. Life-cycle changes also led the collective to expand its educational focus in the companion volumes *Ourselves, Our Children* (1978), *Changing Bodies, Changing Lives* (1980), and *Ourselves, Growing Older* (1987).

The Boston Women's Health Book Collective's commitment to feminism has deepened over the years. Acutely aware of their white, middle-class origins, the collective struggled to become more inclusive by soliciting the help of younger women, poor women, and women of color in subsequent revisions of *Our Bodies, Ourselves*. The collective's feminist politics have also become more sophisticated over the years. Since that initial promise to empower women by providing them with information about their bodies, the Collective has developed a powerful feminist critique of the health care system and its providers. Recognized worldwide as one of the leading feminist health advocacy and activist organizations, the Boston Women's Health Book Collective best exemplifies the philosophy and politics of the women's liberation movement.

## CHAPTER 2: ANATOMY AND PHYSIOLOGY OF SEXUALITY AND REPRODUCTION

### Finding Out About Ourselves

Knowing the facts about our anatomy and physiology helps us become familiar with our bodies. Learning this information has been exciting. . . . It's exhilarating to discover that the material is not as difficult as we once thought. Understanding the medical terminology means that we can understand the things the doctors say. Knowing their language makes medical people less mysterious and frightening. We now feel more confident when asking questions. Sometimes a doctor has been startled to find us speaking "his" language. "How do you know that? Are you a medical student?. . . A pretty girl like you shouldn't be concerned about that."

But we are. Out of our concerns we are acquiring specific medical knowledge. In response to our questions, many doctors have become aware of women's growing interest in medical issues. Some are genuinely coop-erative. Yet many others appear outwardly pleased while continuing to "manage" their patients with new tactics.

## CHAPTER 6: TAKING CARE OF OURSELVES

### Conclusion

One very important concern of women is how we relate to food. Often we find ourselves using food as a reward . . . or we turn to food when we are un-happy. . . . [W]e feel tremendous pressures from society to stay "thin and beautiful" and to diet . . . to maintain these . . . standards. Such standards . . . have little to do with our physical and emotional well-being. . . . Some of us have found it helpful to discuss issues of women and weight with other women. . . . By supporting one another it is sometimes possible for us to re-sist the pressures we resent so much.

. . . We need to make a united demand that our larger stores offer us healthier choices and carry more chemical-free foods. . . . We should also demand that fruits and vegetables not be pre-packaged, so we can examine their quality.

. . . Unfortunately, our system hasn't worked and isn't working now. Money seems to rule everything. . . . The success we have in making more healthful foods available will not . . . come from winning legal battles . . . but from joining with others . . . to put pressure on local markets, boycott harm-ful foods (and let the manufacturers know about it), join food co-ops, grow our own gardens, and help spread accurate information about food and nu-trition. . . . [B]eing in control of our bodies means choosing what we put into them.

## CHAPTER 8: SELF-DEFENSE*

Developing a healthy body makes us happier, more complete women. In this violent society, learning to protect ourselves from attack is an integral part of our physical and psychological health. A *reported* rape occurs every seven minutes in America. . . . Every woman . . . knows the fear of dark, de-serted streets, strange noises in the middle of the night, obscene phone calls, and the everyday humiliation of dirty remarks and gestures. Older women are the particular prey of handbag thieves, and untold numbers of children are sexually molested every year. Many women must face regular beatings from their husbands, boyfriends, fathers at home.

### Learning To Protect Ourselves

*This chapter should be read together with the two preceeding ones on exercise and rape.

For too long . . . [we] had to rely on men, money, or luck for a limited kind of "protection."

. . . We believe it's essential that women . . . take . . . self-defense seriously. . . . [W]e have little sense of the potential power in our own bodies—we don't know our own strength or how to use it to protect ourselves. . . . The physical and mental togetherness that comes from exercise and self-defense training . . . teaches us this . . . [and] gives us added confidence in all areas of our lives.

### Self-Defense Training

We encourage women to learn some basic techniques of self-defense. . . . If you have time and money you can get formal instruction in a school. Check the yellow pages under "Judo" or "Karate" for schools in your area. These are almost always male-run, but you'll have a lot more female company now than a couple of years ago. Try to find one that takes women seriously. . . . Some YWCA's have such classes (ask for one if yours doesn't). . . . These are usually less expensive than the commercial schools. In many areas women's groups have set up cheaper classes . . . and of course, you can start your own. . . . If at all possible, these classes should be taught for women by women who understand where we are coming from physically and emotionally.

### CHAPTER 11: ABORTION

#### Introduction

One of our most fundamental rights as women is the right to choose whether and when to have children. Only when we are in control of that choice are we free to be all that we can be. . . . Birth control is the single best tool for implementing this choice, but as Chapter 10 makes painfully clear, today, in 1975, birth control methods are just not effective enough . . . to avoid unwanted pregnancy. And our society's attitudes toward sexuality, sex education, and health care make it hard . . . to choose, obtain, and use methods of birth control that will work for us. So right now . . . a second indispensable tool for taking control of our fertility is abortion. . . .

The decision to have an abortion is rarely free of conflict. . . . But when an unwanted pregnancy does occur, many of us feel that giving birth to a baby we cannot properly care for would be a greater grief than abortion. . . . So we in our collective believe that women must be free to *choose* abortion. We want all abortions . . . legal, inexpensive (ideally free, as all health care should be), voluntary and safe, done in a supportive atmosphere with sufficient information-sharing and counseling.

Abortion is now legal in the United States. . . . Today, any of us who so choose should be able to end an unwanted pregnancy with a safe and relatively inexpensive abortion. . . . Unfortunately this is not always the case. In many parts of the country abortion is *still* less available than it should be, more expensive than it needs to be, and a more negative experience than it ought to be. And the Supreme Court decision is under attack by a small but powerful anti-abortion movement. . . .

We know that a number of women and men believe . . . that abortion is wrong. To them, abortion violates the "right to life" of an unborn fetus. . . . We cannot agree with them that an unborn fetus has more rights than the pregnant woman who is carrying it. . . .

We defend any woman's right *not* to end a pregnancy if she feels abortion is wrong. . . . But some who are against abortion for themselves want to . . . try to impose their beliefs on us. The "Today" section of this chapter will describe some of the tactics of the anti-abortion movement and ways we can defend our newly established legal right to abortion.

The Boston Women's Health Book Collective, *Our Bodies, Ourselves,* revised and expanded
    (New York: Simon & Schuster, 1976): 25, 110, 162–63, 216.


## Document 13

## FROM "LESBIANS AND WOMEN'S LIBERATION: 'IN ANY TERMS SHE SHALL CHOOSE,' " 1971

As early as 1969 Betty Friedan had voiced some concern about raising the issue of lesbianism within the feminist movement. Well aware that the "lavender menace" had been used historically to discredit feminism, Friedan represented those members of the National Organization for Women (NOW) who preferred silence on this aspect of "sexual politics." Lesbian-feminists, however, were beginning to find this position of silence intolerable; they wanted acceptance from their straight sisters within the movement and they wanted their issues and concerns to be included on the ever-expanding list of items that comprised the feminist agenda.

Lesbianism was a complex and divisive issue for feminists. Both the popular press and the Radical Right used Americans' fear of homosexuality to discredit feminism; as feminists debated how to respond to this practice of "lesbian-baiting," many were forced to confront their own homophobia. Was lesbianism a feminist issue or did it more properly belong to the emerging gay-lesbian movement? If it was a feminist concern, was it an issue of sexuality, or politics, or both? Was the radical feminist critique of monogamy also an attack on sexual conformity (i.e., heterosexuality)? Was a feminist true to the cause only if she identified with, associated with, and loved women? Did this mean that men (gay or straight) could not be feminists?

Between 1972 and 1975, this "woman-centered" view received much stronger support among radical feminists than among liberal feminists. According to several historians, this "gay-straight split" became a significant, contributing factor in the declension of radical feminism as straight feminists abandoned radicalism for liberalism. Even as this shift was underway, NOW was moderating its earlier, ambivalent stance on lesbianism in favor of a policy of choice and tolerance. In 1973 NOW created a Task Force on Sexuality and Lesbianism that linked a woman's sexual self-expression to her right to privacy and personhood.

The following document is from a collection of "observations" on feminism written between 1969 and 1978 by Vivian Gornick, a journalist for the *Village Voice*.

A month ago I spent the weekend in the company of a prominent feminist who spoke out against the recognition of lesbianism in the movement, claiming that the women's movement would destroy its credibility in "middle America" if it should publicly support lesbians as a legitimate element in feminism and the movement. I found this position appalling, and I feel that it raises an issue that must be argued. For just as it seemed transparently certain to that feminist that recognition of lesbianism in the women's movement would imperil [it] so it seems clear to me that denial of lesbianism in the women's movement will ensure [its] death.

Hundreds of women in the feminist movement are lesbians. Many have worked in the movement from its earliest days of organized activity. They were in NOW three and four years ago, working along with heterosexual women for the redress of grievances that affected them all; they are scattered today across the entire political board of women's organizations.

It is the essence of the lesbian's life that she leads an underground existence; that she cannot openly state the nature of her emotional-sexual attachments without enduring the mark of Cain. It is this element[,] separated out from the multiple elements of her experience, that determines the character of the lesbian's life and the shape of her soul. To live with the daily knowledge that what you are is so awful to the society around you that it cannot be revealed is to live with an extraordinary millstone slung from one's neck.

Imagine, the feeling of lesbians who joined the feminist movement only to find themselves unable to be themselves. Here they were, women doubly cast out of society, both as women and as homosexuals, joined together in the feminist struggle for selfhood, being victimized by other women. For there's no mistaking it: the heterosexual feminist who disconnected herself from the homosexual feminist was disavowing that homosexual feminist and thus victimizing her. The irony was that the heterosexual feminist was victimizing herself[,] for that disavowal strikes at the roots of feminism, attacking the movement in its most vital parts, threatening its ideological life at the source.

Feminism has grown out of woman's conviction that she is "invisible," that the life she leads, the characteristics attributed to her, the destiny that is declared her natural one, are not so much the truth of her real being as they are a reflection of culture's willful *need* that she be as she is described. The feminist movement is a rebellious *no* to all that; it is a declaration of independence against false description of the self. The whole *point* of the feminist movement is that each and every woman shall recognize that the burden and the glory of her feminism lie with defining herself honestly *in any terms she shall choose.*

Sexual self-definition is primary to the feminist movement. [T]he movement's entire life is predicated on the idea that woman's experience has been stunted by society's falsifying views of the nature of her sexuality. Feminists are saying to male civilization, "Your definition of my sexuality is false and living inside that falsehood has become intolerable to me." [I]n essence, the feminist's course is really charted on the path of discovery of the sexual self.

Seen in this perspective, homosexuality in women represents a variant of the fundamental search for the sexual self-understanding that is primary in the struggle to alter the position of women in this culture. [S]ome feminists are homosexual, and others are heterosexual; the point is not that it is wrong and frightening to be one and relieving to be the other; the point is that *whatever* a woman's sexual persuasion, it is compelling, and she must be allowed to follow her inclinations openly and honestly without fear of castigation.

That, for me, is the true politics of the feminist movement. It is a woman recognizing that she is a fully developed human being with the responsibility to discover and live with her self. The determination of what the self is, or should be, is a matter of individual choice that must be honored and acknowledged as a legitimate reference to the movement's ultimate aims.

The claim that lesbianism is irrelevant to the movement—that the struggle for recognition as a lesbian belongs to gay liberation and not the women's movement—seems fallacious. The point is not that lesbians in the movement are homosexual; the point is that they are *feminists: fully* participating feminists who are told in a movement predicated on the notion that women are victims of sexism[,] that their sexuality must be kept under wraps because women in "middle America" wouldn't understand.

What I find more distressing than the charge of irrelevancy is the aggressive talk from feminists that admission of lesbianism in the movement is a threat to [its] growth. If anything is a threat to the movement, it is the fear of taking action in the name of political expediency.

Really, this whole thing is bewildering. Three years ago the women's movement was a renegade movement, willing to speak truths nobody wanted to hear. Suddenly, on this issue, it is being told it must speak *only* those truths middle-class America is willing to hear.

In radical circles there is now [an] alarming swing toward the fashionable superiority of lesbianism[,] that the only "true" relationships for a feminist are with other women. I heard a lesbian assert that a woman couldn't be a feminist unless she "related" to women in every way. [T]hat is power politics and it is up to the honesty in both homosexual and heterosexual feminists to keep the central issue uncluttered and free of hysteria.

And the central issue is of self-definition for all women. What must be learned from the acceptance of lesbianism in the movement is that radically different truths inform different lives, and that as long as those truths are not antisocial[,] they must be respected.

In the end, the feminist movement is of necessity the work of a radical feminist sensibility, and the fear of open recognition of lesbianism is the work of a liberal feminist sensibility. The falseness of the liberal is that she offers sympathy when what is needed is courage. By offering sympathy instead of courage, she increases rather than reduces the pain of this world.

Vivian Gornick, "Lesbians and Women's Liberation: 'In Any Terms She Shall Choose,' "in *Essays in Feminism* (New York: Harper and Row, Publishers, 1978), pp. 69–75.

## Document 14

## FROM "ASIAN PACIFIC AMERICAN WOMEN AND FEMINISM," C. 1979

The examples of 1960s activism—dominated by the civil rights movement, the antiwar protest movement, and the women's movement—provided a reference point for other historically disadvantaged minorities within the United States. Although Native Americans, Mexican Americans, and Asian Americans, for example, had a history of organized struggle against their particular brand of oppression and discrimination, the groups that emerged in the 1960s, especially the United Farm Workers (1962), the American Indian Movement (1968), and La Raza Unida (1969), were more militant in their ideology and tactics than their predecessors. Although the particular demands of these ethnic minorities varied, certain overarching themes united them: the fight for economic and social justice, demands for political power, and an end to the cultural superiority of Protestant white America. In an eerie replay of the "second-class" treatment black and white women experienced at the hands of their male counterparts in the civil rights and antiwar movements, Hispanic, Native American, and Asian American women discovered that their contributions and their issues were not accorded the same respect as those of their male counterparts.

The problem of "double jeopardy" that plagued black women in the 1960s and 1970s also afflicted other women of color; but which struggle took precedence when it came time to organize—the shared concerns of the "ethnic minority" or the gender-specific needs of the women? Would it harm the struggle of people of color if women raised the issue of sexism within their respective ethnic movements?

When ethnic women sought common cause with the feminist movement, they, like black women before them, encountered a movement seemingly dominated by white, middle-class women. By 1971, when the National Organization for Women (NOW) formally recognized the "double oppression of minority women," the organization could point with pride to the inclusion of a few "women of color" within the organization's leadership structure. Still, minority women faced an uphill battle in winning the support of middle-class white feminists in ending forced sterilization of poor women of color or in banning the use of agricultural pesticides because of their harmful effects on pregnant women working the fields. Thus, when ethnic women founded their own feminist organizations, like the Mexican-American Women's National Association (1974) or the Organization of Pan-Asian Women (1976), they were following in the footsteps of their black sisters.

Most of the Asian Pacific American women I know agree that we need to make ourselves more visible by speaking out on the condition of our sex and race and on certain political issues. Some of us feel that visibility through the feminist perspective is the only logical step for us. However, this path is fraught with problems which we are unable to solve among us, because in order to do so, we need the help and cooperation of the white feminist leaders, the women who coordinate programs, direct women's buildings, and edit women's publications throughout the country. Women's organizations tell us they would like to have us "join" them and give them "input." These are the better ones; at least they know we exist and feel we might have something of interest to say to them, but every time I read or speak to a group of people about my life it is as if I had never spoken before, as if I were speaking to a brand-new audience of people who had never known an Asian Pacific woman who is other than the passive, sweet stereotype of the "Oriental" woman.

When Third World women are asked to speak representing our racial or ethnic group, we are expected to move, charm, or entertain, but not to educate in ways that are threatening to our audiences. I am weary of starting from scratch each time I speak or write, as if there were no history behind us, of hearing that among women of color, Asian women are the least political, or the least oppressed, or the most polite. As individuals and in groups, we have been more active in community affairs and speaking and writing about our activities. From the highly political writings published in *Asian Women* in 1971 to the more recent voices from the Basement Workshop in New York City to Unbound Feet in San Francisco[,] these all tell us we *have* been active and vocal. And yet, we continue to hear "Asian women are traditionally not attuned to being political," as if most other women are; or that Asian women are too happily bound to their traditional roles as mothers and wives, as if the same cannot be said of number[s] of white American women.

Earlier this year when a group of Asian Pacific American women gathered in San Francisco poet Nellie Wong's home to talk about feminism, I was struck by our general agreement on the subject *as an ideal.* We all believed in equality for women. We agreed that feminism means a commitment to making changes in our lives. [We] knew what we wanted out of feminism and what it was suppose[d] to mean to us. For women to achieve equality in our society we must continue to work for a common goal.

But there was a feeling of disappointment in that living room toward the women's movement as it stands today. One young woman said she had made an effort to join women's groups with high expectations but came away disillusioned because these groups were not receptive to the issues important to her as an Asian woman. Some of the other women present said they felt women's organizations with feminist goals are still "a middle-class women's thing." This pervasive feeling of mistrust toward women in the movement is fairly representative of a large group of women who live in the psychological place we call Asian Pacific America. A movement that fights sexism in the social structure must deal with racism, and we had hoped leaders in the women's movement would see parallels in the lives of women of color and themselves, and would "join" *us* in our struggle and give *us* "input."

Asian Pacific women need to affirm our culture while working within to change it. Many leaders in women's organizations moved from the civil rights politics of the 60's to sexual politics, while few Asian Pacific women involved in radical politics emerged as leaders in these same women's organizations. [Instead, we] have become active in groups promoting ethnic identity. This doesn't mean we placed our loyalties on the side of ethnicity over womanhood. The two are not at war with one another; we shouldn't have to sign a "loyalty oath," favoring one over the other. However, women of color are often made to feel that we must make a choice between the two.

It should not be too difficult for [white feminists] to see why being a feminist activist is more dangerous for women of color[,] that political views held by women of color are often misconstrued as being personal rather than ideological. Views critical of the system held by a person in an "out group" are often seen as expressions of personal anger against the dominant society. (If they hate it so much here, why don't they go back?)

Remembering blatant acts of selective racism in the past three decades in our country, our white sisters should be able to see how tenuous our position in this country is. Many of us are third and fourth generation Americans, but this makes no difference; periodic conflicts involving Third World peoples can abruptly change white American's [sic] attitudes towards us.

Asian Pacific American women will not speak out until we feel secure within ourselves that this is our home too; and until our white sisters indicate by their actions that they want to join us in our struggle because it is theirs also. This means a commitment to a communal education where we learn from each other, the kind of commitment we do not seem to have at the present time. I am still hopeful that women of color in our country will be the link to Third World women throughout the world and that we can help each other broaden our visions.

Mitsuye Yamada, "Asian Pacific American Women and Feminism," in Cherrie Moraga and Gloria Anzaldua, eds., *This Bridge Called My Back: Writings of Radical Women of Color* (Watertown, MA: Persephone Press, 1981), pp. 71–75.

## Document 15

## FROM *WEBSTER V. REPRODUCTIVE HEALTH SERVICES*, 1989 (DECISION BY CHIEF JUSTICE WILLIAM REHNQUIST)

On July 3, 1989, the U.S. Supreme Court handed down a controversial 5–4 decision in the abortion case *Webster v. Reproductive Health Services* that, in the words of one justice, "discard[ed] a landmark case of the last generation [*Roe v. Wade*] and cast into darkness the hopes of every woman in this country who had come to believe that the Constitution guaranteed her the right to exercise some control over her unique ability to bear children." The author of this dissent was Justice Harry Blackmun who, sixteen years earlier, had written the majority decision for the Court in the *Roe* case. Although *Webster* did not completely overturn *Roe*, the decision amounted to an open invitation for states to draft even more restrictive abortion measures that could be used to test the constitutional limits of the 1973 landmark decision. Within the year, dozens of states had taken up the Court's challenge, and by the early 1990s, with several statutes making their way through the appeals process, another Supreme Court showdown on *Roe* seemed imminent.

State challenges to *Roe* were not new, but prior to the mid-1980s, attempts to restrict access to abortion found little support on the Supreme Court. At the most, the Court seemed willing to limit poor women's access to abortion by denying them the use of Medicaid funds to pay for those services. After 1986, however, the Court's majority opinion began shifting in favor of upholding abortion restrictions; by the time the Court rendered its *Webster* decision, the transition was more or less complete.

In part, the Supreme Court's willingness to retreat from *Roe* was a reflection of the American public's changing views on abortion. Although public opinion polls from the 1970s and 1980s consistently indicated that less than one-quarter of those polled supported an end to legal abortion (no matter the circumstances), an increasing number of Americans favored the implementation of state restrictions on abortion. A second factor to consider in the narrowing of the Court's unqualified support for *Roe* was the change in the Court's composition. Between 1981 and 1988, President Ronald Reagan tilted the Court toward the political Right by making three conservative appointments to the Court—Sandra Day O'Connor, Antonin Scalia, and Anthony Kennedy—and by elevating William Rehnquist, one of the Court's more conservative sitting justices, to the position of Chief Justice.

Of the three new appointments, Scalia was the most outspoken opponent of *Roe*, and he knowingly used the occasion of the *Webster* decision to state emphatically his intent to "overrule *Roe v. Wade*." O'Connor was always more equivocal in her support for *Roe*; but she, too, used her written concurrence of *Webster* to signal court watchers that there would be "time enough [in a future case] to reexamine *Roe*. And to do so carefully."

This appeal concerns the constitutionality of a Missouri statute regulating the performance of abortions. The United States Court of Appeals for the Eighth Circuit struck down several provisions of the statute on the ground that they violated the Court's decision in *Roe v. Wade* (1973) and cases following it. We noted probable jurisdiction, and now reverse.

In June 1986, the Governor of Missouri signed into law Missouri Senate Committee Substitute for House Bill No. 1596 (hereinafter Act or statute), which amended existing state laws concerning unborn children and abortions. The Act consisted of 20 provisions, 5 of which are now before the Court. The first provision, or preamble, contains "findings" by the state legislature that '[t]he life of each human being begins at conception," and that "unborn children have protectable interests in life, health, and well-being." The Act further requires that all Missouri laws be interpreted to provide unborn children with the same rights enjoyed by other persons, subject to the Federal Constitution and this Court's precedents. Among its other provisions, the Act requires that, prior to performing an abortion on any woman whom a physician has reason to believe is 20 or more weeks pregnant, the physician ascertain whether the fetus is viable by performing "such medical examinations and tests as are necessary to make a finding of gestational age, weight, and lung maturity of the unborn child." The Act also prohibits the use of public employees and facilities to perform or assist abortions not necessary to save the mother's life, and it prohibits the use of public funds, employees, or facilities for the purpose of "encouraging or counseling" a woman to have an abortion not necessary to save her life.

In July 1986, five health professionals employed by the State and two nonprofit corporations brought this class action in the United States District Court to challenge the constitutionality of the Missouri statute. Plaintiffs sought relief on the ground that certain statutory provisions violated the First, Fourth, Ninth, and Fourteenth Amendments to the Constitution. They asserted violations of various rights, including the "privacy rights of pregnant women seeking abortions"; the "woman's right to an abortion"; the "right to privacy in the physician-patient relationship"; the "physician's righ[t] to practice medicine"; the pregnant woman's "right to life due to inherent risks involved in childbirth"; and the woman's right to "receive adequate medical advice and treatment" concerning abortions.

The Court of Appeals for the Eighth Circuit Court affirmed.

Both [*Webster*] and the United States as *Amicus Curiae* [friends of the court] have urged that we overrule our decision in *Roe v. Wade*. The facts of the present case differ from those at issue in *Roe*. Here, Missouri has determined that viability is the point at which its interest in potential human life must be safeguarded. In *Roe*, the Texas statute criminalized the performance of *all* abortions, except when the mother's life was at stake. This case affords us no occasion to revisit *Roe* and we leave it undisturbed. To the extent indicated in our opinion, we would modify and narrow *Roe*.

Because none of the challenged provisions of the Missouri Act properly before us conflict with the Constitution, the judgment of the Court of Appeals is reversed.

Concurring and dissenting in part from the plurality is Justice Blackmun (joined by Justices Brennan and Marshall).

Today, *Roe v. Wade* and the fundamental constitutional right of women to decide to terminate a pregnancy, survive but are not secure. Although the Court extricates itself from this case without making a single change in the law of abortion, the plurality would overrule *Roe* and return to the States virtually unfettered authority to control the quintessentially intimate, personal, and life-directing decision whether to carry a fetus to term. Although today the Constitution and the decisions of this Court prohibit a State from enacting laws that inhibit women from the meaningful exercise of that right, a plurality implicitly invites every state legislature to enact restrictive abortion regulations in order to provoke test cases, in the hope that sometime down the line the Court will return the law of procreative freedom to the severe limitations that prevailed in this country before January 22, 1973. Never in my memory has a plurality announced a judgment of this Court that forments disregard for the law and for our standing decisions.

Nor in my memory has a plurality gone about its business in such a deceptive fashion. At every level of its review, from its effort to read the real meaning out of the Missouri statute to its intended evisceration of precedents and its deafening silence about the constitutional protections it would jettison, the plurality obscures the portent of its analysis. With feigned restraint, the plurality announces that its analysis leaves *Roe* "undisturbed," albeit "modif[ied and narrow[ed]." But this disclaimer is totally meaningless. The plurality opinion is filled with winks and nods, and knowing glances to those who would do away with *Roe* explicitly, but turns a stone face to anyone in search of what the plurality conceives as the scope of a woman's right under the Due Process Clause to terminate a pregnancy free from the coercive and brooding influence of the State. The simple truth is that *Roe* would not survive the plurality's analysis, and that the plurality provides no substitute for *Roe's* protective umbrella.

I dissent.

The Chief Justice parades through the challenged sections of the Missouri statute [one by one]. There, tucked away at the end of its opinion, the plurality suggests a radical reversal of the law of abortion.

In the plurality's view, the viability-testing provision imposes a burden on second-trimester abortions as a way of furthering the State's interest in protecting the potential life of the fetus. Since under the *Roe* framework, the State may not fully regulate abortion in the interest of potential life (as opposed to maternal health) until the third trimester, the plurality finds it necessary, in order to save the Missouri testing provision, to throw out *Roe's* trimester framework. In flat contradiction to *Roe,* the plurality concludes that the State's interest in potential life is compelling before viability, and upholds the testing provision because it "permissibly furthers" that state interest. [T]he plurality pretends that it leaves *Roe* standing, and refuses to discuss the real issue underlying this case: whether the Constitution includes an unenumerated right to privacy that encompasses a woman's right to decide whether to terminate a pregnancy.

Today's decision involves the most politically divisive domestic legal issue of our time. By refusing to explain or justify its proposed revolutionary revision in the law of abortion, and by refusing to abide not only by our precedents, but also by our canons for reconsidering those precedents, the plurality invites charges of cowardice and illegitimacy to our door. I cannot say that these would be undeserved.

For today, at least, the law of abortion stands undisturbed. For today, the women of this Nation still retain the liberty to control their destinies. But the signs are evident and very ominous, and a chill wind blows.

492 U.S. Reports, 490 (1989).

# Glossary of Selected Terms

**Consciousness-Raising:** A term coined by feminists associated with the radical wing (women's liberation) of the feminist movement. Women engaged in the process of consciousness-raising met regularly in small, intimate groups to share their innermost thoughts about and experiences with male oppression. Consciousness-raising helped women recognize that their problems were political, not personal, and it encouraged women to engage in feminist political activities.

**Cultural Feminism:** Cultural feminism appeared as a variant of radical feminism as early as 1970 but gained ascendancy after 1975. Cultural feminism was based on two premises: first, that women's values were essentially universal (class, color, and sexual orientation mattered little) and in opposition to those of men; and second, that these values were more pure, moral, peaceful, and democratic than men's values. Cultural feminism encouraged women to separate themselves by creating alternative, female institutions. This retreat from male space worried many radical feminists who feared that cultural feminism was escapist and that it gave women permission to abandon political struggle because male institutions were inherently corrupt and therefore unsalvageable.

**Domestic Violence:** An umbrella term used by feminists to include all forms of violence (physical and psychological) within the home. When feminists first identified domestic violence as a problem, they focused on wife beating (also called battering), but over time, feminists recognized that violence in the home was not limited to wife beating. Although women (as wives and girl-friends) still comprise the majority of domestic violence victims, experts and activists in this field now recognize that men, children, and the elderly are also at risk and that domestic violence is not limited to heterosexual couples.

**EEOC (Equal Employment Opportunity Commission):** A federal agency created as part of the landmark 1964 Civil Rights Act, the EEOC was charged with enforcing Title VII (of the same act), which prohibited discrimination in employment on the basis of race, color, religion, national origin, and sex. During its early years, the EEOC's majority was reluctant to enforce the "sex clause" of Title VII (especially in the area of sex-segregated want ads and rulings on protective labor legislation). This foot-dragging sparked women to form the National Organization for Women (NOW) in 1966. NOW led repeated demonstrations against the EEOC and lobbied the Johnson administration to issue an executive order strengthening enforcement (Executive Order 11375 was issued in 1967). By the late 1960s, the agency had reversed its position and began actively pursuing sex discrimination complaints.

**ERA (Equal Rights Amendment):**"Equality of rights under the law shall not be denied or abridged by the United States or by any State on account of sex." First proposed in 1923, the Equal Rights Amendment had a troubled history. Social feminists were among the first to oppose the amendment for fear that it would undermine protective legislation, but by 1972 this concern was moot. That year, the amendment was voted out of Congress and sent to the states for what seemed to be a quick ratification process. By 1975, however, the process appeared stalled as Phyllis Schlafly's STOP ERA movement gained momentum. Feminists rallied briefly in 1978, winning a three-year extension for ratification, but the amendment was defeated in June 1982.

**Equal Rights Feminism:** Equal Rights best describes the philosophy and goals of the liberal wing of second-wave feminism. Equal rights feminists (also described as equality feminists) dismissed the idea that men and women were inherently dissimilar. In the words of the National Organization for Women (the preeminent equal rights organization), "women, first and foremost, are human beings." Equal rights feminists sought an equal partnership with men; their agenda focused simultaneously on including women in the American mainstream and ending sex discrimination in all aspects of public life.

**Feminine Mystique:** Coined by Betty Friedan, this term was immortalized in the title of her 1963 best-seller. The mystique refers to the conflict between the 1950s' image of the "happy suburban housewife" and the discontent that simmered beneath the surface of the domesticated lives led by many middle-class married women.

**Feminism:** A social theory advocating equality between men and women in both public institutions and in private life. As an ideology, feminism is neither defined nor limited to a single issue or organization. Feminist theory does not negate the biological differences between men and women; instead, it emphasizes the cultural implications of these differences in formulating the social, political, and economic roles ascribed to women and men. Feminist theory questions the cultural assumption that because women bear children, they "naturally" bear the primary responsibility for childrearing. At the same time, feminist theory encompasses the tenet that equality between women and men does not always translate into equal treatment before the law. For example, although women and men may share parental responsibilities and therefore may request parental leave for a newborn child, women require special consideration because they need to recuperate from childbirth and because they may choose to breast-feed.

**First-Wave Feminism:** A phrase used to describe the women's movement prior to the passage of the Nineteenth Amendment (woman suffrage) in 1920. Dating the beginning of the first wave is problematic, but many historians point to the formation of the National Woman Suffrage Association and the American Woman Suffrage Association in 1869 (the two groups combined in 1890 as the National American Woman Suffrage Association). First-wave feminism also included, but was not limited to, the Woman's Christian Temperance Union (1874), the National Association of Colored Women (1896), and the National Woman's Party (1916).

**Houston Conference:** The First National Women's Conference was held over four days in mid-November 1977 in Houston, Texas. Chaired by Bella Abzug, the conference brought together over 20,000 individuals, including some 2,000 voting delegates (approximately 19 percent of these delegates represented the antifeminist politics of the New Right). Delegates overwhelmingly approved a twenty-six plank National Plan of Action to be submitted to President Jimmy Carter and Congress. Among the most important planks were those focusing on the needs of women of color and displaced homemakers, protection for reproductive freedom and sexual preference, and support for ratification of the beleaguered Equal Rights Amendment.

**"Lavender Herring/ Lavender Menace":** Betty Friedan used the phrase "lavender herring" (a play on the term "red herring") to warn feminists about the dangers of openly acknowledging the presence of lesbian women within the movement. Friedan worried that "lesbian-baiting" would be used to discredit feminism and that support for lesbian women's concerns would drive straight women from the movement. In May 1970, at the second meeting of the Congress to Unite Women, a score of lesbian feminists (including Rita Mae Brown) channeled their anger with this homophobia by staging a "lavender menace" zap action. Chiding straight feminists with signs ("The Women's Movement is a Lesbian Plot") and wearing "lavender menace" T-shirts, lesbian feminists staked their claim for inclusion within mainstream feminism.

**Liberal Feminism:** *See* Equal Rights Feminism.

***Ms.*:** For over a quarter of a century, *Ms.* has served as a public forum for the feminist movement. By its very name, the magazine served notice that a woman's identity was hers to define (as a Ms.) and that who she was or wanted to be had little to do with her marital status (as a Mrs. or Miss). From 1972 until 1989 *Ms.*'s editorial staff (with founder Gloria Steinem as editor-in chief) tried to balance the demands of maintaining the magazine's feminist reputation with the economic reality of operating a commercial venture. As a "forum for feminism" the magazine showcased some of the best and most outspoken feminist writers (Alice Walker, Marge Piercy, and Kate Millett) and activists (Robin Morgan, Letty Cottin Pogrebin, and Bella Abzug) and pioneered in covering some of the most controversial issues of the day (domestic violence, sexual harassment in the workplace, rape, child abuse, and anorexia). As a commercial venture, the magazine needed to attract advertisers; however, in sprinkling its pages with ads for cosmetics and feminine hygiene products, critics argued that *Ms.* differed little from the more "traditional" women's magazines. Despite a circulation of 350,000 for most of its run, *Ms.* was operating in the red by the late 1980s. In 1987 the magazine was sold to an Australian media firm and Gloria Steinem relinquished her editorial position. *Ms.* ceased publication briefly in November 1989, but with Robin Morgan at the helm as the new editor-in-chief (until 1993 when Marcia Gillespie took over) and new backers (Lang Communications through the early 1990s and more recently MacDonald Communications Corp.), *Ms.* reinvented itself as a bimonthly, ad-free magazine with a more hefty subscription rate ($45 for six issues). What has not changed is the magazine's ongoing commitment to feminism.

**New Right:** A political movement with a conservative social agenda, the New Right (also described as the Radical Right) distinguished itself from the Old Right by targeting feminism (rather than communism) as the root cause of America's problems in the 1970s and 1980s. Decrying the "moral decay" of American society, the New Right drew its strength from the ranks of religious orthodoxy (the Mormon and Catholic churches, Orthodox Judaism, and fundamentalist Protestant denominations). Topping the New Right's political agenda were rescinding the 1973 Supreme Court decision on abortion (*Roe v. Wade*), halting ratification of the Equal Rights Amendment, reversing affirmative action policies, denying equal protection under the law to homosexuals, and securing passage of a Human Life Amendment. This antifeminist political backlash reached its height during the administrations of Presidents Reagan and Bush (1981–1993).

**NOW (National Organization for Women):** Founded in 1966, the National Organization for Women (NOW) has been described as the first modern civil rights organization for women (see Equal Rights Feminism). In its early years, NOW concentrated on removing legal barriers that prevented women's full and equal participation in the economy, education, and civic life. By 1968, NOW's agenda included the two most controversial feminist demands of the period: passage of the Equal Rights Amendment and the repeal of antiabortion statutes. Initially, issues pertaining to sexuality (especially lesbianism), sexual violence, poverty, and racism were not high priorities for NOW, but within a decade of its founding, NOW's membership had become more diverse and its agenda more inclusive.

**Political Feminism/Social Feminism:** Terms used to describe philosophical differences among first-wave feminists about the meaning of equality and how to achieve it. Political feminists dismissed the biological differences between women and men; social feminists emphasized these differences. Political feminists stressed the human qualities shared by women and men; social feminists emphasized the biological differences that separated the sexes. Political feminists favored legislation that reflected equal treatment for women and men; social feminists supported legislation that "protected" women. Both political and social feminists endorsed the woman suffrage amendment, but for vastly different reasons; the former saw the vote as an affirmation of equality between the sexes, the latter saw the vote as a tool for securing protective legislation. They could not, however, find common ground when the National Woman's Party proposed the Equal Rights Amendment this amendment in 1923; for the next forty-five years as feminism ebbed and flowed, this amendment would prove to be the most divisive issue within the feminist movement.

**Politico/Radical Feminist Divide:** This phrase describes an ideological split that characterized the formative years of the women's liberation movement. Politico-feminists dominated women's liberation from its emergence in 1967 until approximately 1969 when the movement became identified with radical feminists. Politico-feminists remained closely tied to the New Left politics of the student and antiwar movements and accepted the notion that "women's issues" were subordinate to the more important revolutionary movement that was centered in class struggle. Radical feminists started from the same New Left position but began questioning this subordination, especially in light of their oppression by New Left men. New Left men's dismissal of women's issues as trivial and their ridicule of the women who persisted in raising "feminist" issues awakened a radical feminist consciousness: patriarchal assumptions and privilege (sexism) would not fall by the wayside if or when the class revolution succeeded. Sexism was as pernicious as racism, and it would have to be attacked separately and directly. Unlike politico-feminists, radical feminists identified women as a "sex-caste" (or class) that stood apart from men.

**Pro-Choice:** The term coined by feminists to describe their continued support for reproductive freedom (a woman's "right to choose") in the face of organized opposition to the 1973 Supreme Court decision, *Roe v. Wade,* by "pro-life" forces.

**Pro-Life:** The term used by activists associated with the National Right-to-Life Committee, Operation Rescue, and the Pro-Life Action Committee to describe their opposition to the legalization of abortion in 1973. Pro-life advocates (dubbed "anti-choice" by many feminists) believe that life begins at conception; "hard-liners" within this movement (also called the right-to-life movement) believe that abortion is tantamount to murder.

**Protective (Labor) Legislation:** An umbrella term used to describe Progressive era (1900–1920) labor legislation that protected women from onerous working conditions because of their unique biological/social roles. Social feminists viewed protective legislation as the centerpiece of their feminist agenda. They were rewarded for their lobbying efforts in the 1908 Supreme Court decision *Muller v. Oregon* and extended their influence on public policy with the creation of the Children's Bureau in 1912, the Women's Bureau in 1920, and passage of the Sheppard-Towner Act in 1921.

**Radical Feminism:** Radical feminism became synonymous with the women's liberation wing of second-wave feminism. Unlike their liberal feminist counterparts, radical feminists identified patriarchy as the foundation of women's oppression. Liberal feminists joined national organizations such as the National Organization for Women, the Women's Equity Action League, and the National Women's Political Caucus. Radial feminists organized at the grass roots; their groups were localized. Some of the more "famous" groups included New York Radical Women, Redstockings, the Boston Women's Health Book Collective, Bread and Roses, Radicalesbians, and the Women's International Terrorist Conspiracy from Hell. Radical feminists viewed the legislative and judicial tactics of liberal feminists as a band-aid solution designed to lessen but not eradicate sexism. Instead, radical feminism was predicated on a fundamental reordering of American institutions. Radical feminists were among the first to criticize the institution of marriage and the family; to challenge deeply held myths about female sexuality; and to identify rape, wife abuse, and pornography as problems stemming from male violence.

**Radical Right:** *See* New Right.

**Right-to-Life Movement:** *See* Pro-Life.

**Roe v. Wade:** This landmark 1973 Supreme Court decision determined that a woman's constitutional right to privacy included her right to terminate a pregnancy. Contrary to popular belief, this decision did not guarantee a woman's right to "abortion on demand." Instead, a woman's right to choose this medical procedure during the first trimester of the pregnancy was balanced against the state's right to protect her life during the second trimester, and the potential life of the fetus during the third trimester.

**Second-Wave Feminism:** A phrase used to describe the reemergence of feminism as a significant political and social force in American life beginning in the mid-1960s. Until the mid-1970s, second-wave feminism included two distinct wings—liberal, or equal rights feminism and radical feminism, or women's liberation; after 1975, the ideological line separating liberals and radicals began to blur. Second-wave feminism reached its zenith between

1970 and 1980 (when many items on the feminist agenda were incorporated into American society); the decade of the 1980s also witnessed the formation of a concerted backlash against second-wave feminism.

**Sexual Politics:** Popularized by Kate Millett in her 1970 exposé on the "patriarchal bias" in the literary works of D. H. Lawrence, Henry Miller, and Norman Mailer, the term redefined the symbolic depiction of sexual expression in Western culture. According to Millett, sexual activity did not exist in a "vacuum," instead, it reflected issues of power and domination (i.e., politics). The implication of this revisioning was revolutionary. If literary descriptions of sexual relations reflected power relations between fictional actors, did the same theory apply in real life? Feminists certainly thought so, and they acted on this assumption in their critiques of rape, pornography, domestic violence, incest, and homophobia.

**Title VII:** Sometimes referred to as the "sex amendment," Title VII of the 1964 Civil Rights Act banned discrimination in employment on the basis of race, color, religion, national origin, and sex. Subsequent amendments to Title VII during the Johnson and Nixon administrations have broadened its scope, strengthened the agency (the Equal Employment Opportunity Commission) created to enforce it, and made possible several precedent-setting Supreme Court decisions during the 1970s (for example, the 1971 decision *Phillips v. Martin Marietta* overturned state laws excluding women with young children from holding certain jobs, and the 1974 decision *Cleveland Board of Education v. LaFleur* ended mandatory and unpaid maternity leave for teachers).

**Title IX:** Included as a provision of the 1972 Educational Amendments Act, Title IX prohibited sex discrimination in institutions of higher education receiving federal assistance for any program or activity. Although Title IX is most frequently identified with ending discrimination in college athletics programs (eventually the ban extended to high school programs), it also covered admissions policies (an exception was made for private undergraduate colleges), course restrictions, financial aid, health services, housing, and other special programs. Title IX was intended to include faculty, staff, and students but was met with several challenges until a decision favoring broad coverage was reached in a 1982 Supreme Court decision (*North Haven Board of Education v. Hogan*). In 1984, opponents of Title IX won a victory when the Supreme Court (in *Grove City College v. Bell*) applied a "program-specific" interpretation to the sex discrimination ban (programs that did not directly receive federal funds could practice sex discrimination). This decision was reversed in 1988 when Congress passed the Civil Rights Restoration Act over President Reagan's veto.

**Women's Liberation:** Although this term was used indiscriminately by the media to describe second-wave feminism, feminist scholars use it to describe the radical wing of the movement. Women's liberation groups began forming in

1967, but as a concept, "women's lib" caught the nation's attention at the mythic "bra-burning" demonstration held at the 1968 Miss America Beauty Pageant. The heyday of radical feminism was probably between 1968 and 1975. After 1975, as cultural feminism began to eclipse radical feminism, many liberation groups disbanded; by the time of the 1977 Houston Conference, liberal feminism had become the dominant force within the movement. Still, in the minds of most Americans, feminism will always be equated with the radicalism of the "women's libbers."

# Annotated Bibliography

## BOOKS

Abzug, Bella S. *Bella!: Ms. Abzug Goes to Washington*. New York: Saturday Review Press, 1972. A highly personal and entertaining chronicle of Representative Bella Abzug's first year in Congress.

Asian Women United of California. *Making Waves: An Anthology of Writings by and about Asian Women*. Boston: Beacon Press, 1989. Excellent sampling of Asian American women's views on ethnicity and feminism.

Berry, Mary Frances. *Why ERA Failed: Politics, Women's Rights, and the Amending Process of the Constitution*. Bloomington: Indiana University Press, 1986. Analyzes the defeat of the Equal Rights Amendment from a legal and historical perspective.

Boles, Janet K. *The Politics of the Equal Rights Amendment: Conflict and the Decision Process*. New York: Longman, 1979. Early analysis of the political conflicts generated by the campaign for ratification of the Equal Rights Amendment.

Boston Women's Health Book Collective. *Our Bodies, Ourselves*. New York: Simon & Schuster, revised and expanded second edition, 1976. Revised edition of the famous text that helped launch the feminist health movement.

_____. *Our Bodies, Ourselves for the New Century*. New York: Simon & Schuster, 1998. The most recent edition on women's health issues by the feminist collective.

Brown, Rita Mae. *Rita Will: Memoir of a Literary Rabble-Rouser*. New York: Bantam Books, 1997. Frank and funny memoir of lesbian activist and writer Rita Mae Brown. See, especially, her retelling of the conflicts between straight and lesbian feminists during the early days of the movement.

Brownmiller, Susan. *Against Our Will: Men, Women, and Rape.* New York: Simon & Schuster, 1975. One of the first historical overviews of rape.

Cade, Toni, ed. *The Black Woman, An Anthology.* New York: New American Library, 1970. Early example of essays on black feminist theory and black women's problematic relationship with (white women's) feminism.

Carabillo, Toni, Judith Meuli, and June Bundy Csida. *Feminist Chronicles, 1953–1993.* Los Angeles: Women's Graphics, 1993. A yearly chronicle of the leading events and personalities that shaped feminism from 1953 to 1993.

Caraway, Nancie. *Segregated Sisterhood: Racism and the Politics of American Feminism.* Knoxville: University of Tennessee Press, 1991. Implications of white racism on feminism with special emphasis on the theoretical critique developed by black feminists.

Carden, Maren Lockwood. *The New Feminist Movement.* New York: Russell Sage Foundation, 1974. An early study of second-wave feminism that delineates the differences between the movement's two branches: women's rights and women's liberation.

Castillo-Speed, Lillian, ed. *Latina: Women's Voices from the Borderlands.* New York: Touchstone Press, 1995. A current sample of Hispanic women's thoughts on race, class, gender and identity.

Chisholm, Shirley. *The Good Fight.* New York: Harper and Row Publishers, 1973. Chisholm's account of her historic campaign for the presidency in 1972.

———. *Unbought and Unbossed.* Boston: Houghton Mifflin Company, 1970. Autobiographical account of the life and early political career of the first black woman elected to Congress.

Collins, Patricia Hill. *Black Feminist Thought: Knowledge, Consciousness, and the Politics of Empowerment.* New York: Routledge, 1991. Traces the development of black feminist thought in the works of nineteenth- and twentieth-century women writers.

Connell, Noreen, and Cassandra Wilson, eds. *Rape: The First Sourcebook for Women.* New York: New American Library, 1974. Written by members of New York Radical Feminists, this text explores the reasons for rape, criticizes the legal treatment of rape victims, and offers a feminist solution to the problem.

Coontz, Stephanie. *The Way We Never Were: American Families and the Nostalgia Trap.* New York: Basic Books, 1992. Revisionist interpretation of American family life.

Cott, Nancy F. *The Grounding of Modern Feminism.* New Haven: Yale University Press, 1987. A path-breaking study of modern feminism both as a theory and as a broad-based social movement.

Daly, Mary. *Beyond God the Father: Toward a Philosophy of Women's Liberation.* Boston: Beacon Press, second revised edition 1976. Rejects the
   concept of a male God within Christianity and envisions a new female-
   centered religion based on radical feminist theory.
————. *The Church and the Second Sex.* New York: Harper and Row, 1968. Daly's earliest criticism of antifeminism within the Catholic church, this
   text reflects her soon-to-be-rejected reformist philosophy.
Davis, Flora. *Moving the Mountain: The Women's Movement in America since
   1960.* New York: Simon & Schuster, 1991. A detailed study of second-
   wave feminism from its origins in the early 1960s to the backlash in the
   1980s.
Deckard, Barbara Sinclair. *The Women's Movement: Political, Socioeconomic,
   and Psychological Issues.* 3rd edition. New York: Harper and Row,
   1983. A useful sourcebook on contemporary feminist issues.
Donnerstein, Edward, Daniel Linz, and Steven Penrod. *The Question of Pornography: Research Findings and Policy Implications.* New York: The Free
   Press, 1987. A balanced analysis of current research on pornography, es-
   pecially its relationship to promoting violence.
Dworkin, Andrea. *Pornography: Men Possessing Women.* New York: Plume
   Books, 1981. A classic example of the radical feminist's argument
   against pornography.
Echols, Alice. *Daring to Be Bad: Radical Feminism in America, 1967–1975.*
   Minneapolis: University of Minnesota Press, 1989. A brilliant historical
   analysis of the rise and fall of the women's liberation movement in
   America.
Evans, Sara M. *Personal Politics: The Roots of Women's Liberation in the Civil
   Rights Movement and the New Left.* New York: Vintage Books 1980.
   One of the earliest histories linking the emergence of the women's lib-
   eration movement to the sexism women experienced in the civil rights
   and New Left movements (written by a participant).
Faludi, Susan. *Backlash: The Undeclared War against American Women.* New
   York: Doubleday and Company, Inc. 1991. Chronicles the rising tide of
   antifeminism in the 1980s.
Felsenthal, Carol. *The Sweetheart of the Silent Majority: The Biography of Phyl-
   lis Schlafly.* Garden City, NY: Doubleday and Company, Inc. 1981. A
   portrait of Phyllis Schlafly, a leading figure in the anti-ERA movement.
Ferraro, Geraldine A., with Linda Bird Francke. *Ferraro: My Story.* New York:
   Bantam Books, 1985. An account of the historic 1984 presidential campaign told from the perspective of the first woman nominated for the
   number two spot by a major political party.
Firestone, Shulamith. *The Dialectic of Sex: The Case for Feminist Revolution.*
   New York: Bantam Books, 1979. A provocative analysis of radical
   feminist theory by one of the movement's founders.

Friedan, Betty. *It Changed My Life: Writings on the Women's Movement*. New York: Random House, 1976. An autobiographical account of second-wave feminism by one of the movement's founders.

———. *The Feminine Mystique*. New York: W.W. Norton and Company, Inc. 1963. The classic text that identified the domestic trap (the feminine mystique) ensnaring middle-class American housewives in the years immediately following World War II.

———. *The Second Stage*. New York: Summit Books, 1981. This controversial sequel to *The Feminine Mystique* criticizes feminists for replacing the feminine mystique with a "feminist mystique."

Giddings, Paula. *When and Where I Enter: The Impact of Black Women on Race and Sex in America*. New York: William Morrow and Company, 1984. The historical experiences of African-American women with specific reference to racism within the mainstream feminist movement.

Gordan, Linda. *Birth Control in America: Woman's Body, Woman's Right*. New York: Penguin Books, 1976. Revised and updated, New York: Penguin Books, 1990. Historical account of the birth control movement in the United States from the perspective of a radical feminist historian.

———. *Heroes of Their Own: The Politics and History of Family Violence, Boston, 1880–1960*. New York: Viking Press, 1988. Excellent historical case study of family violence from the Progressive era to the eve of second-wave feminism.

Gornick, Vivian. *Essays in Feminism*. New York: Harper and Row, 1978. Invaluable collection of essays on feminism (1969–1978) written by a writer for the *Village Voice*.

Harrison, Cynthia. *On Account of Sex: The Politics of Women's Issues, 1945–1968*. Berkeley: University of California Press, 1988. A penetrating analysis of feminism and public policy prior to the formation of the National Organization for Women.

Hartmann, Susan M. *From Margin to Mainstream: American Women and Politics since 1960*. Philadelphia: Temple University Press, 1989. Excellent study of women's increased participation in politics, the effects of feminism on the political process, and the consequences of antifeminism on American politics.

Heilbrun, Carolyn G. *The Education of a Woman: The Life of Gloria Steinem*. New York: The Dial Press, 1995. An excellent biography of Gloria Steinem and the movement she helped create by a renowned feminist literary critic and feminist mystery writer (under the pseudonym Amanda Cross).

Hewlett, Sylvia Ann. *A Lesser Life: The Myth of Women's Liberation in America*. New York: Warner Books, 1987. A highly critical view of feminism by a "former feminist" to be read as a companion piece to Betty Friedan's *Second Stage*.

Hoff, Joan. *Law, Gender, and Injustice: A Legal History of U.S. Women.* New York: New York University Press, 1991. Impressive historical study of women's unequal status before the law and feminists' legal efforts to extend the rights and privileges of citizenship to all women.

Hoff-Wilson, Joan, ed. *Rights of Passage: The Past and Future of the ERA.* Bloomington: Indiana University Press, 1986. Anthology explores the origins and early controversies blocking acceptance of the Equal Rights Amendment until 1972; offers several explanations for the amendment's defeat in 1982.

Hole, Judith, and Ellen Levine. *Rebirth of Feminism.* New York: Quadrangle Books, Inc., 1971. Invaluable early history of the origins, organizations, and goals of second-wave feminism.

hooks, bell. *Ain't I a Woman: Black Women and Feminism.* Boston: South End Press, 1981. Historical overview of black women's struggles with racism and sexism.

Horowitz, Daniel. *Betty Friedan and the Making of 'The Feminist Mystique': The American Left, the Cold War, and Modern Feminism (Culture, Politics, and the Cold War).* Amherst: University of Massachusetts Press, 1998. Revisionist biography of Betty Friedan linking the origins of modern feminism to labor radicalism and the American Left.

King, Mary. *Freedom Song: A Personal Story of the 1960s Civil Rights Movement.* New York: William Morrow and Company, 1987. Chapter 13 explores the growing tensions over race and gender that contributed to the writing of the "anonymous" 1964 position paper on the "place of women" within the civil rights movement.

Klatch, Rebecca E. *Women of the New Right.* Philadelphia: Temple University Press, 1987. Excellent study of New Right women activists with special emphasis on the division within the political Right between "laissez-faire conservatives" and "social conservatives."

Koedt, Anne, Ellen Levine, and Anita Rapone, eds. *Radical Feminism.* New York: Quadrangle Books Inc., 1973. Collection of some of the earliest and most influential essays on radical feminism, including "The Myth of the Vaginal Orgasm," byAnne Koedt, "Women-Identified Women," by Radicalesbians, and "The Tyranny of Structurelessness," by Jo Freeman.

Lederer, Laura, ed. *Take Back the Night: Women on Pornography.* New York: William Morrow and Company, 1980. Excellent collection of essays and reports by feminist activists on the relationship between pornography and violence.

Linden-Ward, Blanche, and Carol Hurd Green. *Changing the Future: American Women in the 1960s.* New York: Twayne Publishers, 1993. Part of Twayne Publishers' chronological series on American Women in the Twentieth Century, this volume provides a wealth of information on the emergence of second-wave feminism.

Luker, Kristin. *Abortion and the Politics of Motherhood.* Berkeley: University of California Press, 1984. Balanced analysis of the pro- and antiabortion movements in California, prior to and after legalization.

McLaughlin, Steven D., et al. *The Changing Lives of American Women.* Chapel Hill: University of North Carolina Press, 1988. Study compares socio-economic changes across three generations of American women: the women who gave birth to the baby-boom generation, the baby-boomers, and their daughters.

Mansbridge, Jane J. *Why We Lost the ERA.* Chicago: University of Chicago Press, 1986. This analysis of the Equal Rights Amendment's defeat views the ratification process as a political contest between pro- and anti-ERA forces.

Martin, Del. *Battered Wives.* San Francisco: Glide Publications, 1976. The first major report on domestic violence written by the coordinator of the National Organization for Women's Task Force on Household Violence.

Martin, Del, and Phyllis Lyon. *Lesbian/Woman.* San Francisco: Glide Publications, 1972. An important early source on lesbianism.

Mathews, Donald G., and Jane Sherron De Hart. *Sex, Gender, and the Politics of ERA: A State and a Nation.* New York: Oxford University Press, 1990. Invaluable study of the pro– and anti–Equal Rights Amendment ratification battle in a keysouthern state (North Carolina).

Mead, Margaret. *American Women: The Report of the President's Commission on the Status of Women and Other Publications of the Commission.* New York: Charles Scribner's Sons, 1965. Reprint of the 1963 report of the President's Commission on the Status of Women; includes final reports of the individual committees (also contains an introduction by Margaret Mead).

Meyerowitz, Joanne, ed. *Not June Cleaver: Women and Gender in Postwar America, 1945–1960.* Philadelphia: Temple University Press, 1994. Revisionist essays countering the stereotype of female complacency, docility, and domesticity during the era when the "feminine mystique" supposedly reigned supreme.

Millett, Kate. *Flying.* New York: Alfred A. Knopf, 1974. Autobiographical account of Millett's experiences following the publicity that surrounded her coming out as a lesbian.

———. *Sexual Politics.* Garden City, NY: Doubleday Press, 1970. Millett's brilliant exposé of the patriarchal bias inherent in Western culture and reflected in the literary works of D. H. Lawrence, Norman Mailer, and Henry Miller.

Moraga, Cherrie, and Gloria Anzaldua, eds. *This Bridge Called My Back: Writings by Radical Women of Color.* Watertown: Persephone Press, 1981. Rare collection of early prose, poetry, and personal reflections by women of color on their views toward and relationship with contemporary feminism.

Morgan, Robin. *Going Too Far: The Personal Chronicle of a Feminist*. New York: Random House, 1977. Collection of Robin Morgan's most influential essays and private musings on feminism.

———, ed. *Sisterhood Is Global: The International Women's Movement Anthology,* updated and revised. New York: The Feminist Press, 1996. Contains a new preface and updated material covering international feminism from Afghanistan to Zambia.

———, ed. *Sisterhood Is Powerful: An Anthology of Writings from the Women's Liberation Movement*. New York: Random House, 1970. The first collection of essays on radical feminism.

Morrison, Toni, ed. *Race-ing Justice, En-gendering Power: Essays on Anita Hill, Clarence Thomas and the Construction of Social Reality*. New York: Pantheon Books, 1992. Excellent collection of articles on the politics of race and gender concerns in the confirmation hearings of Supreme Court Justice Clarence Thomas.

Murray, Pauli. *Song in a Weary Throat: An American Pilgrimage*. New York: Harper and Row, 1987. Published posthumously, an excellent autobiography of the civil rights and feminist activist Pauli Murray.

Orenstein, Peggy. *Schoolgirls: Young Women, Self-Esteem, and the Confidence Gap*. New York: Doubleday, 1994. Excellent source on gender bias in schools.

Pagila, Camille. *Sexual Personae: Art and Decadence from Nefertiti to Emily Dickinson*. New Haven: Yale University Press, 1990. A neofeminist's critique of feminist theory.

Petchesky, Rosalind Pollack. *Abortion and Woman's Choice: The State, Sexuality, and Reproductive Freedom*. New York: Longman, 1984. Revised edition, Boston: Northeastern University Press, 1990. Well-researched and cogently argued analysis of the abortion debate from a feminist perspective.

Peterson, Esther, with Winifred Conkling. *Restless: The Memoirs of Labor and Consumer Activist Esther Peterson*. Washington, DC: Caring Publishing, 1995. Autobiography of Esther Peterson, the point person for John F. Kennedy's President's Commission on the Status of Women.

Pizzey, Erin. *Scream Quietly or the Neighbors Will Hear*. Short Hills, NJ: Ridley Enslow Publishers, 1974. First book to call attention to the problem of wife beating; used by Pizzey to raise public awareness of domestic violence.

Pleck, Elizabeth. *Domestic Tyranny: The Making of Social Policy against Family Violence from Colonial Times to the Present*. New York: Oxford University Press, 1987. Excellent historical study of social policy and family violence.

Reagan, Leslie J. *When Abortion Was a Crime: Women, Medicine, and Law in the United States, 1867–1973*. Berkeley: University of California Press, 1997. Brilliant historical study of the "practice and policing" of abortion in the United States during the hundred-year period in which it was illegal.

Roiphe, Katie. *The Morning After: Sex, Fear, and Feminism on the American Campus.* Boston: Little, Brown and Company, 1993. Blames feminists for fostering a climate of "victimization" and for poisoning male-female relationships on college campuses.

Rudy, Kathy. *Beyond Pro-Life and Pro-Choice: Moral Diversity in the Abortion Debate*. Boston: Beacon Press, 1996. Places the debate over abortion by pro-life and pro-choice advocates within the context of four competing religious and philosophical prespectives: Catholicism, evangelical Protestantism, feminism, and classic liberalism.

Rupp, Lelia J., and Verta Taylor. *Survival in the Doldrums: The American Women's Rights Movement, 1945 to the 1960s*. Columbus: Ohio State University Press, 1990. Examination of organized feminism's persistence during an era of political conservatism (1945–1960).

Scharf, Lois, and Joan M. Jensen, eds. *Decades of Discontent: The Women's Movement, 1920–1940.* Boston: Northeastern University Press, 1987. Part IV, "Organizational and Ideological Struggles," contains five essays on the ebb and flow of organized feminism between World Wars I and II.

Schlafly, Phyllis. *The Power of the Positive Woman*. New Rochelle, NY: Arlington House Publishers, 1977. Schlafly's critique of women's liberation.

Scott, Anne Firor. *Natural Allies: Women's Voluntary Associations in American History*. Urbana: University of Illinois Press, 1991. Excellent historical overview of American women's voluntary organizations from the colonial era to the present (inclusive of race, ethnic, and class differences).

Snitow, Ann, Christine Stansell, and Sharon Thompson, eds. *Powers of Desire: The Politics of Sexuality*. New York: Monthly Review Press, 1983. Collection contains some classic articles, as well as fiction and autobiographical views exploring the range of female/feminist sexual theory and practices.

Stern, Sydney Ladensohn. *Gloria Steinem: Her Passions, Politics, and Mystique.* Secaucus, NJ: Carol Publishing Group, 1997. Based on interviews with Gloria Steinem, this biography should be read in tandem with Carol Heilbrun's interpretation of Steinem's life and contributions to feminism.

Thom, Mary ed. *Letters to Ms., 1972–1987*. New York: Henry Holt and Company, 1987. An excellent sampling of the response *Ms*. generated from its readers as reflected in the letters written to the magazine's editors.

Vance, Carol, ed. *Pleasure and Danger: Exploring Female Sexuality*. Boston: Routledge and Kegan Paul, 1984. Contributions focus on the theory and history of sexuality and the links between sexuality, fear, danger, and pleasure.

Vidal, Mirta. *Women, New Voice of La Raza*. New York: Pathfinder Press, 1971. Early example of the political consciousness of Hispanic women.

Wandersee, Winifred D. *On the Move: American Women in the 1970s*. Boston: Twayne Publishers, 1988. Part of Twayne Publishers' chronological series on American Women in the Twentieth Century, this volume provides a wealth of information on both wings of the feminist movement (equal rights and women's liberation).

Ware, Susan. *Holding Their Own: American Women in the 1930s* Boston: Twayne Publishers, 1982. Part of Twayne Publishers' chronological series on American Women in the Twentieth Century. This volume explores the persistence of feminism during the Great Depression.

Weitzman, Lenore J. *The Divorce Revolution: The Unexpected Social and Economic Consequences for Women and Children in America*. New York: The Free Press, 1985. Sociologist Weitzman's flawed analysis of the negative effects of "no-fault" divorce laws on women and children.

White, Evelyn C. *The Black Women's Health Book: Speaking for Oursleves*. Seattle, WA: Seal Press, 1990. Excellent source on women's health issues and the health care system from the perspective of black women.

## ELECTRONIC RESOURCES (WEB SITES)

Documents from the Women's Liberation Movement: Duke Special Collections. http://scriptorium.lib.duke.edu/wlm. On-line archival collection of primary documents from the late 1960s and early 1970s on the women's liberation movement in the United States

Feminist Research Center. http://www.feminist.org/research/1_public. html. Maintained by the Feminist Majority Foundation, this site provides information on government research, feminist classics and journals, recent books, and the foundation's reports.

General History of Feminism: http://www.nau.edu/~wst/access/fhist/fhist-sub.html. Information on general studies of feminism (first-wave, history of second-wave, and feminist theory).

H-GIG Women's History. http://www.ucr.edu/h-gig/hist-topics/women.html. Maintained by UC Riverside's History Department, this site provides links to sites related to women's history.

The Lesbian History Project: http://www-lib.usc.edu/~retter/main.html. Information on lesbian history and links to related sites (e.g., journals, archives, dissertations, bibliographies).

ViVa Women's History. http://www.iisg.nl/~womhist/index.html. Maintains current bibliography of articles about women and gender history; links to women's history institutions, organizations, and archival and library collections.

Voices from the Gaps: Women Writers of Color. http://english.cla.umn. edu/lkd/vfg. Links to sites about women writers of color (e.g., African American, Native American, Chicana/Latina, General Women's Lit.).

Women's Studies—American Studies: http://www.georgetown.edu/cross-roads/asw/wmst.html. Links to women's history/gender issues sites (e.g., women's liberation movement documents, domestic violence resources, feminist film reviews, demographic and health surveys).

## ARTICLES

Abrams, Kathryn. "The Reasonable Woman: Sense and Sensibility in Sexual Harassment Law." *Dissent* 42 (Winter 1995): 48–54. Common sense application of sexual harassment law.

Arrington, Theodore S., and Patricia A. Kyle. "Equal Rights Amendment Activists in North Carolina." *Signs: Journal of Women in Culture and Society* 3 (Spring 1978): 660–80. An analysis of pro– and anti–Equal Rights Amendment activists in a progressive southern state.

Brady, David W., and Kent L. Tedin. "Ladies in Pink: Religion and Political Ideology in the Anti-ERA Movement." *Social Science Quarterly* 56 (March 1976): 564–77. Compares the social characteristics of anti–Equal Rights Amendment women activists with those of activists in the political Right.

Brauer, Carl M. "Women Activists, Southern Conservatives, and the Prohibition of Sex Discrimination in Title VII of the 1964 Civil Rights Act." *Journal of Southern History* 49 (February 1983): 37–56. Describes the political maneuvering that led to the inclusion of the "sex amendment" in the 1964 Civil Rights Act.

Burris, Val. "Who Opposed the ERA? An Analysis of the Social Bases of Anti-feminism." *Social Science Quarterly* 64 (June 1983): 305–17. Based on an analysis of the 1980 National Election Study, identifies three factors that may have contributed to the eventual defeat of the Equal Rights Amendment.

Chafe, William H. "Women's History and Political History: Some Thoughts on Progressivism and the New Deal." In *Visible Women: New Essays on American Activism*, edited by Nancy A. Hewitt and Suzanne Lebsock, 101–18. Urbana: University of Illinois Press, 1993. Traces the connection between Progressive era feminism and public policy during the era of the New Deal in the figure of Eleanor Roosevelt and the women she brought to Washington, D.C.

Combahee River Collective, "A Black Feminist Statement." In *Capitalist Patriarchy and the Case for Socialist Feminism*, edited by Zillah Eisenstein, 362–72. New York: Monthly Review Press, 1979. Summary of black feminist theory, circa 1977, by a black lesbian feminist collective from Boston.

Daniels, Mark, Robert Darcy, and Joseph Westphal. "The ERA Won—At Least in the Opinion Polls." *Political Science 15* (1982): 578–84. Analysis of public opinion polling and the Equal Rights Amendment.

De Hart, Jane Sherron. "Rights and Representation: Women, Politics, and Power in the Contemporary United States." In *U.S. History as Women's History: New Feminist Essays*, edited by Linda K. Kerber, Alice Kessler-Harris, and Kathryn Kish Sklar, 214–42. Chapel Hill: University of North Carolina Press, 1995. Compares and contrasts political styles and strategies of women candidates during the 1970s with those of the late 1980s and early 1990s.

Dill, Bonnie Thornton. "Race, Class, and Gender: Prospects for an All-Inclusive Sisterhood." *Feminist Studies* 9 (Spring 1993): 130–50. Scholarly critique of the (white) feminist theory of "sisterhood" from the perspective of women of color.

Farrell, Amy Erdman. "A Social Experiment in Publishing: *Ms*. Magazine, 1972–1989." *Human Relations* 47 (1994): 707–30. Analyzes the history of *Ms*. magazine as as social experiment in running a business venture informed by feminist principles.

Joffe, Carole. "Portraits of Three 'Physicians of Conscience': Abortion before Legalization in the United States." *Journal of the History of Sexuality* 2 (July 1991): 45–67. Case study of strategies employed by three physicians who provided abortion services prior to *Roe v. Wade*.

King, Mary C. "Occupational Segregation by Race and Sex, 1940–1988." *Monthly Labor Review* (April 1991): 30–35. Comprehensive overview of race and gender patterns in employment opportunities between 1940 and 1988.

Radicalesbians. "The Woman-Identified Woman." In *Radical Feminism,* edited by Anne Koedt, Ellen Levine, and Anita Rapone, 240–43. New York: Quadrangle Books, 1973. Position paper on the relationship between lesbianism and feminism.

Rich, Adrienne. "Compulsory Heterosexuality and Lesbian Experience." *Signs: A Journal of Women in Culture and Society* 5 (Summer 1980): 631–60. An essay on the politics of sexuality and the relationship between lesbianism and feminism.

Rosen, Ruth. "The Female Generation Gap": Daughters of the Fifties and the Origins of Contemporary Feminism." In the previously cited *U.S. History As Women's History* by Kerber, Kessler-Harris, and Sklar, 313–34. Locates the roots of second-wave feminism in the "gendered" generation gap between 1950s mothers and their activist daughters.

Rothschild, Mary Aickin. "White Women Volunteers in the Freedom Summers: Their Life and Work in a Movement for Social Change." *Feminist Studies* 5 (Fall 1979): 466–95. Examines the emergence of race and gender tensions among civil rights workers during the summers of 1964 and 1965.

Scully, Diane, and Pauline Bart. "A Funny Thing Happened on the Way to the Orifice: Women in Gynecology Textbooks." *American Journal of Sociology* 78 (January 1973): 1045–50. Reveals the patriarchal bias prevalent in medical textbooks prior to the advent of the feminist health movement.

Sealander, Judith, and Dorothy Smith. "The Rise and Fall of Feminist Organizations in the 1970s: Dayton as a Case Study." *Feminist Studies* 12 (Summer 1986): 321–41. An invaluable case study of radical feminism in the American heartland.

Shanley, Kate. "Thoughts on Indian Feminism." In *A Gathering of Spirit*, edited by Beth Brant, 213–15. Ithaca, NY: Cornell University Press, 1984. A view of feminism from the perspective of Native American women.

Strosen, Nadine. "The Perils of Pornophobia." *The Humanist* 55 (May–June 1995): 7–9. A critique of the pro-censorship position advocated by radical feminists.

Tierney, Kathleen. "The Battered Women Movement and the Creation of the Wife Beating Problem." *Social Problems* 29 (February 1982): 207–20. Analysis of organized feminism's role in addressing domestic violence.

Toolin, Cynthia. "Attitudes toward Pornography: What Have the Feminists Missed?" *Journal of Popular Culture* 17 (Fall 1983): 167–74. Analysis of Catherine MacKinnon's and Andrea Dworkin's views on pornography.

Valverde, Mariana. "Beyond Gender Dangers and Private Pleasures: Theory and Ethics in the Sex Debates." *Feminist Studies* 15 (Summer 1989): 235–54. Analysis of divergent feminist theories on sexuality, rape, pornography, and abortion.

Wootton, Barbara H. "Gender Differences in Occupational Employment." *Monthly Labor Review* (April 1997): 15–24. Analyzes the persistence of gender differences in employment opportunities between 1975 and 1995.

# Index

## About the Author

KATHLEEN C. BERKELEY is Professor of History at the University of North Carolina at Wilmington. She is the author of *Like a Plague of Locusts: From an Antebellum Town to a New South City, Memphis, Tennessee, 1850–1880* (1991) and numerous articles including the 1986 History of Education Society's prize-winning selection "The Ladies Want to Bring About Reform in the Public Schools: Public Education and Women's Rights in the Post–Civil War South." She is currently working on a biography of Charlotte Hawkins Brown, an African-American educator and race leader from North Carolina.